D1499061

MITCHELL BEAZLEY WINE GUIDES

MICHAEL BROADBENT'S

Wine Tasting

Michael Broadbent's Wine Tasting

Published in Great Britain in 2003 by Mitchell Beazley,
an imprint of Octopus Publishing Group Ltd,
2–4 Heron Quays, London E14 4JP.

First published as *Wine Tasting* by Wine & Spirit Publications Ltd 1968.

Revised editions 1982, 1983, 1988, 1991, 1992, 1995, 1998, 2000, 2003

A CIP catalogue record for this book is available from the British Library.

ISBN 1 84000 854 7

Commissioning Editor: Hilary Lumsden
Executive Art Editor: Yasia Williams
Editor: Juanne Branquinho
Designer: Colin Goody
Index: Ann Parry
Production Controller: Alexis Coogan

Typeset in Verailles and Helvetica

Printed and bound by Toppan Printing Company in China

Contents

Foreword to new edition

I was convinced forty years ago – and the conviction remains to this day – that in winetasting and winetalk there is an enormous amount of humbug.

T. G. Shaw

WINE, THE VINE AND THE CELLAR, 1863

This, I can assure you, really is, yet again, a fully revised and updated edition of a work that has been in print, and through many editions, for thirty-five years. Has anything changed over this period? After all, tasting is pretty basic. All I can answer is that one lives and learns. Indeed, for the whole of the time I have been writing about wine I have also been tasting, have organized, and taken part in tastings, have "moderated" – as the Americans say – great tastings of old wines, horizontal and vertical tastings of châteaux, estates, and vintages, and have conducted endless courses. And I can honestly say that, for me, every tasting is a revelation; the feedback is as enlightening as it is invariable. Believe me, the best way to learn is to teach.

The feedback has always made me look at what I have written with fresh eyes. It has obliged me to question the relevance of methods and techniques, to filter, or amend. In short, I have re-read every word, for I have long adopted the motto of my old firm, Harveys of Bristol, "That and better will do". Perhaps I can also reassure readers – or perhaps disappoint some – that I am not an oenologist, a chemist, or any sort of technician. I like to think of myself as an "amateur" in the French sense: a wine lover and a wine enthusiast. Moreover, for the whole of the time I have been engaged in the wine trade – over half a century – I have through necessity always had the consumer in mind. I am also a regular wine drinker; indeed, I can scarcely contemplate any meal except breakfast without wine, in which situation I have the full support of my wife!

In the final analysis, the wine we study, taste, criticize, write about, or toy with, has been produced simply to be consumed. Happily, we do not need to be experts to enjoy drinking wine. Drinking wine mellows, loosens the tongue and inhibitions; drinking wine with food is good for digestion, it is healthy and natural. Drinking good wine with good food and in good company is one of life's most civilized pleasures. Moreover, the more one tastes, the more one learns, understands, and appreciates – leading to deeper enjoyment.

What follows ambitiously targets both the beginner and the more experienced wine lover; its purpose is to awaken the interest of newcomers and to encourage even the hard-nosed professionals to think more carefully about the methods and words they use. Above all, as I have written in every edition, I aim to encourage those teetering on the brink to plunge into the unfathomable depths of wine.

The approach to tasting

The difference in a trial of wine by the consumer and the expert, is that the former seeks for something agreeable, something to praise; whilst the latter seeks for a fault, a blemish, or something to condemn.

Arpad Haraszthy
WINES AND VINES OF CALIFORNIA, 1889

It is not necessary to know all about the internal combustion engine in order to drive a car. It is, however, generally agreed that driving lessons are essential and, in the final analysis, practice makes perfect. In the same way, a detailed knowledge of viniculture and viticulture is not a prerequisite for the enjoyment of wine. However, an understanding of basic principles, a degree of experience, and a fairly discerning palate are essential if wine is to be appreciated as something more than just an ordinary drink.

ABILITY TO TASTE

If one can taste food, one can taste wine. Generally, what is good smells and tastes good; what smells "off" and has a nasty taste is bad. I believe this is the reason why most people are able, correctly, to judge that one wine is better than another simply on the basis that it taste or smells nicer: that elementary hedonistic judgement will fairly accurately pin down the relative quality of the wines in question. Saying why one is better than another is a different matter. There are, however, exceptions to the above rule: an over-mature wine, like an overripe cheese or well-hung game bird, sometimes has a putrid overtone to the smell and taste which can be unattractive, even repellent, to the uninitiated, though appreciated, sometimes sought after, by a connoisseur. It is all a matter of taste, and experience. Experience, as always, takes time; it cannot be bought or simply read about.

FIRST PRINCIPLES

But what about the first principles? In the course of some pretty voracious reading, up to the time I originally wrote this work, I had come across not a book, hardly a chapter, which dealt with what I considered a fairly basic subject: taste. This is not to say that background information about districts, soil, grape varieties, winemaking, and winemakers is not interesting or valuable; indeed, later chapters deal with the influence of such elements on taste. The history of wine, of firms, and people adds to one's awareness, but such vital fringe activities are apt to obscure the main object of the exercise: the appreciation of wine, its colour, bouquet, and flavour. Over the past few years there has been a positive spate of attempts, more and less successful, to deal with the subject. The French, in particular, seem to be making up for lost time (as witnessed by the number of books listed in the Appendix).

There are, of course, difficulties in getting down to brass tacks. Tasting is subjective, and the language needed for describing wine smells and flavours is still singularly ill-defined and anything but universally accepted. What perhaps is needed is something approaching musical notation, for in many ways the problems are similar. Both music and wine appeal to the senses; both are fleeting, in the sense that actual sounds and flavours cannot be retained by the receptive ear or palate; both, on the other hand, can be appreciated, even greatly loved, by those who lack technical knowledge or who are without a deep interest. But to reach the heights of full understanding and to convey this to others, rather more is required.

The first stage is an awareness of first principles; the second is a detailed understanding of what lies behind the colour, smell, and taste of any wine; and the third is plenty of practice.

PRACTICE, MEMORY, AND NOTES

Although wine can be consumed with enjoyment without a lot of fuss and nonsense, reasoned judgment of the finer wines must be based on knowledge, and this can only be acquired by the sort of practice in tasting that will help a vinous memory – a memory that will hold in store the great touchstones, the standard norms, and the exceptions to the rule.

Some people are no doubt endowed with a more delicate and sensitive palate than others, but this alone is less useful than a normal but well-trained and experienced palate. Mind you, a sensitive palate and an excellent memory will give the new taster a head start. The greatest tasters will surely be those with all the physical attributes, wide experience, and a flawless memory. In the end it is almost always memory which lets one down, which is why it is advisable to make notes – a subject dealt with at length in the chapters "The use of words" and "How to taste – a practical recapitulation".

PERSPECTIVE AND COMMON SENSE

The important thing is to keep tasting in perspective, to spend time and effort only on those wines that are worthy of attention, and to talk intensely about wine only with those who are of like mind. In short, don't get carried away: use a little common sense.

Need to taste

In passing the lips, crossing the tongue, and descending the throat, wine is to some extent tasted, whether or not a comment or judgment is made. The word "tasting" in relation to wine refers to a deliberate, conscious, and subjective act, the object of which is to assess the qualities of the wine under review. Incidentally, the word "tasting" is used here (as the French use dégustation) in the broader conventional sense, which I prefer to the more academic terms "sensory" and "organoleptic" examination.

Does all wine need to be tasted in this sense? The answer is no. For of the millions of gallons produced and marketed, by far the largest proportion is the plainest of ordinary beverage wine, made to be consumed as an adequate accompaniment to a meal or merely as a refreshing drink. This sort of wine is not intended to be sipped reverently; nor is it meant to provide the basis of intellectual discussion. It is immaterial that one of the end products of its consumption may be the mellowing of the drinkers and loosening of their tongues to discuss other subjects with new enlightenment. Ordinary wine is for talking over, not about.

Before finally dismissing plain, honest-to-goodness *vin de table*, a word about mass-produced wines may not come amiss.

OENOLOGY, COMMERCE, AND MEDIOCRITY

We are living in a world where, whether we like it or not, standards are concertinaing. Thanks to new pesticides, new methods of controlling fermentation, and other new techniques, less is now left to chance. Although fine vintages cannot be created artificially, certainly poor vintages are less disastrous than they used to be. This is a mixed blessing. If oenologists can rightly take credit for much of the improvement in the overall standard of winemaking, they are also accountable for some of the decrease in character and individuality of fine wines in certain classic areas. If more wine is made, then more is to be marketed, and the production of wine is as subject to the law of supply and demand as any other commodity.

It is not coincidence that we live in the era of the "light" and "mild", subjected to a relatively new set of standards which applies to nearly all consumer products from "mild-flavoured" cornflakes to light whiskies. Unhappily, commercial necessity forces this pace, taking character and stuffing out of the raw material, reducing the awareness of the consumer to any elements of positive taste. What is not sufficiently realized is that mixing individual flavours can have a similar effect to mixing colours: the more they are mixed, the greyer the result.

Mass-marketed wines have to be blended. Blended wines, of necessity and by design, lose much of their individuality and character and a neutral wine often results. Neutral wines are inoffensive and therefore will not displease the majority. This, unfortunately, is just one more example of how commercial necessity can become a marketing virtue.

THE NEW "GLOBAL" TASTE

Whilst it seems that the whole world is now busily making and drinking wine – surely a healthy sign? – there is a downside.

The overall standard of winemaking has improved; more producers have the knowledge and ability to cultivate good grapes, and new technology enables them to make good wine. The tendency and temptation is to adapt what they grow and make to match international demand, hence the plethora of wines made from a limited number of fashionable grape varieties such as Sauvignon Blanc, Chardonnay, Cabernet Sauvignon, Merlot, and Pinot Noir. This results in a homogeneity of styles making it difficult for even experienced tasters to tell the difference, or at least detect the origin of, for example a Sauvignon Blanc made in New Zealand or Bordeaux, a Chardonnay from Italy or California. As for reds, it seems that the aim is to produce an anonymous, deeply coloured, full of fruit, soft, sweet, and easy to taste wine which appeals to brand retailers and a gullible and uninformed public, the new global clientele.

Pure quality, subtlety, and finesse are considered "old hat". A mistake. My recommendation is to avoid the obvious and seek out the well made, well crafted wines. They are more distinctive, more interesting and need not be expensive.

VITAL CRITICAL STANDARDS

It is in the context of maintaining interest and positive standards that critical tasting must be kept alive. It would be a pity to allow our finer perceptions (and resultant range of pleasures) to atrophy. Moreover, I do not think we should feel obliged to re-evaluate, lower, our standards in the light of technical "improvements".

Reasons for tasting What, then, are the main reasons for tasting? The important thing to realize is that wine will be tasted throughout its life in different places, by different people, and for a variety of practical reasons. Here are some of them:

1 In the *chai* (*keller*, *cantina*, whatever local name is given to the producer's cellar), the winemaker, *maître de chai*, or the proprietor will be acting as nurse and midwife. He or she will taste from the moment the grape juice is fermented into wine, watching its condition, balance, and development until it is sold or bottled.

2 Prior to making a purchase the broker and the merchant will also taste from the producer's casks during this period. For the amateur, tasting young wine from a barrel in a *chai* – such a romantic-sounding occupation – may be sadly disappointing. Few things can be so starkly raw and scouring as a mouthful of purple new wine. It is much better at this stage to leave it to the professionals.

3 Samples may have to be submitted by the producer to an official body for a seal of approval. For example, regulations issued in 1974 by the French Government introduced analysis and tasting for all *appellation contrôlée* wines.* The finer German wines are also tasted by a panel before they are awarded a quality seal and a proof number.

4 In the cellars of the local merchant, négociant, or shipper, the selected wine may be nursed a little further up to the stage of shipment in cask or bottling. During this period, it is tasted by professional buyers with a keen eye on price, style, and potential.

5 There are competitive tastings at wine fairs and conventions. These are fairly common in wine-producing countries, particularly in California and Australia. There are also "International" winetasting competitions to which producers and marketeers submit samples to be judged by mixed tasting panels who award gold and silver medals and commendations. These are of increasing importance.

6 After shipment in cask† it will rest in the cellar of the shipper or merchant until it is ready for bottling. The firm's tasters – and the analyst, if there is a laboratory – will examine its condition prior to bottling. Thereafter, from time to time, quality-control personnel will monitor the behaviour and development of the wine in bottle.

**The main provisions of Decree 74-871, are as follows:*

ARTICLE 1: the wines for which an AOC is claimed cannot be put into circulation without a "certificate of agreement" issued by the Institut National des Appellations d'Origine des Vins et Eaux-de-Vie (INAO) *after an examination conforming to the terms of Article II of EEC regulation No. 817/70 of the Council of 28 April 1970.*

ARTICLE 2: the examination, organized by INAO *or local wine-growing syndicates, consists of any analysis and tasting, the latter carried out by a Commission, following officially laid-down procedures.*

†To the UK or elsewhere in Europe. The volume of quality wine being bottled at source has increased enormously and in many wine areas this is now mandatory. Shipment in cask is not permitted by some countries, notably the USA.

7 The next category is the trade tasting, where the merchant, wholesaler, or restaurateur selects wine for re-sale. This sort of function may be of the headline-hitting variety in a vast candle-lit cellar, or it may take the form of a quiet, down-to-earth event in a rather clinical-looking tasting room. In either case, the buyer is looking for wines either to lay down or to offer for laying down, or, of course, for immediate consumption.

8 Relatively new are the tastings organized for, or by, journalists – some self-styled "wine critics" whose judgement can have considerable influence on what is bought and consumed (*see* page 85).

9 Between trade and consumer come educational tastings and tutorials organized by merchants, societies, and tasting clubs.

10 Lastly, keen amateurs with good cellars will taste their own wines to see how they are progressing and to choose wines suitable for a particular occasion, guest, or type of food. They will also taste the wine, before serving, to make sure that its condition and temperature are right.

TASTING CONTEXTS

In all the above instances, it will be seen that each taster will be examining a wine in a different context and with a particular point of view: the winemaker with a parental eye, the buyer with price and market uppermost, the quality-control taster or chemist for condition and stability, the salesman for attractive qualities of price and style, the club member for education and amusement, and the ultimate consumer with palate, pocket, and future entertaining plans in mind. From the second stage to the penultimate, the value of the tasting to the participants will increase roughly proportionately to the range of wines on show. Even at a dinner party, the qualities of a really fine wine will be more fully apparent if paired off with, or preceded by, a lesser but comparable wine.

It follows, however, that as each category of taster is apt to be concerned with a limited aspect of wines, their perspective in general will narrow, and it is only too easy for the professional and the amateur to adopt, out of habit, a blinkered, one-sided approach. Professional tasters, with limited time at their disposal and a narrow objective, cannot be expected to probe and analyse the hidden depths of sixty young wines at 10 am. Nevertheless, they should be conscious of the dangers of slipping into a rut. Equally, amateurs will enrich their experience by taking more than a superficial glimpse at the wonderful liquids that nature, with man's aid, has contrived for their pleasure.

When to taste

The best time for doing anything constructive and creative is when the mental and physical states are freshest. This, for most people (whether they appreciate it or not), is in the morning. It is said, incidentally, that the palate is sharpened by hunger, which would indicate the benefits of pre-luncheon tasting sessions.

In point of fact, the majority of trade tastings are held in the morning. The most quiet and business-like tastings may be held around 10 am, possibly at 12 noon. Tastings to which trade or private customers are invited usually begin about 11.30 am and may end with a buffet or light luncheon, during the course of which selected wines are shown off against appropriate food. (It is not without significance that the simpler and more wholesome the repast, the better the wines show; there are fewer distractions of flavour. Simple cold roast beef and mild English cheeses provide the most perfect foil for good French reds.)

Early evening tastings are also popular. They are generally held by the trade between 6 and 8 pm to attract customers who would otherwise find it difficult to attend during their working day. These evening tastings tend to be less serious – people are tired after a day's work and feel more in need of a reviver than the concentration needed to taste in earnest. Or they have had time to go home and change, and may treat the whole affair as a rather jolly social occasion. The wine-merchant host dispensing his or her stock-in-trade may not particularly mind, so long as the party-goer leaves in a sufficiently sober state to remember the firm's name.

Wine society tastings tend to be held in the early evenings for similar reasons, though the degree of serious attention is often higher – perhaps because the members have paid to attend?

GENERAL POINTS TO OBSERVE

Before getting down to the serious business of tasting, there are quite a number of general points to watch out for. Not all are appropriate for professionals and amateurs alike. Some are quite basic, some merely minor details, some may even appear quite trivial. Not necessarily in order of importance, they are listed as follows:

No smoking Smoking in a tasting room is not only considered inconsiderate and offensive, it will also seriously reduce the effectiveness of other tasters, particularly if they are non-smokers. It is difficult enough as it is to detect subtleties of bouquet without a nullifying smoke-screen attacking one's nostrils at the same time. For those who doubt this, try puffing smoke into a glass of wine, then sniffing it.

It should be said immediately that the rule of "no smoking" in the tasting room does not mean that a taster should not smoke at all. There seems little evidence that a smoker's tasting abilities are less than a non-smoker's. The palate appears to compensate for this regular coating of tobacco smoke and nicotine, and there are numerous examples in the trade of fairly heavy smokers being good tasters. Some are even reputed to have a drag at a strong French cigarette between tasting sessions.

Make notes Remembering the taste of a wine, but forgetting its name, and vice versa, is very tiresome. It is astonishing how easy it is to forget the name of even an outstanding wine only an hour or so after tasting. These blank spots are experienced by the professional, whose memory is cluttered with multitudinous examples, as well as by the novice. It is particularly frustrating for a merchant to recommend a range of wines to a customer and for the latter to say that he or she thought one of them outstanding – only to forget its name.

The answer is, make a note. At least scribble on a piece of paper or in your diary the name of the wine and vintage, and whether is was agreeable or not.

Note-making can turn into a fetish; it can become a hobby like collecting stamps. The moderate use of intelligible notes is, however, invaluable, and even a good memory is better served by the briefest record of name, description, and opinion. Various methods of note-making are dealt with in the chapter "How to record tasting notes".

Good company An exchange of views helps to shape and strengthen a hazy impression, revealing aspects of a wine that might not otherwise have been noticed. It goes without saying that the company in question must be equally interested – a large party of casual observers or hard drinkers is merely off-putting.

An organized tasting group is often the best solution, not the least of its virtues being the increased purchasing power of pooled resources which makes it possible to accumulate a wider range of better-class wines.

The main snag about a free-for-all tasting is the distraction of general chatterboxes. It is difficult enough as it is without being interrupted between sniffing and note-making.

Quite the best advice I can give the newcomer is to taste in the company of an expert, or at least with a taster of some experience.

Related wines It is perfectly possible to judge a fine wine on its own, but its true qualities will be thrown into much sharper perspective when it is tasted alongside another wine, even if dissimilar in style. By far the most revealing type of tasting is one where comparisons can be made between wines of the same vintage but from different districts, or from the same vineyard but of different vintages (*see* pages 69–70).

Appropriate order of tasting Dry before sweet; young before old; modest before fine. Whether red wines are tasted before white depends on their relative "weights". Light, dry whites are better before fuller-bodied reds, but light young red wine must be tasted before full-bodied, sweet white wine with high extract and residual sugar.

It is perfectly possible for a professional taster to assess the relative qualities of a large range of related wines, say thirty to sixty, in a session. It is doubtful, however, whether more than an essential facet or two can be obtained by tasting on this scale, and certainly for beginners, six to ten wines are usually as many as they can effectively cope with. Over this number, the taste-buds can become tired and the mind confused.

Try to relate the time spent per wine to the total time available and, if necessary, be selective: concentrate on those wines you particularly wish to taste. Nothing is more frustrating than to find that you have spent nearly all the tasting session on a handful of wines at the lower end of a range, invariably the least interesting, leaving yourself neither time nor energy for the best at the end.

Temperature and presentation Present the wines appropriately: red wines at room temperature, white wines, rosé, Champagne, sherry at cellar temperatures or cooler still (*see* pages 123–25). Do not draw the corks too far in advance; up to one hour before tasting is a reasonable average. Decant old and mature wines, as the sediment will swirl up in the bottle after a couple of pourings.

Taste blind "A sight of the label is worth fifty years' experience" – a cynical truism, for what an impressionable lot we are! Even the most disciplined taster is biased by the merest glimpse of the label, even by the shape of the bottle. One can also be swayed by the appreciative – or otherwise – noises and looks of other tasters.

For a completely objective assessment, arrange the wines to be tasted in numbered glasses (use a wax pencil or stick self-adhesive labels to the upper side of the base), the numbers being related to the bottles which are, of course, out of sight. Alternatively, cover up the bottles, standing the glasses in front. Failing this, turn the bottles round so that the labels cannot be seen.

Don't drink, spit It is nothing short of ridiculous to drink one's way through a tasting. How can the last few wines yield more than a hazy impression? This is particularly important when tasting fortified wines.

To taste critically is one thing; to enjoy wines with a meal is another. So when tasting, spit out the wine, don't swallow it. It is not considered rude, nor need it be undignified: purse the lips, draw in the cheeks, and expel the wine with enough force to project it into the spittoon. It is considered a normal thing to do.

In a wine producer's cellar it is considered perfectly acceptable to spit on the floor, which is often of earth, or, if of concrete, perhaps strewn with sand or sawdust. Most professional tasting rooms are furnished with spittoons, often with running water. If a tasting is held in a public building, or in a private room, spittoons must be provided. A wooden wine box lined with plastic containing sawdust is simple to prepare and has the advantage of dimensions generous enough to accommodate all but the very worst shots. It is advisable not to dribble or spit on your host's carpet!

Taste the best Straightforward, ordinary wines are for drinking, not for philosophical deliberation. Moderate-quality wines afford good practice and can be interesting, but they are often indefinable and rarely clear-cut in character. The most vivid characteristics of a district or a vintage are best exemplified by wines of good quality. Those who are fortunate enough to afford, and restrict their interest to, only the finest wines will tend to undervalue the quality of much lesser wines. The opposite does not, however, obtain. Regular drinkers of ordinary table wine do not tend to overvalue a fine wine when it is put before them; if anything, they are more likely to be unappreciative of its subtleties and to wonder why anyone would be crazy enough to pay, for one bottle, a sum that might cover their daily fare for a month. Do not be an inverted snob; occasionally buy a top class wine and try to see what extra dimensions it has to offer.

Physical hazards Do not waste time trying to taste if you have a streaming cold. Catarrh doesn't help, either. Clear your nostrils. Do not try to taste with traces of alien matter in the mouth. Alkaline toothpaste interacts with the acidity of wine. Fruit, with its high acid content, will affect taste, too; so will highly spiced breakfast sausages. Crabmeat sticks in the teeth.

Order and discipline Taste in a regular sequence; examine the appearance of the wine first, its bouquet next, and finally its taste. And within these three main subdivisions, look out for the salient factors, (*see* "The elements of tasting").

A prepared tasting sheet or notebook can be a great help in this respect, and moreover guards against the temptation to leapfrog from wine to wine in a haphazard fashion. This does not mean that one should never dodge back and forth. Indeed, when tasting wines in ascending order of quality or descending order of age, the earlier wines can be seen in sharper perspective if one retastes them after completing the range.

Awareness of context This is highly important and usually underrated. There are several relevant aspects. The climate as well as the food has to be considered. For example, a charming light wine with refreshingly high acidity drunk with fresh trout on the banks of the Loire in mid-summer, or a Vinho Verde enjoyed with a rich pork dish in the Minho can taste entirely different on home ground; quite apart from the need to match wine with food, the temperature, humidity, and time of year have a bearing. The colder the climate, the more full-bodied the wine needs to be, or can be tolerated, and vice versa.

WINE AND FOOD

The interrelationship of wine and food is too well known to be restated here. Many books deal with the subject. Suffice it to say that a good wine can be wasted in a wrong food context. It may seem unenterprising, but it is usually safer and more sensible to follow the conventional rules.

However, there are two conventions I like to overturn: red wine and cheese, sweet wines with desserts. Unless the cheese is mild and the red wine reasonably robust and not of fine quality the cheese spoils the taste of the wine. At all costs avoid pairing good quality red wine, burgundy in particular, with a fancy restaurant's *"sélection des fromages"*: blue cheese, ripe and runny cheese, goat's cheese. Try instead white wine, in particular semi-sweet white wine. As for desserts, a rich crème brûlée will destroy a fine Sauternes, turning it into a dry wine. If faced with, say Château d'Yquem with a rich "pudding", at least serve and taste the Yquem first.

Origins of taste characteristics

O for a draught of vintage! that hath been Cool'd a long age in the deep-delvèd earth.

Keats

I now propose to deal briefly – and necessarily inadequately, for it is a huge subject – with those factors at the growth and production end which create and influence the taste of wine.

It is helpful to have some knowledge of grape varieties, soil, climate, methods of cultivation, and winemaking to understand the effects they all have on colour, bouquet, and flavour. All this is not, however, necessary for the pure and simple appreciation and enjoyment of wine, so please do not think that you have to read about, let alone master, this subject in order to be numbered among the world's happy band of wine-lovers.

But if you do want to learn more, where do you begin? What has the greatest bearing on the style and flavour of wine? The variety of grape. Is it constant? No, it depends on the soil in which it is grown. Is this combination constant? Again, no; the latitude, climate, the care of the vine and length of fermentation, and, of course, level of human skill at every turn... all these have a bearing. However, before going into more detail it is important to realize that although it is convenient to break these elements down and study them separately, they can never, in practice, be completely isolated. They interact to create the end product.

Grape varieties

Grape varieties are all-important. They have to suit the soil, the climate, and the economy of the region. Many good wine books name and describe the main species and varieties; some also deal with vine diseases and pests, grafting, and so on; but only a few relate all these to end taste.* What I propose to do here is to list the main varieties in alphabetical order (denoting the most important "noble" varieties with a star), giving examples of the wine they make. But before I do so, there are a few points worth bearing in mind. First, it is important to remember that the bulk of the world's wines are of ordinary quality, made from comparatively easy-to-grow, high-yielding vines. Grapes from different varieties may be blended, just as final wines may be. The resulting appearance, smell, and taste are usually unremarkable.

Second, the great wines of the world, being those with exceptionally distinctive and refined taste characteristics and quality, are made from a limited range of noble grape varieties, the four leading ones being Cabernet Sauvignon, Riesling, Pinot Noir, and Chardonnay. These are produced mainly on difficult, sometimes almost barren, soils and terrains, in delicately uncertain, not to say risky, climates. Familiarize yourself with these; they give the highest satisfaction to the senses, and their

**Outstandingly the best book on the subject is* Vines, Grapes and Wines *by Jancis Robinson (Mitchell Beazley, 1997).*

characteristics, once mastered, can be more easily memorized than those of lesser varieties.† The latter may well be interesting and pleasant, but they rarely merit a second glance. Their role is to provide an agreeable accompaniment to a well-cooked meal.

Finally, a highly important factor and one that is often overlooked is the age of the vine. A newly planted vine does not bear wine-making fruit for three years. Thereafter the quality of the fruit increases steadily with age as the roots grow deeper through soil and subsoil; then, for a period, the vine combines high quality and substantial yield. Eventually the plant loses vigour and its crop falls to uneconomic levels.

Aligoté White grape producing minor white wines in Burgundy. Pale; pleasant but undistinguished aroma; dry and light.

Albariño In Spain, aromatic white; Alvarinho in Portugal, mainly Vinho Verde.

Aramon Prolific "ordinaire", was grown extensively in the Midi.

Auxerrois Red; synonym for Malbec (in Cahors).

Baco Noir Crossing, once widely planted in France; now also in North America.

Baga Most-planted red variety in Portugal, particularly Bairrada.

Barbera An important, versatile red, particularly in Piedmont.

Blanc Fumé *See* Sauvignon Blanc.

Blaufränkisch Fruity Austrian red.

Brunello Major clone of Sangiovese, grown in Montalcino.

Bual or Boal White grape for medium-sweet madeira.

Cabernet Franc One of the main Bordeaux varieties. A close relation to the Cabernet Sauvignon, fairly similar in style. Known as Bouchet in St-Emilion. Somewhat underrated but particularly successful in Chinon (Loire), Villány (Hungary), and Virginia (USA).

★ **Cabernet Sauvignon** Without hesitation, I put Cabernet Sauvignon at the head of the great red wine grapes of the world, not because I am dogmatic enough to place the finest claret, which it produces, above the finest burgundy, but because it maintains a recognizable style and character even when transplanted out of its classic home region, Bordeaux. A well-made Cabernet Sauvignon from Australia, California, or Chile will have a family resemblance despite overtones produced by differences of soils, climate, and vinification.

The Cabernet Sauvignon gives red Bordeaux (claret) its quality; its depth and richness of colour, aroma and wealth of bouquet; its firm, hard, keeping qualities, and length of flavour. The three keys to its recognition are its deep colour, its characteristic aroma of fresh blackcurrants or cedar, and its particular concentrated, fruity flavour combined with tannin and acidity. These may all vary in strength and intensity, not only because of differences of soil and microclimate within the Bordeaux area, but because the Cabernet Sauvignon is rarely used alone but is grown alongside and combined with other Bordeaux grapes, mainly Cabernet Franc and Merlot.

†*"Many centuries of experience indicates that only relatively few of the several hundred grape varieties used in making the world's wines are capable of developing the complex aromas and bouquets of the ideal, perfect wine." Professor A. Dinsmoor Webb, Department of Viticulture and Ecology of the University of California, Davis.*

I think it is useful practice to familiarize yourself with the Cabernet Sauvignon characteristics at their most pronounced. First-growth red Bordeaux has an opacity of colour, an opulence of bouquet, and a concentration of flavour that characterize great claret. If finances do not run to this, try a lower-classed growth of good reputation and a respectable year. Memorize the grape aroma in particular.

Carignan Prolific and rather neutral red wine grape (France, North Africa, and elsewhere).

★**Chardonnay** This is the white relative of the Pinot and makes the great white burgundies of the Côte de Beaune and Chablis (not to forget Champagne). It also produces some of the finest varietal wines in California, and it has achieved great success in Australia, New Zealand, and elsewhere. It thrives on chalky soil and produces a wine varying in colour from very pale straw to a fairly pronounced straw-yellow (a feature of many Meursaults and "New World" wines). A good example will have a fresh, crisp, sometimes smoky, fruity (but not grapey) bouquet – very hard to describe. It will be dry; from the firm, steely dryness of Chablis, and to some extent of Puligny-Montrachet, to the softer dryness of Meursault, and the nutty dryness of Corton-Charlemagne. It will have a fair amount of acidity and body, and a subtlety and austerity of flavour that understandably, but paradoxically, attracts lovers of red Bordeaux. Where high-quality white burgundies have a rich, yet understated flavour, poor ones can be thin and dull.

Chasselas Neutral, ubiquitous, prolific; the most-planted vine in Switzerland, best known as Fendant.

★**Chenin Blanc** A major variety making the dry, medium-sweet, and sweet white wines of the mid-Loire. A pleasant waxy aroma, plenty of refreshing acidity. Also grown in California, Australia, and South Africa (where it is also known as Steen).

Cinsaut or Cinsault Good red grape of the Midi; one of the permitted varieties used in Châteauneuf-du-Pape.

Concord American vine of species *Vitis labrusca* native to New York State, making red wine with inimitable "foxy" taste.

Dolcetto Makes important but minor red wine in Piedmont.

Fendant The same as Chasselas. Grown in Switzerland.

Folle Blanche White and ordinary (often used for brandy).

Freisa Light red, in Piedmont.

Fumé Blanc A Californian version of Sauvignon Blanc.

Furmint Hungarian white grape, producing one of Europe's least well-known great classic wines: Tokay. Straw-coloured wines, with a distinctive old-apple-like aroma when young, richly honeyed when aged. Ranging from dry to sweet to concentrated "essence".

Gamay This is not a noble grape, but in one region, Beaujolais, it excels and produces a wine of such a distinct character that it ranks only just below Pinot Noir in flavour. The Gamay produces mainly light red wine; often lightish pink-purple in colour, its most marked characteristics are a charmingly forthcoming and fruity, jammy bouquet, unique in character. Lightweight and fresh in the mouth, with little tannin but quite a lot of acidity.

★**Gewürztraminer** (no umlaut in Alsace) In some ways, the most idiosyncratic of the noble grapes. It has an immediately attractive and recognizable style; easy (perhaps too easy) to appreciate and drink, for all its opulent flavour tends to overplay its hand and sometimes begins to pall; a white wine, at its best in southern Germany (the Pfalz particularly) and Alsace. In colour it is sometimes deeper and more yellow than the Riesling; its most noticeable feature is a rose-petal scented aroma, reminiscent of lychees, herbs, and spice (*Gewürz*). It ranges from fairly dry to medium-dry, has an equally flowery flavour, but is soft and velvety, lacking the tinglingly refreshing acidity of Riesling.

Of all wine districts, Alsace has the most consistent and reliable producers. It is invidious to recommend just one, but for copybook Gewurztraminer try one of Trimbach's. The old classic Gewürztraminer of the Pfalz have never been very popular outside Germany and are even losing favour there, being rather earthy, heavyweight, and sometimes clumsy in style. They can, of course, be magnificent. Take the advice of a specialist Rhine-wine shipper if you want a good example.

Grauburgunder Synonym for Pinot Gris, grown in Germany, also known as Ruländer, making pleasant, soft, agreeable whites.

Grenache A Spanish grape known there as Garnacha, making fruity, pleasant red wines: lightish in colour but not in alcohol; agreeable, lightly fruity aroma. Grown in the southern Rhône, the Midi, California, and Australia.

Gros Plant A synonym for Folle Blanche, making a useful, rather neutral, dry wine in the lower Loire.

Grüner Veltliner Dependable, dry white wine from Austria.

Hárslevelü Important, aromatic Hungarian white.

Huxelrebe White: a flowery, grapey German crossing.

Kadarka Red grape grown in Hungary (principal ingredient of Bull's Blood); also in Austria and the former Yugoslavia.

Kerner White: a more recent and very successful German crossing. Also grown in England.

Lambrusco Makes robust reds, mainly in Central Italy.

Macabeo Widely planted white in northern Spain and southern France.

Malbec Still the most important red grape in the Argentine; also in Cahors.

Malmsey White grape grown in Madeira, making a deep, amber-brown, sweet dessert wine with a characteristically warm and tangy bouquet.

Malvasia Versatile, ubiquitous white grape in Italy and Madeira.

Manseng Gros and Petit, making the lovely white Pacherenc in Madiran; also Jurançon.

Marsanne Important white, in northern Rhône and Châteauneuf.

★**Merlot** A major variety grown in Bordeaux, giving red Bordeaux flesh and roundness, complementing Cabernet Sauvignon; dominant in Pomerol. Not widely used in California and elsewhere.

Meunier Prolific French black grape, used in Champagne blends.

Montepulciano Much-planted red in central Italy.

Morio-Muskat Popular grapey white, in Germany and Austria.

Moscatel, Moscato Widely planted grapey, scented white.

Müller-Thurgau A Riesling/Sylvaner cross producing a pale-coloured, grapey-scented white wine of easy and attractive character in most German wine districts, particularly in Rheinhessen. Also grown in England.

Muscadelle A familiar-sounding grape name. One might expect it to be raisiny in smell and flavour, and it is. Usually of very pronounced character, it is used to add particular savour, in small quantities, to sweet white Bordeaux.

Muscadet Name of grape and type of wine: pale, bone-dry, white, from the lower Loire. Somewhat neutral.

★**Muscat** Grape producing rich, amber-coloured, fortified dessert wine, with tangy aroma, penetrating taste, and madeira-like acidity. Grown in several parts of the world but reaching its summit in northeast Victoria (Australia).

Muscat (d'Alsace) This is a somewhat unusual relation of Muscadelle. It looks like any dry white wine, smells overpoweringly grapey and sweet, but is usually bone-dry on the palate. The best seem to combine the grapeyness and richness of a Traminer with the dryness and crispness of a Riesling.

★**Nebbiolo** One of the great red grapes of Italy, making the deep, powerful, firm, and classic Barolo and Barbaresco.

Optima An early ripening German white crossing.

Ortega Useful German crossing, full-flavoured whites for blending.

Palomino The sherry grape: pale, dry, refined. With *flor* culture develops characteristic zestful bouquet (difficult to describe).

Pedro Ximénez (PX) Classic sherry grape used for blending. Has often been drunk as a dessert wine: brown, almost opaque; rich, burnt, tangy nose; excessively sweet, rich, and heavy.

Petit Sirah A red California varietal.

Petit Verdot Often used as the fourth component, albeit in a small proportion, of red Bordeaux. Adds a touch of zest. Slow ripener. A somewhat acidic grape which tends to be green and tart in lesser years.

Pinotage A red grape, a cross between Pinot Noir and Cinsault, grown in South Africa, producing a rather jammy, inelegant, alcoholic wine. Better in cool vintages.

Pinot Blanc Once confused with Chardonnay but, although of similar style, less distinguished.

Pinot Grigio The dry Italian version of Pinot Gris.

Pinot Gris Sometimes underestimated classic, mainly dry white in Alsace. *See also* Tokay-Pinot Gris.

★**Pinot Noir** I place this second among the red grapes of the world, for though (at its best) in Burgundy it produces wines of sublime richness and quality, it does not always seem to make wine of so recognizable a character when grown in other districts – though wines of pronounced Pinot Noir character are now being made in California, in Oregon, and most recently, in New Zealand. It is also (with Chardonnay) the principal grape of Champagne.

A ripe Pinot Noir, vinified in a traditional way, from a good *climat* in the Côte de Nuits, will have a velvety depth of colour (true burgundy red) with pronounced viscosity ("legs"). However, depth of colour is not a major factor. Pinot Noir has a thinner skin than Cabernet Sauvignon, hence less pigment and less colour. Its bouquet will be sweeter and more opulent than the Cabernet Sauvignon in Bordeaux: and it will have a consistency on the palate that is both full and soft, alcoholic and velvety. The first main recognition signal is detected by the nose, in particular the Pinot grape aroma which I, personally, find impossible to describe (though the head of a wine school once suggested boiled beetroot as a memory trigger). The Pinot smell must be identified, isolated, and memorized. It is only from ripe grapes that the true Pinot aroma emanates.

The next key factor is the weight of the wine, allied to softness. There is much less of the searingly mouth-drying tannin of its great rival, the Cabernet Sauvignon – a characteristic which makes a Pinot Noir much easier to drink even when young. Traditionally served at a slightly cooler temperature (cellar temperature in Burgundy) than red Bordeaux, the warmth of the mouth brings out the flavour. It is the hardest thing in the world to recommend perfect examples in the modest to middle-priced ranges; perhaps it is a bit easier in the slightly pricier realms. To discover the flavour and character of a good, true Pinot Noir from the Côte de Nuits, one should buy a fine vintage wine bottled by a leading grower.

Primitivo Deeply coloured southern Italian grape.

Rieslaner White crossing, making racy, acidic whites in Franconia.

★**Riesling** Certainly the most versatile and ubiquitous fine white grape, being grown in several European wine districts as well as in almost every major region on other continents. Like Cabernet Sauvignon, it has a fairly consistent flavour and character, showing through even after transplanting.

The Riesling makes a wine with a colour ranging from very pale straw with a hint of green, through pale yellow to deep gold (the latter would be a rich dessert wine, particularly with bottle-age). Its bouquet will be fruity but not grapey, forthcoming, refreshing, and clean as a whistle; sometimes flowery, honeyed, and, when made from fully ripe grapes, almost Muscat-scented. Most Rieslings are dry to medium-dry, but – another proof of its versatility – it can make the richest and sweetest dessert wines of the world. Another marked feature is a firmness, almost steeliness, of body, and fresh, crisp fruity acidity. In Germany it is never very high in alcohol but has an excellent balance and finish. The Riesling scales the greatest heights in the Rheingau, Pfalz, and Mosel districts, but can often be seen at its most recogniszably straightforward in Alsace. If I were to suggest a copybook specimen I would choose a Riesling *réserve spéciale* or *exceptionnelle* bottled by a top Alsace producer. These wines are remarkably pure and very good value.

Roussanne Aromatic white used in northern Rhône and the Midi.

Ruländer Synonym for Pinot Gris making a pleasant, slightly innocuous white wine in the Rhinelands of Germany. Pale-coloured, grass-like aroma, mild.

★**Sangiovese** One of the noble grapes of Italy, Sangiovese is the principal variety of Chianti. Firm, full, long-lasting, and with a distinctive dry, almost bitter finish.

★**Sauvignon Blanc** Dry white grape now producing one of the world's most distinctive and popular styles of wine. It combines a spicy, whitecurrant, cat's pee aroma with mouth wateringly refreshing acidity. Fashionable, but can be thin if poor. It is grown under this name in Bordeaux and is one of the components of Graves and Sauternes, adding the necessary crispness and acidity. Of the same grape family but called Blanc Fumé it is responsible for the wonderfully crisp, dry, fruity wines of Pouilly-sur-Loire and for those over the river at Sancerre.

Scheurebe A successful crossing used in Germany, particularly in Rheinhessen and the Pfalz, producing a dramatically grapey aroma and rather facile flavour to match. Lacks the firmness and balance of the Riesling.

★**Sémillon** A white grape, one of the major components of Sauternes and Graves. It has quality and style, a soft lanolin nose, and a solid dependability invigorated by the fruity acidity of Sauvignon Blanc. Also used in New World blends and for late picked dessert wines.

★**Sercial** Riesling descendant; makes the palest and driest madeira.

Seyval Blanc A white hybrid quite widely grown in England and making a clean, dry, somewhat neutral, ungrapey, but often very satisfactory wine.

Shiraz (synonym for Syrah) A red variety extremely at home in Australia and South Africa, making deep-coloured, swiftly maturing yet long-lasting, soft but alcoholic wines, sometimes with an unmistakable and, at first, strange, tangy aroma aptly described as "sweaty saddle".

Siegerrebe Another somewhat exotic, grapey-smelling white crossing grown in Germany.

Silvaner *See* Sylvaner.

Steen A long-planted variety, similar, probably identical, to the Chenin Blanc, grown in the Cape vineyards of South Africa and certainly making their most characteristic dry whites.

Sylvaner Though making a familiar Alsatian wine type, this is not a noble grape. It is a more humble but nevertheless distinct variety. It would be unkind and misleading to describe it as "the poor man's Riesling", but it makes a useful dry wine of less marked character. It is also grown in Germany, producing a second-rank wine, lacking the finesse and crispness of the Riesling, except in Franconia where, known as Silvaner, it produces great wines.

Syrah Fine variety grown in the Rhône Valley, responsible for red Hermitage and Côte-Rôtie. Also used in Châteauneuf-du-Pape, the Midi, Australia, and California, (*see also* Shiraz).

Tannat Makes tough, tannic reds in Madiran, south west France.

Tempranillo The most important Spanish red grape.

Terrantez Small yielding, the rarest madeira.

Tinta Portuguese for red. Tinta Negra Mole, the most versatile grape used in Madeira.

Tokay-Pinot Gris Pinot Gris grown in Alsace, previously simply called Tokay. A firm, very satisfactory, dry white wine, yet with few marked characteristics. Not to be confused with Hungarian Tokay.

Touriga Francesca and **Nacional** Two major Douro port wine grapes.

Traminer *See* Gewürztraminer.

Trebbiano A major Italian white-wine grape used in Soave, Orvieto, Chianti, and elsewhere, the style depending on the vinification but often straw-yellow in colour, with a waxy, rather unfruity, nose; dry, foursquare, and rather unexciting flavour and finish.

Ugni Blanc (Trebbiano in Italy) France's most planted white grape variety, mainly in southern France. A high proportion used for distillation (cognac, armagnac).

Verdelho Used to produce medium-sweet madeira.

Viognier An unusual grape which, in the Rhône Valley, notably Condrieu and Château-Grillet, makes dry whites of crispness, style, and distinction. Also grown in California and the Midi.

Weissburgunder German synonym for Pinot Blanc.

Welschriesling Not related to the classic Riesling; grown in Austria, Hungary (Olasz Rizling), Yugoslavia (Laski Riesling).

Zinfandel A grape peculiar, and well-suited, to California,making reds of distinction, many with potential staying power.

Soil

The taster can comfort himself in the knowledge that conventional – historical trial and error – and more recent research work has established exactly what variety of vine flourishes in which type of soil (at any rate in the classic European districts). It is interesting to note that the best wines are made from vines grown in uncompromising terrain; often upon ground too poor to support any other crop: schistous rock (port), gravel (claret), slate (Mosel), large pebbles (Châteauneuf-du-Pape), and so on.

It seems that soil plays a major but subdued supporting role, at best when unobtrusive, supplying just those minerals, storing moisture and so forth, to allow the vine to struggle for existence but no more. Certainly good fertile soil encourages the vine to become overprolific, producing quantity at the expense of quality. Excess use of fertilizers has a similar effect and, in addition, gives undesirable off-tastes to the wine.

Fine white wines, requiring freshness and acidity, thrive on chalk (*e.g.* fino sherry and Champagne). In Burgundy, along the Côte de Beaune, the natural adaptation of vines to soils can be seen dramatically by walking from the red wine *climats* of Corton round to the white-wine chalky slope of Corton-Charlemagne. Some wines – red Graves, some Rhône, and Pfalz wines – smell and taste "earthy". Some, as in parts of St-Emilion, reflect the high iron content of the soil by having a taste reminiscent of an iron tonic. Some Napa Valley soils give their red wines a distinct and recognizable volcanic richness and earthiness.

The importance of the subsoil cannot be overstressed. Much of the richness and extract of a fine wine is drawn from the right sort of subsoil by the deeply thrusting roots of the mature vine.

There are often subtle and complex differences between two red wines made in the same way, from the same grapes, but from neighbouring vineyards. These differences of flavour and bouquet are mainly due to the make-up of soil and subsoil and the balance of minerals. The drainage and the aspect also play a part, mainly in the disposition of moisture and the retention of heat.

Rarely, however, are the effects of soil on taste direct, and when they are these tend to be in the nature of overtones of bouquet and taste, which make their origin the more difficult to pin down. I readily admit to being ill-equipped to delve deeply into the fascinating substrata of soil and mineral tastes. At least the taster should be aware of their presence and influence, and should try to recognize those soil characteristics that are pronounced.

Climate

After the indefinable complexities of soils, the effects of climatic variations in wine producing areas are more frequently documented and more easily understood.

Like soil, climate influences the taste of wine through its effect on the grape. Understand the reaction of the grape to climate, and it is easier to recognize the end product of a vintage. Geographical influences – the limits of latitude, proximity of rivers and bodies of water, and height above sea level – can take a back seat from the taster's point of view. The wines we normally come across will not be grown in climatically unsuitable areas. Climatic variations, however, are of considerable interest and significance. There are four broad aspects of climate in so far as they affect wine.

Zones The first concerns the consideration and comparison of the effects of two quite different climes: the gentle but significant variations in a temperature zone, the northern half of Europe, for example, and the less variable, hotter, and drier zones exemplified by North Africa, the uplands of South Africa, the irrigated areas of South Australia, and southern California.* The comparative uniformity and reliability of the warmer areas make life less hazardous for the grower but somewhat less interesting for the discerning drinker, as the wine is of a more even quality, with fewer surprises, and rarely if ever, scales the heights. The motto of fine wine could well be *nil sine labore*, for it is the struggle against the elements that kindles quality.

Annual differences The second aspect of climate is confined mainly to the temperate zones. It consists of the annual variation and is of enormous importance to the entire concept of vintage wines†. This aspect will be dealt with in some detail below.

Macroclimate Or, more popularly, but incorrectly, microclimate ("microclimate" strictly speaking refers to variations within the vine itself) encapsulates the variations due to the lie of the land – sun traps, the susceptibility to pockets of frost and fog, etc. – which occur within wine areas and from vineyard to vineyard.

Variations The connoisseur will mainly be concerned with vintage variations but in the process of describing the general effects of too much sun and rain, the implications will throw light on the extremes of the first aspect: that is to say, the character of wines made at the edges of the permissible vine-growing latitudes will reflect the characteristics outlined below. Too much sun and too little rain will reduce the quantity of juice in the grape, thicken the skins, and maximize the sugar content, thus producing excess colouring matter, tannin, and alcohol. In some northern zones, at the end of the ripening period the skins may shrivel and crack, letting in undesirable ferments. The first fermentation may be hard to control, risking spoilage. (Choice of grape, soil, irrigation, and vat cooling systems are counter factors in hot, dry areas.) As a result, the wines, if red, will be full of colour, alcohol, and tannin; they well also be heavy, coarse, and hard. If white they will lack acidity and, in consequence, be heavy, flat, flabby, and charmless with little bouquet.

Too much rain and insufficient sun will increase the volume of juice. However, the grapes will not ripen fully, so the sugar content will low, and the wrong sort of acidity high. This will result in a low alcoholic content and pale colour (if red). The wine will be thin and tart, unbalanced and short-lived. If steps are taken during vinification

**California has been scientifically divided into five climatic regions based on average sun/heat levels.*

†This important subject is exhaustively covered in The Great Vintage Wine Book II *by Michael Broadbent (Mitchell Beazley, 1991) and succinctly summarized in the pocket guide* Michael Broadbent's Wine Vintages *(Mitchell Beazley, 2003).*

to increase the sugar content artificially, it can be made into a tolerable beverage but will never be fine.

VINTAGE CHARTS

Those much maligned aids, vintage charts, do at least provide a handy *aide-mémoire*, for their ratings, in effect, summarize the overall weather conditions which have affected a particular area in a given year. For example, the year 1991 rates two out of seven under the "Red Bordeaux" heading of the current International Wine & Food Society Vintage Chart. This low rating reflects the poor weather prevailing that year in Bordeaux resulting in equally poor wine. However, the north of Portugal enjoyed an excellent combination of sun and rainfall which resulted in a very good vintage for port.

It is with vintages like 1964 that generalizations become dangerous. Heavy rainstorms in the middle of the vintage were disastrous for some Bordeaux growers who were holding on for further ripening. Charts can be useful, but watch out for the exceptions. But, better a generalization than no information at all. My tip for beginners is not to be bamboozled and bedazzled by airy-fairy vintage talk. Forget the bottle and label for a minute and remember the precious liquid inside stems from a crop affected by weather conditions like other crops. It would all come more naturally if we were to realize that when we British enjoyed a hot summer the odds are that the rest of northern Europe has too; the vintage will probably be particularly good, and vice versa.

Winemaking

Whereas the care of the vine – the annual toil in the vineyards – varies from grower to grower, we can reasonably assume that they achieve a tolerable standard to enable them to earn a living. Their husbandry will affect quality and quantity; the overuse of certain fertilizers may also affect the taste, but it is when we come to winemaking that the skills and techniques of the owner, manager, or cellar-master will have a direct bearing on the colour, bouquet, and flavour of the wine produced.

IMPROVEMENTS

Thanks to the activity of schools of oenology and viticulture, to governmental and local institutes and advisory bodies, much less bad wine need now be made. However, great wines were made before oenology (as an exact science) was conceived – just as wine was sold before marketing concepts were devised. The sciences and pseudosciences are servants and modern aids; rarely the originators, rarely the masters.

Nevertheless, in the more ignorant and uncontrolled days of the past, galloping fermentation by wild yeasts would frequently give an off-taste to the wine; over-hot fermentation might breed microbes and the heat would usually "cook" the wines; sulphur would be overused, and so on. All these errors and omissions could spoil the smell and taste in some detectable way. Nowadays, so far as red wines are concerned, the principal worry is that the demands of commerce are being met by standardization of production methods to meet the most acceptable "international" taste.

CARE

Care of the wine prior to bottling – or the lack of it – can have a direct effect on taste. For example, there is the sharp spiciness which comes from wines being kept too long in new casks, or the musty woodiness from too long in old ones; the acrid effect of over-sulphuring; the sour overtones of a wine left on the lees too long; and the vinegary smell of a pricked, probably neglected, wine.

The effect of age

It is a useful oversimplification to say that wine is a living thing. It implies that wine, once made, is in a constant state of development. It is, of course, possible to stabilize lesser quality wines, but my terms of reference here are limited to the ageing of good quality vintage wines, in so far as they affect taste.

QUALITY AND MATURITY

"Quality vintage wine" is a wine made from the grapes grown in a well-established vineyard* of one vintage whose young components need time in cask, then in bottle, to mature and harmonize.

Red wines Young red wine will start life with a deep colour, noticeable, often bitter tannins, acidity, and alcohol. Over a period of time, depending on the strength and degree of these basic elements, the colouring matter will be precipitated by the tannins (*see* pages 55–6), which themselves gradually lose their harshness. The acidity will be less intrusive and the whole ensemble will look more mellow, smell sweeter and richer, with subtler overtones and scents. The effect in the mouth will also be soft, mellow, and harmonious – no discordant edges – with layers of flavour and a long finish and fragrant aftertaste.

Red wines repay keeping best. But do all red wines benefit from keeping? The answer is no. Inexpensive branded and blended wines are not meant to be kept. Minor clarets and burgundies will probably improve with a few months' to a couple of years' bottle-age in your cellar (do not rely on the merchant to give lesser wines bottle-age; he will endeavour to sell them soon after bottling). Even well-made but minor *bourgeois* wines, red Bordeaux in particular, are not worth holding overlong. It is important to keep things in perspective and realize that a twenty-year-old *bourgeois* red Bordeaux will not have improved to classed-growth quality simply by keeping. It may have softened and mellowed a little, but in the final analysis it will only taste like a minor claret: not finer but older, more tired, and possibly sadder!

White wines It is commonly accepted that dry white wines are not meant to be kept, but to be drunk while young and fresh. What is little known is that the really good dry whites, particularly from classic districts, not only keep well but with bottle-age will develop distinctive qualities of colour, bouquet, and flavour. For example, a 1971 Montrachet, a 1952 Corton-

**The grapes from which a particular brand of vintage port or Champagne is made might come from one or more vineyards, but will be under the control of a single firm.*

Charlemagne, a 1947 Vouvray and many 1971 Rhine wines of quality from a good cold cellar can still be on the plateau of perfection now. In financial terms, unlike their red equivalents, they may not have appreciated proportionately in value, but in sensory terms they can be a revelation. This is really what tasting is all about.

Elders and betters? Do not expect age to confer upon an ordinary wine qualities it never had to begin with. The only wines that will keep and develop are those with an impeccable pedigree: classed-growth red Bordeaux and some of the other classified growths of Bordeaux, single-vineyard burgundies bottled at the domaine, Chiantis of Riserva quality, Barolos, Barbarescos; vintage port, Tokay Aszú, Sauternes, sweet Loire wines (particularly Coteaux du Layon), and Rhine and Mosel wines of Auslese, Beerenauslese, and Trockenbeerenauslese (TBA) quality; and also the really top-quality premium wines of Australia, California, and elsewhere.

Main regional characteristics

Planting a vineyard and making wine is a gentleman's occupation, and the highest type of agriculture.

Frona Eunice Wait

WINES AND VINES OF CALIFORNIA, 1889

This chapter is an attempt to give an indication of what to expect when faced with a wine from a major region, district, or type.

Rather than give a blow-by-blow description of each wine – which would require a gazetteer, not a chapter – I will endeavour to point out those salient features which are most characteristic, most distinctive, or unusual. It might be helpful to keep a marker in the grape variety section of the chapter "Origins of taste characteristics" and another in the "Full glossary of tasting terms".

The following arrangement is by country, district, and type. Good, bad, and indifferent vintages are listed, and finally, in chart form, there is a breakdown of wines into dry, sweet, light, and heavy. If the structure is rather rigid and the generalizations too broad, nevertheless I feel that some guidance is better than none at all. As tasting is so subjective, it is up to you, the reader, to develop your own pattern of knowledge and to clothe it with your own tasting experiences.

Regarding the overall quality of vintages I prefer a broad brush, the 5-star system which I first introduced in the 1980 edition of *The Great Vintage Wine Book* (Mitchell Beazley):
Even in a good vintage year, poor wine can be made.

★★★★★	Outstanding (vintage or wine)
★★★★	Very good
★★★	Good
★★	Moderately good
★	Not very good, but not bad
~	Poor
v	Variable

France

Red, white, dry, sweet, sparkling, fortified with brandy, *liquoreux*, spice-augmented, common-or-garden to finest and rarest: France produces the whole gamut. Here is a brief description of the major districts and the types of wine produced.

RED BORDEAUX

"Claret", the English name for any red Bordeaux, is the ideal table wine. It can vary from deep-coloured and fairly substantial to less deep and lighter in body, depending on district, vintage, weather, vineyard site, and vinification.

Médoc

The classic "claret" area: firm, dry wines, purple and tannic when young, elegant and harmonious when mature. Life span depends on vintage, weight, and class of wine. These are the main districts:

Pauillac Depth and concentration of colour, opaque, and purple when young; pronounced and concentrated Cabernet Sauvignon aroma and flavour (*see* page 15), very noticeable tannin and acidity when immature. The greatest wines for long keeping and development. Home of three first-growths: Châteaux Lafite, Latour, and Mouton-Rothschild.

St-Estèphe Fairly deep in colour; fruity, sometimes raw on the nose, Cabernet Sauvignon less marked; classic châteaux offer firm, tannic, slow-developing wines from heavier clay soil. More Merlot being used nowadays to make the wines softer and more amenable.

St-Julien "Copybook" claret. Cedary bouquet; balance, elegance, harmony. Not the longest-living but capable of great finesse.

Margaux A more diffused district, quite variable in style but, on the whole, similar in colour and weight to St-Julien; bouquet complex and fragrant. Develops well.

Moulis, Listrac, Soussans, and St-Laurent These middle-Médoc and hinterland districts, noted mainly for good *bourgeois* growths, produce fruity and dry wines but without the strongly marked characteristics of greater districts and vineyards. Will keep, but generally not worth keeping too long.

Graves

Similar weight to Médoc, but develops more quickly. Garnet-coloured, showing red-brown tinge sooner. Bouquet and flavour often notably earthy, loose-knit, soft, and rounded.

Pomerol

Two styles: one is deep and firm but with a full, fleshy Merlot richness, slow in developing; the other is paler in colour, sweeter and easier, quicker-maturing. Each has a noticeably velvety texture in the mouth.

St-Emilion

Two styles. From the "Côtes" around the town: deepish-coloured, but quick-maturing wines; loose-knit, sweeter on bouquet and palate; easy, flavoursome. From the "Graves" plateau next to Pomerol: firm, fine fruity wines, with depth of colour and flavour and hints of iron/earth character detectable on nose and palate.

Fronsac

Good, deep-coloured wines; hard, fruity bouquet and flavour, tannic, and needing bottle-age though rarely capable of great development. Like a firm, hard Pomerol. Sometimes austere but pure and characterful wines.

Bourg and Blaye

"The poor man's Médoc" – if I may so categorize without wishing to give offence. Dry, straightforward, rather robust wines; plain but honest. Need a little bottle-age but not worth cellaring for too long.

Red Bordeaux vintages

★★★★★ 2000, 1990, 1989, 1985, 1982, 1961, 1959, 1953, 1949, 1947, 1945, 1929, 1928, 1920. ★★★★ 2002, 2001, 1998**v**, 1997**v**, 1995, 1988, 1986, 1970, 1966, 1964**v**, 1962, 1955, 1934, 1926, 1921. ★★★ 1999**v**, 1996**v**, 1994, 1983, 1981**v**, 1978, 1976**v**, 1975**v**, 1971**v**, 1952**v**, 1948, 1943, 1937, 1924. ★★ 1993**v**, 1991**v**, 1987, 1979, 1958, 1950, 1946. ★ 1992, 1984, 1980, 1973, 1969, 1967, 1960, 1957. ~ 1977, 1974, 1972, 1968, 1965, 1963, 1956, 1951.

Maturity span

Major châteaux, vintages ★★★★ and above: twelve to thirty years.
Good châteaux, vintages ★★★: eight to twenty.
Minor châteaux: four to eight years.

WHITE BORDEAUX

Two ranges: from very dry to medium-dry, and from medium-sweet to very sweet; colour from very pale, greenish tinge/golden-tinged with bottle-age, to the deep old-gold of venerable Sauternes. Note the soft lanolin fragrance of the Sémillon grape, the fresh and mouth-watering Sauvignon Blanc, which in combination become deep, rich, and honeyed when fully matured.

Graves (the best from Pessac-Léognan)

Colour range: pale, with youthful lime-green tinge, to straw-yellow. Very dry to medium-dry, with more body and usually less of the strident acidity of Loire whites and less fruity-fragrant than German Rieslings. At best, refined; improves with five to ten years' bottle-age. All but the few top growths should be drunk young.

Sauternes

Positive yellow colour, tinged with gold that deepens with bottle age. Characteristic honeyed, overripe-grape smell from *pourriture noble* (noble rot). Essentially sweet, luscious, and full-bodied though varying in weight and richness, depending on the vintage; neatly counter-balanced by acidity. Note particularly the concentration, length, and aftertaste of the really great wines. Fine Sauternes not only keep well, they develop extra dimensions.

Barsac

Similar in style though sometimes paler and green-tinged when young; often with a more refreshingly forthcoming bouquet. Slightly lighter bodied and less rich, particularly in minor vintages.

Sauternes vintages

★★★★★ 2001, 1996, 1995, 1990, 1989, 1988, 1983, 1975, 1971, 1967, 1959, 1955, 1949, 1947, 1945, 1937, 1929, 1928, 1921. ★★★★ 2002, 1998, 1997, 1986, 1976, 1962, 1953, 1943, 1934, 1926. ★★★ 1999, 1985, 1982, 1981, 1979, 1970, 1966, 1961, 1957, 1952, 1950. ★★ 2000**v**, 1994**v**, 1984, 1980, 1978, 1973, 1969**v**, 1958, 1948. ★ 1992, 1991, 1987, 1974, 1972, 1960, 1946. ~ 1977, 1968, 1965, 1964, 1963, 1954, 1951.

Maturity span

Great Sauternes: ten to one hundred years; at peak twenty to thirty. Good Sauternes: eight to forty; at peak ten to twenty. Lesser wines: three to ten; peak four to eight. Finest dry white Bordeaux from Pessac-Léognan districts of very good vintages have a five to fifteen year life span.

RED BURGUNDY

It is difficult to generalize about burgundies.The dominant factor is the reputation of the individual domaine or merchant. Nevertheless, burgundy is essentially different in character, weight, and development to red Bordeaux and subject to great variations of colour, weight, and quality. At best, it is richly coloured but not necessarily deep; boasts a fine, ripe Pinot Noir aroma and fragrance; is fairly alcoholic yet velvety and quicker-developing thanks to less tannic astringency – the result jof the Pinot grape variety, climate, and vinification methods.

Côte de Nuits

The main classic red burgundy area capable of producing full, firm, long-lasting wines. By commune or village-district:

Gevrey-Chambertin At its best – good vintage, great vineyard, top grower – the wines are deep coloured, with an inimitable bouquet: rich, masculine, complex, with meaty Pinot aroma; full-bodied, firm yet velvety, and long-lasting.

Chambolle-Musigny Almost the opposite to the above: lighter, more gentle, feminine, elegant; noted for fragrance of bouquet – the "Margaux" of the Côte de Nuits.

Morey-St-Denis Two styles: one big and fruity, the other lighter and looser-textured. At best, firm and elegant.

Vougeot The famous Clos is much subdivided and variable. Hope for a full, firm, flavoursome, and long-lasting wine.

Echézeaux Just above Vougeot, more close-knit and elegant; refined, with some delicacy.

Vosne-Romanée The centre, the heart of the Côte de Nuits. Colour is variable in depth; the bouquet is rich, fragrant, and capable of extraordinary opulence, even spicy. The palate is deep, rich, velvety but not heavy – at best the epitome of Burgundian elegance and style.

Nuits-St-Georges At best "copybook", but without the majesty of Gevrey-Chambertin or regal opulence of Vosne-Romanée. Agreeable, fullish, firm, and flavoursome. Note the smoky, oak-reminiscent Pinot aroma and flavour of some of the finer domaines.

Côte de Beaune

Generally more loose-grained, less concentrated, and with a shorter life span than Côte de Nuits. Easy and agreeable, but as with all burgundy, only the best domaines will give a true picture of the Pinot grape and district styles.

Aloxe-Corton Pleasant, medium-weight wines except for Le Corton, with its full, meaty, slightly roasted Pinot aroma and flavour. Long-lasting.

Beaune The centre, geographically and in style. At best, not too full, but elegant, with good Pinot flavour and balance.

Pommard Not dissimilar, but Epenots and Rugiens produce very distinguished, fruity wines which develop and keep well.
Volnay Often lighter in colour and style; firm, elegant, with some delicacy. Equivalent to Chambolle-Musigny in the Côte de Nuits, but lower-keyed.
Santenay The most southerly of the Côtes and relatively minor. True Santenay is fairly pale in colour and agreeable, but do not expect great depth or finesse.

Red burgundy vintages

★★★★★ 1990, 1988, 1985, 1978, 1969, 1959, 1952, 1949, 1945, 1937, 1929, 1920. ★★★★ 2002, 1999, 1998, 1996, 1995, 1989, 1986, 1976, 1971, 1966, 1964, 1962, 1953, 1947, 1943, 1928, 1926, 1923, 1921. ★★★ 2001, 2000, 1994, 1993, 1992, 1987, 1983, 1979, 1972, 1961, 1957, 1955, 1954. ★★ 1991, 1982**v**, 1981, 1980, 1970, 1967, 1958, 1948**v**. ★ 1984, 1974, 1963, 1950, 1946. ~ 1977, 1975, 1973, 1968, 1965, 1960, 1956, 1951.

Maturity span

Great wines: eight to thirty years. Good wines: six to fifteen. Lesser wines: three to eight.

WHITE BURGUNDY

Virtually all white burgundy is pale in colour and dry. Exceptionally hot vintage years will produce a more positive yellow colour, more body, and a touch of sweetness.

Chablis

Noted for its appealing, pale straw-yellow colour with greenish tinge; its firm, steely bouquet and in particular, its dry, crisp, rapier-like quality. The best are austere yet subtle and long-flavoured.

Côte de Beaune

Puligny-Montrachet In weight and style not unlike Chablis but the best have a noticeable and very fragrant, smoky, Chardonnay aroma. Firm, crisp, refreshing on the palate – "copybook" white burgundy.
Le Montrachet Rich, yellow colour, shot with gold as it matures; deep, complex, rich, smoky bouquet. Dry, warm, nutty, and long in flavour, with a fragrant aftertaste. Small production. Expensive.
Bâtard-Montrachet Fine, full, dry, oaky; substantial; high quality.
Chevalier-Montrachet Refined, elegant; also high quality.
Chassagne-Montrachet Not unlike its neighbouring commune Puligny-Montrachet, but perhaps slightly less elegant, less austere. (Also some excellent red wine.)
Meursault Often yellower in colour; boasts a fine bouquet; broader texture and character.
Corton-Charlemagne Noted for its full, nutty, vanilla-oak aroma and flavour. Full-bodied and long-lasting.

White burgundy vintages

★★★★★ 1996, 1986, 1978, 1971, 1969, 1962, 1928, 1921. ★★★★ 2002, 1999, 1998, 1995, 1990, 1985, 1983, 1979, 1976, 1966, 1961, 1955, 1953, 1952, 1949,

1947, 1945, 1937, 1934, 1929. ★★★ 2000, 1994, 1993**v**, 1992, 1989, 1988, 1973**v**, 1967, 1964, 1959, 1957, 1950. ★★ 2001, 1987, 1982**v**, 1972, 1970**v**, 1963, 1948, 1946. ★ 1991, 1984, 1981, 1980, 1977, 1974, 1958, 1954. ~ 1975, 1968, 1965, 1960, 1956, 1950.

SOUTHERN BURGUNDY

South of the Côte d'Or, between Chagny and Lyon, are a string of relatively minor districts producing pleasing, fairly distinctive, reasonably priced red and white wines for early consumption.

Chalonnais

Rully and Mercurey make stylish, medium-light red wines of a generally Burgundian character; fruity and best drunk fairly young. Montagny makes good, well-balanced, dry white wine.

Mâconnais

Mâcon rouge and Mâcon blanc are at best agreeable, clean and wholesome, lightish red, and dry white. Do not expect more. Pouilly-Fuissé produces the best-quality dry white wine.

Beaujolais

There are two sorts of Beaujolais. Currently fashionable, the modern-vinified, whole-fruit wines follow Beaujolais Nouveau. They are a palish, pink-red colour; with a pronounced, scented, strawberry-like Gamay aroma; dry, flavoursome, and with refreshing acidity. To be drunk young.

However, the finest, worth seeking out, are still the unblended single-vineyard wines made by older methods. They possess more substantial colour and body, with a deep, elegant, more vinous Gamay bouquet and flavour, which improve with some bottle-age.

Beaujolais *blanc* is pale and dry, often with slightly more body than Mâcon *blanc* or even Pouilly-Fuissé.

RED RHONE

The main characteristics of the Rhône reflect the nature of the region's terrain and sun. The wines are deep and very purple when young; full, heavy, alcoholic, less elegant, and with less acidity than burgundy. Bouquet is the least interesting feature. Body and flavour are more interesting.

Châteauneuf-du-Pape

Most people's idea of a Rhône wine: deep-coloured (unless a poor year or hasty vinification); foursquare, hefty, fruity, soft yet with good balance. The bouquet is vinous, but no strong varietal aroma owing to the mixture of grapes (up to thirteen permitted varieties). Tannin and acidity are less marked than in red Bordeaux.

Hermitage

Although these wines are deep and purple when young, they are a contrast to Châteauneuf-du-Pape in style: less heavy, with a more distinctive bouquet, considerable fruit concentration, more refinement, and, at best, perfect balance. Sometimes claret-like. Improves with age.

Côte-Rôtie

Deeply coloured, substantial wine, with ageing potential. Now fashionable and highly priced.

Lirac, Ventoux, Gigondas

Although from the hot southern Rhône, lighter, almost Beaujolais-like wines. At best, these are delightful, fruity, and not too serious, but often lack depth and finesse.

Tavel rosé

Nearest rosé to red wine. Tavel's most notable feature is dryness, body, and a certain austerity. Less frivolous than most rosés.

WHITE RHONE

Fairly pale in colour, more body than white burgundies and less acidity. The bouquet is not very marked, save for really good Hermitage *blanc*, Condrieu, and Château-Grillet.

Condrieu

Made with the richly subtle Viognier grape. Fine and rare; dry and nutty; complex, with great length.

Château Grillet

Unusual wine, and deserving its unique appellation. In a good year deep yellow in colour; vinous, rich, slightly smoky in bouquet; dryish, fairly full, stylish, and with a slight caramel-tinged flavour.

Hermitage blanc

A lemon-tinged, straw colour; a squeeze of lemon peel in the often stylish bouquet and flavour. Dry, often refined.

Châteauneuf-du-Pape blanc

Not often seen, but in a good year slightly sweet and with unusual character. Fullish colour and body; deep and rich.

Rhône (red) vintages

★★★★★ 1998, 1995, 1990, 1985, 1983, 1978, 1971, 1969, 1964, 1961, 1959, 1953, 1949, 1945. ★★★★ 1999, 1997**v**, 1992**v**, 1989, 1988, 1986**v**, 1982, 1976**v**, 1970**v**, 1966, 1955, 1952, 1947. ★★★ 2001, 2000, 1996**v**, 1994**v**, 1992**v**, 1980, 1979**v**, 1967, 1962, 1957. ★★ 1993**v**, 1991, 1987**v**, 1984, 1981, 1973. ★ 2002, 1977, 1975.

LOIRE

A total contrast to the Rhône. Mainly white, very dry to sweet; lighter, with pronounced refreshing acidity.

Sancerre and Pouilly-Fumé

Both pale, slightly green-tinged; forthcoming, piquant, raw whitecurrant Sauvignon Blanc aroma; very dry and light (thin and sharp in poor years), with a piquant fruitiness and high acidity.

Vouvray

Although with high acidity, the Chenin Blanc grape produces wines much broader in style than Sancerre, with pleasant, not very pronounced, waxy-vanilla aroma. Both dry, medium-dry (*demi-sec*), *moelleux*, and *doux* in style; the latter can be long-lasting, developing a honeyed richness. Also pleasing *pétillant* and sparkling wines.

Saumur

Often thin but flavoursome white and red (Champigny). Excellent sparkling wines, lively with an attractive grapey aroma, medium-dry, light, and clean.

Chinon and Bourgueil

The two main red wine producing areas. Medium, Beaujolais-like colour and violet when young. The Cabernet Franc grape provides the marked piquant, raspberry-like aroma. Dry, light, very flavoursome, and fruity, but tart and thin in lesser years.

Savennières

Yellow, with an elegant and waxy bouquet; dry, firm, often austere, but elegant and finely balanced.

Coteaux du Layon

Shows a yellow, rather underplayed lanolin aroma that deepens and improves with age. Main features: delectable sweetness, rich, ripe, attractive fruitiness, and marked acidity. Bonnezeaux and Quarts de Chaume keep magnificently; indeed they need bottle-age.

Muscadet

Near to nondescript in colour and bouquet; pretty low-keyed in flavour, too. Main feature bone-dryness, but clean and zestful; only the best are refined.

Sweet Loire vintages

★★★★★ 1997, 1990, 1989, 1964, 1959, 1947, 1937, 1928. ★★★★ 2002, 1996, 1995, 1988, 1986, 1985, 1976, 1949, 1945, 1934. ★★★ 2000, 1999, 1998, 1993, 1982, 1979, 1978, 1975, 1971. ★★ 2001**v**, 1994, 1992, 1983, 1981, 1980, 1973, 1970. ★ 1987, 1984, 1974. ~ 1977, 1972.

ALSACE

In Alsace, the wines are named after the grape variety and not the district. The name of the producer is important. Virtually all are white, most are dry and, overall, honest and reliable. Some excellent sweeter, late-harvest wines are produced and, in certain years, outstandingly rich Sélection des Grains Nobles (SGN).

Riesling Main features: fragrance, firm fruit, and steeliness of flavour; dry, crisp acidity.

Gewurztraminer (No umlaut) spicy-grapey, scented bouquet and flavour. Soft, fatter, less acid. Dry to medium.

Muscat Main features: assertive grapey bouquet, but surprisingly dry, and sometimes austere.

Tokay-Pinot Gris Less distinctive but good, underrated, dry food wines, often fairly substantial.

Sylvaner Less pronounced characteristics. Dry, mild.

Alsace vintages

★★★★★ 2002, 1998, 1995, 1990, 1989, 1983, 1976, 1971, 1961, 1959, 1945, 1937, 1921. ★★★★ 2000, 1997, 1996, 1993, 1988**v**, 1985, 1981, 1967, 1964, 1952, 1949, 1947. ★★★ 2001, 1999**v**, 1994, 1992, 1986**v**, 1975, 1973. ★★ 1987**v**, 1982, 1979, 1978. ~ 1972.

CHAMPAGNE

All-important is the name of the *marque*, though most major Champagne houses produce a *de luxe* blend of some refinement and distinction. Whether the full, meaty classics or pale, light blanc de blancs, the essential characteristics of a fine Champagne are:

Appearance: appealing palish colour with a steady, continuous flow of small, evenly spaced bubbles. With age, the colour deepens to gold; sparkle less lively.

Bouquet: firm, creamy, vinous, with either a rich, meaty style or a nutty, crusty, smoky-charred Chardonnay aroma.

Palate: bone-dry to dryish; light and firm to full, depending on the house style. What distinguishes fine Champagne from other sparkling wines is finesse, elegance, and length of flavour.

Champagne vintages

★★★★★ 2002, 1996, 1990, 1989, 1985, 1971, 1964, 1959, 1945, 1937, 1928, 1921, 1911. ★★★★ 1999, 1998, 1995, 1992, 1988, 1982, 1979, 1970, 1966, 1962, 1961, 1955, 1953, 1952, 1949, 1947, 1943, 1934, 1933, 1929, 1923, 1920, 1914. ★★★ 1993, 1986**v**, 1983, 1981, 1976, 1973, 1969, 1942, 1926, 1919, 1915. ★★ 1994, 1991, 1978, 1975, 1960, 1941. ★ 2001, 2000, 1997, 1987, 1984, 1980. ~ 1984, 1977, 1972, 1968, 1967, 1965, 1963.

CAHORS

Although recently upgraded, the wines from this famous old area are rarely seen outside France, the "black" Cahors almost never. At best, deep, characterful, substantial reds; soft, full, long-lasting.

MIDI

The Gard, Hérault, Aude, and the Corbières areas produce a vast amount of white and red – but until recently little for the connoisseur to linger over. Some, like Fitou, have character and flavour. One or two boutique vineyards now produce remarkable quality. Little seen outside France, are the *vins doux naturels*: muted sweet dessert wines such as Lunel and Muscat de Frontignan – palish tawny in colour; with an attractive, Muscat/grapey aroma; sweet and fullish on the palate, but not heavy like port; easy, raisiny wines with refreshing end acidity

PROVENCE

Solid, respectable reds; dry, rather unexciting whites; dry, artless rosés – the main attraction being a fancy bottle. Fine for drinking on the spot.

JURA

The red, white, rosé, and sparkling wines from this area, with a few exceptions, are sound, quite appealing but often commercially bland and fairly undistinguished. The Jura is, however, the cradle of one of the most original wines in the world: the *vin jaune* of Château-Chalon. Yellow in colour, with a strange, nutty bouquet; dry, austere, and fairly full-bodied taste – a cross between an old fino sherry and Tokay Szamorodni.

SOUTH WEST FRANCE

Madiran Tannic reds and gently sweet whites with a difficult name; Pacherenc du Vic Bilh.

Jurançon Fairly rare but excellent sweet whites from near Pau. Jurançon *see* the dry version.

Germany

From the point of view of the connoisseur, German wines are white, ranging from dry and light to exceptionally sweet; in quality and style from insubstantial and short to deep; rich, refined, and long-flavoured. However, the market is diluted, and German wines devalued, by much bland commercial "sugar and water" wine. Real character and quality depend on dedicated growers. Happily, there are many left and increasing. The finest wines are made from the "noble" Riesling, arguably the finest and certainly the most versatile of the world's grape varieties. The essential thing to bear in mind is that the German winemakers' ideal is "fruity acidity" – a combination of delicacy, ripe, grapey quality, fragrance, low alcohol, and refreshing acidity.

Thanks to efficient winemaking techniques, the ideal is now too easily reached at the expense of character and individuality. Nevertheless, the great estates continue to produce the finest wines. Quality and vintage variations are still important. The drinkers of German wines should confine themselves to either the Erstes Gewächs fine, dry wines or those in the ascending *"Qualitätswein mit Prädikat"* order:

Kabinett Natural, unsugared wines of some quality.

Spätlese "Late-picked". Intensity, weight, character, and sweetness vary from district to district, grower to grower, year to year, but generally speaking, these are palish in colour, dry to medium-dry.

Auslese From selected riper bunches. As with Spätlese, variations of sweetness and body depend on place and vintage. This wine is usually richer, riper, not necessarily sweeter, and of fine quality.

Beerenauslese From individually selected, ultra-ripe grapes. Usually deeper yellow-gold in colour; a most characteristic bouquet: rich, ripe, honeyed scent of *edelfäule* (noble rot). On the palate: sweet, rich, ripe, often grapey, with fine balancing acidity.

Eiswein Very sweet wine from frozen grapes.

Trockenbeerenauslese (TBA) If the late-harvest conditions are suitable very sweet, rich, highly concentrated wines, often with low alcohol but high degrees of residual sugar and acidity. The world's rarest and richest dessert wines. Extremely long-lasting.

Trocken and Halbtrocken Not to be confused with the TBAs just referred to; dry and half- (semi-) dry wines made from more fully fermented grape juice, with a higher alcoholic content.

RHEINGAU

Riesling reigns supreme in this district and produces fine, firm, steely wines with intense bouquet and fragrance; dry to medium-dry, long finish. Also, in suitably fine years, outstanding sweet wines with incredible concentration, richness, and refinement are produced; long-lasting. Districts provide thematic variations: for example, Eltville wines are light but firm and elegant; Rauenthal – rich, almost spicy; Hochheim – masculine, foursquare, more earthy.

RHEINHESSEN

Generally softer, less-condensed; attractive, ripe, and fruity wines.

PFALZ

Germany's most southerly great wine district, just north of Alsace. Essentially more substantial, deep, grapey wines. Even the dry Rieslings have a touch more body and richness; the more old-fashioned Pfalz wines have a weight and earthiness of their own. Also good, spicy Gewürztraminer.

NAHE

Fruit-salad bouquet; firm, medium-light, crisp-bodied Rieslings. Can be quite dry. Halfway, geographically and in style, between the Rheingau and Mosel.

MOSEL-SAAR-RUWER

Pale, sometimes almost colourless, green-tinged, and *spritzig* (very slight effervescence); fruity, light, high-toned Riesling aroma; dry to medium-dry, usually light, low in alcohol, but enormously appealing with characteristic refreshing acidity. In exceptional years, Beerenauslese and Trockenbeerenauslese quality wines can be made. In essence, both Saar and Ruwer are Mosel in style. Special characteristics: peach-like bouquet; often very dry and with fine, steely acidity, delicacy, and subtlety.

BADEN AND WURTTEMBURG

To the east of Alsace, these two regions produce a large quantity of wine, both commercial and good red and white, though rarely of fine quality. Rather foursquare in style; with an agreeable bouquet and flavour but overall undistinguished. The reds are variable, there are some impressive wines from Spätburgunder (Pinot Noir).

FRANCONIA

Fine, dry, steely wines from the area around Würzburg, like *grand cru* Chablis, yet with Germanic fruit and acidity. Silvaner thrives here, producing wines of unusual firmness and quality; also racy Rieslaners in good years.

German vintages

★★★★★ 2001, 1998, 1997, 1990, 1989, 1971, 1959, 1953, 1949, 1945, 1937, 1921, 1911. ★★★★ 2002, 1995, 1994**v**, 1988, 1983, 1976, 1975, 1967, 1964, 1947, 1934, 1929, 1900. ★★★ 1999, 1996, 1993**v**, 1992**v**, 1991**v**, 1985, 1979, 1966, 1961, 1933, 1925, 1920. ★★ 2000**v**, 1986**v**, 1981, 1978, 1973, 1970, 1969**v**, 1963**v**, 1962, 1958, 1957, 1955, 1952, 1950, 1948, 1946. ★ 1982, 1977, 1972, 1960. ~ 1987, 1984, 1980, 1974, 1968, 1965, 1956, 1954, 1951.

Austria

Although there is a family resemblance, it is a mistake to compare Austrian wines with German Rhine wines. They look similar, have variations of a delicate, grapey bouquet, and are lightish in style but soft-edged, yet the fine wines display distinguished fruity acidity and length. The Grüner Veltliner grape grown in and around the Wachau district typifies the easy Austrian style. Some remarkably good Rieslings are made, and excellent Trockenbeerenauslese wines from around Rust, near the Hungarian border. There are some outstanding individual growers in a surprisingly wide range of districts. Austrian wines are currently enjoying a well deserved renaissance. Recent vintages now rated:

Austrian vintages

★★★★ 2000. ★★★ 2001**v**. ★ 2002.

Hungary

This once most characterful and varied wine country suffered post-war, until the departure of the Russians, from the deadening hand of state-controlled production and marketing. Happily, quality has improved; certainly the table wines are good value. Robust reds from Eger and decent dry Rieslings from Badacsony.

TOKAJI (OR TOKAY)

This area stands out; it produces one of the great classic wines of the world, which is famed for its longevity, and, was once the preferred wine of the Polish and Russian courts and aristocracy. Thanks to an influx of new capital and more sophisticated winemaking, Tokaji is enjoying a revival.

Szamorodni The natural white wine of the region. Pale yellow in colour, it has the characteristic appley nose of the Furmint grape, and is quite dry or slightly sweet. Boasts an unusual flavour and is generally something of an aquired taste.

Aszú Ranges in colour from straw to deep yellow, golden-tinged with age. Pronounced appley, wet-straw nose, unlike any other wine aroma. Gradations of sweetness range from two *puttonyos* slightly sweet, three "putts" roughly medium-sweet, four and five "putts" rich dessert wines, fairly full-bodied but not heavy; rich, attractive, with a spicy-straw flavour, good acidity, and finish.

Essence No longer made for sale, though a very rich Aszú-Eszencia, which is somewhat on a par with the former six *puttonyos*, is now marketed – like a rich Aszú but more luscious.

Tokaji essence of old vintages varies from deep amber to deep tawny, and has a very heavy sediment; a magnificent concentrated, raisiny, almost pungent nose (a cross between old Malmsey and a TBA); very sweet on the palate, rich, and concentrated with high acidity and a penetrating, lingering flavour and aromatic aftertaste. It also appears to have unlimited life.

Tokaji Aszu vintages

★★★★★ 2000, 1999, 1995**v**, 1993, 1983, 1972, 1968, 1963, 1957, 1952, 1947, 1945. ★★★★ 1996, 1992, 1991, 1988, 1981, 1975, 1964, 1961. ★★★ 1997, 1990, 1973, 1956, 1943. ★★ 2002, 2001, 1998, 1994. ~ 1989.

Switzerland

There are three main areas: the Suisse-Romande, the German-speaking areas, and the Italian-speaking areas. They produce a variety of reds and whites ranging from commercial to moderately good; for local drinking.

In the Suisse-Romande, the best reds, made from the Pinot Noir grown on the chalky soil of the upper Rhône, are soft, mild, and of a burgundy character. The whites, from the Chasselas grown on the shores of Lac Léman, are often rather yellow, have fruit but tend to lack zest.

Reds from the German-speaking areas are generally light and unimpressive, though some excellent Spätburgunders are being made. The whites, from the Riesling and Müller-Thurgau grapes, are fresh and pleasant for early drinking.

The Italian-speaking areas produce wines of little interest except for a pleasant, rather mild Merlot which comes from the canton of Tessin (Ticino).

Italy

An immense range of wines in terms of colour, type, and strength. The increase in quality over the past twenty years has been notable, with excellent, floral dry whites from Trentino in the north to greatly improved reds as far south as Sicily, and much in between. Nevertheless, connoisseurs still head for the two great classic areas, Tuscany and Piedmont.

TUSCANY

The home of Chianti, once associated more with cheap and cheerful red wine in *fiascos*, now enjoying a renaissance. Giving a kick-start to quality has been the Super Tuscan Vino de Tavola and the fashionable Brunello di Montalcino. Once again, the Sangiovese grape variety and Chianti Classicos are reasserting themselves. They have a rich garnet hue, are deep when young, warm brick-red when mature, and show a deep, slightly earthy, and complex flavour with a characteristically dry, tannic finish.

Tuscan vintages

★★★★★ 1997, 1995, 1990, 1985, 1978, 1961 1947. ★★★★ 2001, 2000**v**, 1999, 1998, 1996, 1994, 1983, 1982, 1971**v**, 1964, 1962. ★★★ 1998, 1993**v**, 1989**v**, 1987, 1986, 1981**v**, 1979**v**, 1977, 1975**v**, 1973**v**, 1970, 1968, 1967, 1957. ★★ 2002, 1992, 1980, 1974. ★ 1991, 1984. ~ 1976, 1972.

PIEDMONT OR PIEMONTE

Here the noble Nebbiolo grape reigns supreme, producing the fine, long-lasting Barolos and Barbarescos. Both keep well, have a fine deep colour, fruit and finesse on the nose and palate, and are full-bodied yet finely balanced. Tannic when young, need ageing.

Piedmont vintages

★★★★★ 1997, 1990, 1988, 1985, 1978, 1971, 1961, 1952. ★★★★ 2001, 2000, 1999, 1996, 1995, 1989, 1986, 1982, 1979, 1974, 1970, 1964, 1958. ★★★ 1998, 1994, 1993**v**, 1981. ★★ 2002, 1992, 1987**v**, 1983, 1975**v**, 1973. ★ 1991, 1984, 1980, 1976. ~ 1977, 1972.

VALPOLICELLA

A lighter, elegant red from near Verona.

SOAVE

One of the best-known dry whites. They used to be yellow and flat; now they are fresher and altogether more pleasant and reliable.

MARSALA

One of the world's classic fortified wines. Deep, plummy-purple in colour when young. Sweet, meaty, almost malty on the nose; rich, with an earthy-volcanic burnt flavour followed by a tangy, acidic, slightly bitter finish.

Portugal

A wide range of table wines, many with character and above-ordinary quality. The reds are particularly interesting and are generally well-made and of good value. The whites vary from the light, refreshing Vinho Verdes to the strange *madura* (mature) wines little seen outside the country, with some innocuous commercial dry whites in between.

MINHO

Vinho Verde can be white or red. Both are light, with a slight to marked effervescent prickle and fairly high acidity. Commercial wines are slightly sweeter, with the acidity toned down. The raw reds are rarely exported.

DAO

Reliable reds and whites. The best red Dão is full in colour and body, with positive bouquet – classic, but a little earthy – and good flavour and finish. The whites are dry, sound, and dependable.

BAIRRADA

Newest delimited region producing very good reds. Excellent value wines.

SETUBAL

The Moscatel de Setúbal is a classic, grapey, dessert wine. Pale tawny-brown in colour, it has a light, clear Muscatel-grape aroma and flavour; sweet, of course, but not heavy in style.

PORT

All port is fortified with brandy, full-bodied, and with a high alcoholic content. Red port is sweet, white is dryish. These are the main styles:

Ruby A true ruby in colour, with a fruity, peppery nose, not unlike young vintage port; invariably sweet, full, and fruity. Once the standby of "pub" ports and now mainly used for blending or exporting to France.

Tawny A true tawny, aged in the wood, is surprisingly pale in colour, with an attractive amber-tawny hue and a positive, sometimes lemon-yellow rim. Its next most noticeable feature is the soft nutty bouquet – sweet and harmonious. Now mainly marketed as ten- or twenty-year-old tawnies of dependable quality and excellent value.

White Palish, yellow-tinged; the nose is somewhat characterless; rarely truly dry, usually medium-dry, and a trifle heavy and unexciting. Pleasant, though lacking the freshness of fino sherry and the rich tang of a dry madeira. Serve very cold.

Late-bottled vintage and single-quinta The middle-quality market is more and more dominated by "LBVs", port usually of a good but not "declared" vintage that spends more time maturing in wood. Also, mainly in undeclared vintages, port made in a given year at individual *quintas*.

Vintage Bottled two years after the vintage and matured in bottle. Modulations depend on the vintage, age, and shipper's house style; quality is reliably high among the major port houses. Young vintage port is deep and purple, often opaque; rather peppery, alcoholic, and unyielding on the nose; sweet, very full-bodied, fruity but slightly rasping.

As vintage port ages it becomes less deep and much more tawny-hued; the bouquet ripens and develops overtones, sometimes of liquorice. When very old, fruit fades leaving the brandy exposed; it dries out, becoming lighter in body, softer, more harmonious. Styles vary from a lighter style to full-bodied wines with firm backbone, great power, depth, and longevity.

Port vintages

★★★★★ 2000, 1977, 1970, 1966, 1963, 1955, 1948, 1945, 1935, 1931, 1927, 1912, 1908, 1900. ★★★★ 1997, 1995, 1994, 1991, 1985, 1983, 1960, 1947, 1934, 1920, 1904. ★★★ 2002**v**, 2001, 1999, 1998**v**, 1996, 1992**v**, 1990, 1987, 1982, 1980, 1978, 1975, 1958, 1924, 1922, 1917, 1911. ★★ 1988, 1986, 1984, 1979, 1968, 1967, 1962, 1950. ★ 1981, 1976, 1965, 1964 ~ 1993.

Maturity span

Great classics: twelve to eighty years, at peak fifteen to forty. Good vintages: ten to thirty years.

MADEIRA

One of the three great, traditional fortified wines of the world. They range from fairly dry to very sweet. The rare top-quality wines have remarkable longevity. The best are named after the four major white grape varieties.

Sercial The palest, deep "fino" yellow, sometimes amber; the freshest, most mouth-watering aroma, but still with burnt-tangy character; dry to medium-dry, the lightest, yet still with a fair amount of body. Finer and older wines are very acidic.

Verdelho Varying amber-brown shades; nose deeper, richer, more tangy; medium-dry to medium-sweet, medium-bodied, fairly rich, attractive, zesty wine with good acidity. Very versatile.

Bual Deeper, warm amber-brown; rich, with a more volcanic, meaty, and assertive madeira tang; sweet, rich, and fine-flavoured.

Malmsey The sweetest and softest, with a rather more grapey-rich, chocolatey flavour added to the burnt-volcanic character. Intensely rich and attractive dessert wine.

Tinta Negra Mole Not a noble variety. Red grapes, prolific, less expensive, but which are capable of making remarkable "lookalike" styles and labelled as dry, medium-dry and sweet.

Old vintage and old solera The many authentic old *solera* and vintage madeiras have a common denominator: great richness of colour, a powerful bouquet, and length of flavour. A true old madeira has a positive tawny-brown colour with ruddy hue in the middle and a pronounced greeny-amber rim; a strong burnt aroma, high acidity; sometimes the sweetness fades, but maintains a rich, complex flavour, dense, with an extraordinarily powerful tang, and extended finish. The longest-living wine after Tokaji Eszencia and often still full of character after one hundred years or more.

Spain

Almost as ancient, and with an even larger acreage of vines than Italy, Spain until recent times was best-known for its undistinguished reds and often poor white wines – the honourable exception being sherry. Since the 1970s, enormous strides have been made, particularly in northern districts, with wines of dependability and good value.

RIOJA

Although acheiving considerable success in the second half of the nineteenth century, there came a long decline, followed in the late 1960s by a revival. It was the red Riojas that rescued Spain's tainted reputation. Originally with Bordeaux character, many successful *bodegas* now produce a vast amount of wine of different styles, mostly dependable and good value, for early consumption. But the Gran Reservas attain a distinctive tawny smoothness with age.

PENEDES

In the hills overlooking the Mediterranean, south of Barcelona, one family firm, Torres, put the wines of this region on the international map. Using classic Franch varieties – notably Cabernet Sauvignon and Chardonnay as well as local varieties – a wide range of styles and qualities are produced, all dependable, all good value, mainly for early to mid-term drinking.

NAVARRA

Bordering on Rioja to the north, another ancient wine-producing area that has only recently been making its mark with excellent red and dry white wines.

DUERO AND RUEDA

These twin districts in the northwest of Spain share the banks of the river Duero before the latter, after it crosses the Portuguese border, becomes the Douro of port wine fame. For nearly a century, the Duero was known only for one great classic red wine, Vega Sicilia, but in the mid-1970s to early 1980s a new style of red wine began to emerge: full, fairly rich, and fashionable. Rueda, in the west, is best-known for its excellent dry whites made, since the 1970s, from a combination of modern vinification methods and the traditional Verdejo grape.

SHERRY

Basically dry white wine, but with a wide range of styles within the two basic families, fino and oloroso. The former are usually dry and the latter (though starting dry), generally have sweetening wine added to them.

Fino Pale colour, fine lemon/straw-yellow; refined, positive, mouthwatering, and with a distinctive *flor* aroma less marked on lower quality wines; dry, light, fresh, with a long, crisp finish. Moderate alcoholic content: 15.5 per cent.

Manzanilla A fino from Sanlúcar, usually very dry and with a fine, tangy, almost salty, flavour.

Amontillado Deeper in colour; light amber-brown. Fine-quality amontillados have a very slight fino-reminiscent smell but are richer and distinctly nutty. Dry to medium-dry, slightly fuller in body and nutty-flavoured.

Palo Cortado A rarer and refined version of amontillado: similar in colour and weight; dryish but with a certain richness, nuttiness, vinosity, and length of flavour.

Oloroso A total contrast to fino: deeper in colour, ranging from deep amber to warm amber-brown; complete absence of *flor* tang; softer, richer on nose and palate. The best are unsweetened, but most are sweet. Medium- to full-bodied.

Cream Commercial version of oloroso, sometimes paler; certainly very sweet and soft.

Brown Now almost totally out of fashion. Deep and brown-coloured with a burnt, oloroso aroma; very sweet and heavy.

Pedro Ximénez The ultimate brown sherry: opaque in colour; powerful, and tangy. Very sweet, heavy, and highly concentrated but fine acidity. Magnificent in its way but rarely seen.

United States of America

Once condescendingly known as "domestic" and lacking the snob appeal of imported wines, the tables have turned and the development over the past thirty years has been astonishing. Virtually every state now produces wine.

CALIFORNIA

The scale, variety, and quality of California wines are not to be underestimated: red, white, rosé, sparkling, fortified, and flavoured; mass-produced, sound, commercial, refined, even rarefied. Until recently, grape variety and winemaking has taken precedence over area. Though the Napa is undoubtedly the "Mecca", a wide range of other districts produce an equally wide range of styles – and qualities.

Cabernet Sauvignon The finest red, widely planted, still mainly used alone, unblended. Characteristics: more consistently deep-coloured than in Bordeaux, often opaque and very purple when young, maintains its depth of colour better than red Bordeaux with age; often a pronounced blackcurrant, recognizably Cabernet aroma but with richer, riper, often spicy overtones; less dry than claret, often full-bodied, hefty wines full of fruit, rich in iron, and quite tannic. Can be magnificent; long-lasting.

Zinfandel Unique to California: variable, but mainly satisfactory, fruity red, not unlike Cabernet in weight, character, and longevity. Possibly nearest to a Barolo in style.

Pinot Noir In California, Pinot Noir often produces a deepish-coloured, full-bodied, rich, rounded wine. Some are remarkably good examples of the Pinot varietal aroma and flavour.

Chardonnay Outstandingly the most successful varietal in terms of style and quality. Colour: palish to buttercup-yellow; remarkable aroma: oak-vanilla tang, rich and fresh; dry to medium-dry. Old-style: yellow in colour, buttery, oaky, and alcoholic. Moves to lighter, Chablis-style wines are discernible. The best are clean with true varietal flavour.

Riesling Frankly, not successful in California, lacking the fruity acidity of the German ideal. However, some outstanding sweet wines are made with late-picked and botrytis-induced grapes up to finest Beerenauslese quality.

Fumé Blanc Not absolutely comparable with the light, acidic Blanc Fumé of the Loire, but there are some consistently successful versions: pale; fresh, fruity aroma; dry, appetizing, crisp finish.

Sauvignon Blanc Synonym for Fumé Blanc.

Napa vintages

★★★★★ 2001, 1997, 1991, 1985, 1974, 1968. ★★★★ 1999, 1992, 1990, 1987, 1980, 1978, 1973, 1970. ★★★ 2002, 2000**v**, 1996, 1995**v**, 1994**v**, 1988, 1984, 1983**v**, 1979, 1976, 1975, 1972**v**, 1971**v**. ★★ 1998**v**, 1993, 1989, 1986, 1982, 1981, 1977.

OREGON

As with Washington State,a comparitively late starter. Serious wine growing is barely thirty years old, yet remarkable strides have been made. Cooler and more temperate climate than California to the south. Oregon is producing some outstanding Pinot Noirs, full of flavour and varietal character, good Chardonnays, and racy Rieslings.

WASHINGTON STATE

More northerly still and with double Oregon's acreage, Washington State's vines endure a hotter, more arid continental climate east of the Cascade Mountains and produce a surprisingly wide range of wines of variable quality: Pinot Noir, Cabernet Sauvignon, Merlot, Chardonnay, Riesling, Sémillon, and Gewürztraminer.

NEW YORK STATE

The Finger Lakes district that stretches north to the Canadian border produces strange-tasting white wine from native American vinestock and from hybrids but also some excellent Rieslings and Gewürztraminers which thrive in this harsh climate. The Hudson River valley to the south, and Long Island, within driving distance north of Manhattan, are new thrusting areas, the latter producing much good Chardonnay, Sauvignon Blanc, reds, and whites from other classic varieties.

Canada

BRITISH COLUMBIA

British Columbia is a small vineyard area some 200 miles (320 km) to the east of Canada's Pacific seaboard, close to the Washington State border, still planted with hybrids as well as the newer *Vitis vinifera* varieties. Outside the local market, best-known for Ice Wines.

ONTARIO

The vines of the Niagara Falls peninsula and the Canadian shores of Lake Ontario struggle with a short growing season. It is not much over twenty years since success was achieved with Chardonnay and Gewürztraminer, and more recent still with some varietal reds. But the most successful of all – and hardly surprising – are the intensely sweet Ice Wines.

Australia

A vast continent with widely spaced vineyard areas producing a vast quantity of wine of all types: white, red, sparkling, and dessert. Production is shared by very large and dependable pan-Australian companies and smaller, often family owned, wineries. The practice of blending wines of different grape varieties, most commonly Cabernet Sauvignon and Shiraz, from different regions can add to the profusion and confusion. Weather conditions can veer from great heat, drought, and fires to torrential rains, so vintages can vary. But usually there is a satisfactory balance of quality and price.

HUNTER VALLEY

The oldest classic district in New South Wales, north of Sydney. The home of the Shiraz, producing a rich, earthy, Rhône-style wine with highly evocative aroma: "sweaty saddle"; also of Semillon (no é), and excellent Chardonnay.

BAROSSA

A vast, broad, vine-clad valley in South Australia, north of the city of Adelaide. This area houses long-established family businesses producing excellent reds from Shiraz and Cabernet varieties, also good Rieslings.

CLARE/WATERVALE

Also north of Adelaide, growing Cabernet, Shiraz, Riesling, and making good "sherries".

ADELAIDE AND SOUTHERN VALES

Born in a small vineyard on the slopes above Adelaide was the famous Grange: deep, rich, and magnificent, the Château Latour of the southern hemisphere. To the south of Adelaide are small family wineries and large companies, all producing a wide range of wines from excellent Chardonnays to surprisingly good "ports".

COONAWARRA

An extraordinary strip of red earth in the middle of nowhere, first planted early this century, now recognized as the "Médoc" of Australia. Magnificent Cabernet Sauvignon, Shiraz reds, and some good Rieslings are created.

RUTHERGLEN AND NORTHEAST VICTORIA

An old-established, classic area making a variety of wines, but famed for its magnificent rich, tangy Liqueur Muscats, the great classic dessert wines of Australia. Also a wide range of table wines, including excellent Rhine Rieslings, Shiraz, Cabernet Sauvignons, also interesting Semillon and Marsanne wines.

MELBOURNE AND YARRA VALLEY

Old districts that have been resuscitated and are now making some superb wines, most notably Pinot Noirs and Chardonnays.

Australia red vintages

★★★★★ 1998, 1996**v**, 1995, 1986, 1982, 1975, 1971, 1966, 1962. ★★★★ 2002**v**, 2001, 1994, 1991, 1990, 1988**v**, 1987**v**, 1985, 1984, 1980, 1979, 1978, 1976, 1973, 1963. ★★★ 2000**v**, 1999**v**, 1997**v**, 1983**v**, 1977, 1967. ★★ 2001**v**, 1993**v**, 1992**v**, 1989**v**, 1981, 1965, 1960. ★ 1974. ~ 1972.

South Africa

Perhaps the most beautiful of all winelands, the Cape, once the home of some very fashionable dessert wines, went into a long decline. Its post-war reputation was built upon its excellent "sherries", but now many fine wines are being made – magnificent Rieslings and interesting reds at many individual estates. The most at-home white grape variety is the Steen (Chenin Blanc), and of the reds, Pinotage. But successful wines are now made from Pinot Noir, Cabernet Sauvignon, Chardonnay, and Sauvignon Blanc.

South America

CHILE

A great success story, partly due to the climate, partly due to the good fortune of having original French vinestock which has not been attacked by phylloxera, and a good deal to do with good winemaking and marketing. In the central section of this attenuated country, the vineyards, wedged between the Pacific Ocean and its benevolent breezes and the shelter of the mighty Andes, is produced excellent Cabernet Sauvignon, top class Chardonnay, Merlot, and Sauvignon Blanc; all expressive of their varietal origin, and good value.

ARGENTINA

Astonishingly, for long a prolific producer of wine, the fifth biggest in the world, only recently have the Argentinians made wine to an acceptable international standard. In the inland Mendoza region, to the east of the Andes, the principal red has been made from the Malbec grape though Cabernet Sauvignon and other better known varietals are more and more used. A country whose wines are improving fast.

England

Pioneered in the 1950s, small vineyards now abound in southern England, the best sweeping from Norfolk in the east to Wiltshire in the west. Unfortunately, the main hazard for the English grower is still the weather – grapes rarely ripen fully. Several early ripening white grapes are grown, among which Müller-Thurgau has been the most popular, also Seyval or Seyve-Villard. The best have decent fruit and zestful acidity. Reds are not a success.

The senses of sight, smell, and taste

Tasting is the introduction of wine to our senses: sight, smell and taste.
Emile Peynaud

Sense of sight

Those fortunate to have eyesight employ this sense every minute of their waking day. Our eyes have plenty of practice. Even colour awareness, for example, which may not be as fully developed as an artist's, is normally at a high level, mainly because of constant use. The enormous advantage that colour has over smell and taste is that it can be so much more easily described, recorded or matched, and conveyed from one person to another.* In the last resort it can be accurately reproduced.

On the other hand, the senses of smell and taste are rarely so high or so continuously employed. Indeed, the level of awareness can be abysmally low. This is partly owing to the fact that the sense of smell is easily fatigued (after only a short time a worker in a chocolate factory or a tannery does not notice the smell) and partly because it is less frequently exercised.

Flavour is a compound of taste and smell, yet although the sensitivity and selectivity of the latter sense is infinitely high, it is the least consciously applied. In relation to wine, most people "taste" – in a superficially literal sense – but very few deliberately and consciously smell the wine first, let alone derive any positive information or pleasure from that act. What is far too little known is that a great deal of what one wants, or needs, to know about wine can be detected from its appearance and bouquet alone. The actual taste on the palate basically confirms the impressions that sight and smell have previously conveyed and adds to the sum total.

Sense of smell

Smell is perhaps the most basic and most primitive of all the senses; more than any other it invokes memory in a particularly direct manner. The "smell-brain", due to its direct contact with the memory areas, can act as an immediate catalyst to recognition and identification. This accounts for the value of the first impression that, justifiably, can be relied upon by experienced tasters.

Let me deal now in some detail with the mechanics of smell. Physically, this is what happens: the stimulus that excites the sense of smell results from certain substances, in solution, coming into contact with myriads of

**A complete and universally accepted scientific analysis, classification, and description of smells and tastes, despite a mass of multidisciplinary research and enquiries, appears to defy solution. Perhaps, slightly out of context, I can quote the last sentence of the epilogue of Dr Roland Harper's* Odour Description and Odour Classification: *"Perhaps at present this remains more of an art than a science."*

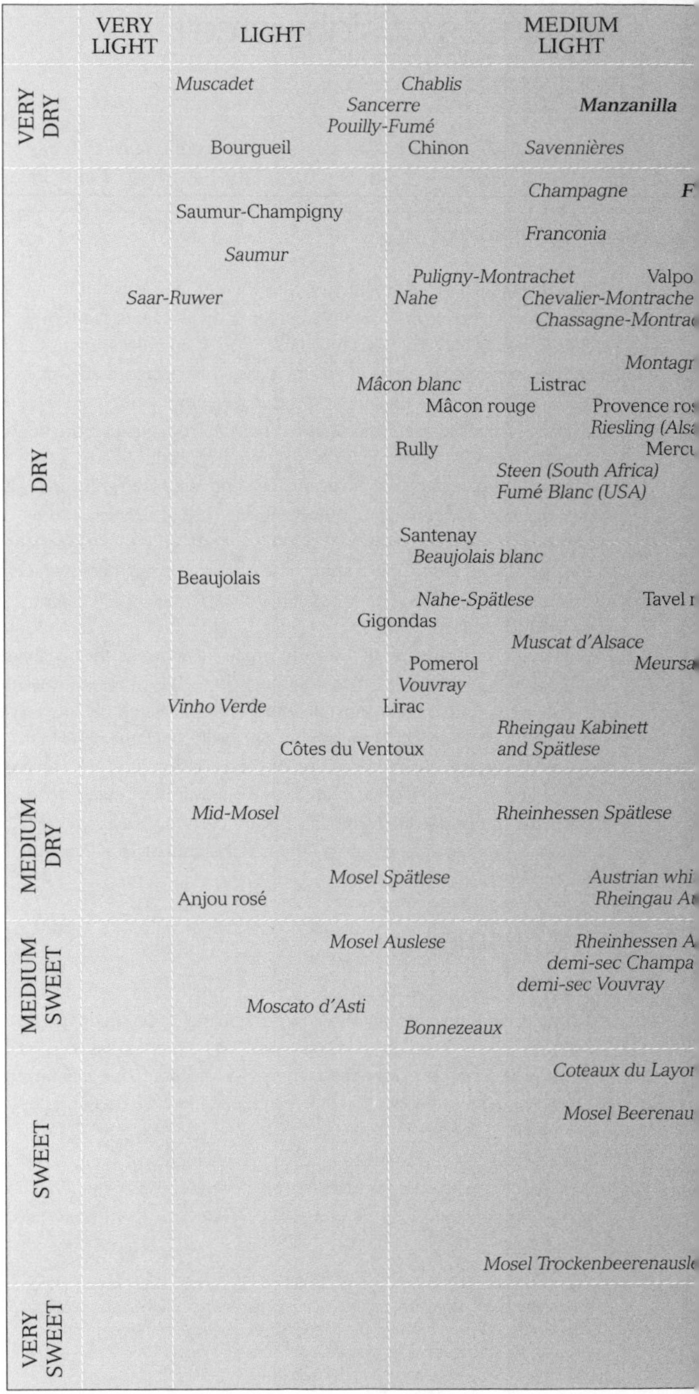

	VERY LIGHT	LIGHT	MEDIUM LIGHT
VERY DRY		*Muscadet* *Sancerre* *Pouilly-Fumé* Bourgueil	*Chablis* ***Manzanilla*** Chinon *Savennières*
DRY	*Saar-Ruwer*	Saumur-Champigny *Saumur* *Mâcon blanc* Beaujolais Gigondas *Vinho Verde* Lirac Côtes du Ventoux	*Champagne* ***F*** *Franconia* *Puligny-Montrachet* Valpo *Nahe* *Chevalier-Montrache* *Chassagne-Montra* *Montagr* Listrac Mâcon rouge Provence ro *Riesling (Als* Rully Merc *Steen (South Africa)* *Fumé Blanc (USA)* Santenay *Beaujolais blanc* *Nahe-Spätlese* Tavel r *Muscat d'Alsace* Pomerol *Meursa* *Vouvray* *Rheingau Kabinett and Spätlese*
MEDIUM DRY		*Mid-Mosel* *Mosel Spätlese* Anjou rosé	*Rheinhessen Spätlese* *Austrian whi* *Rheingau A*
MEDIUM SWEET		*Mosel Auslese* *Moscato d'Asti*	*Rheinhessen A* *demi-sec Champa* *demi-sec Vouvray* *Bonnezeaux*
SWEET			*Coteaux du Layo* *Mosel Beerenau* *Mosel Trockenbeerenausl*
VERY SWEET			

Key to typefaces: Red and rosé wine; *white wine;* **red fortified wine;** ***white fortified***

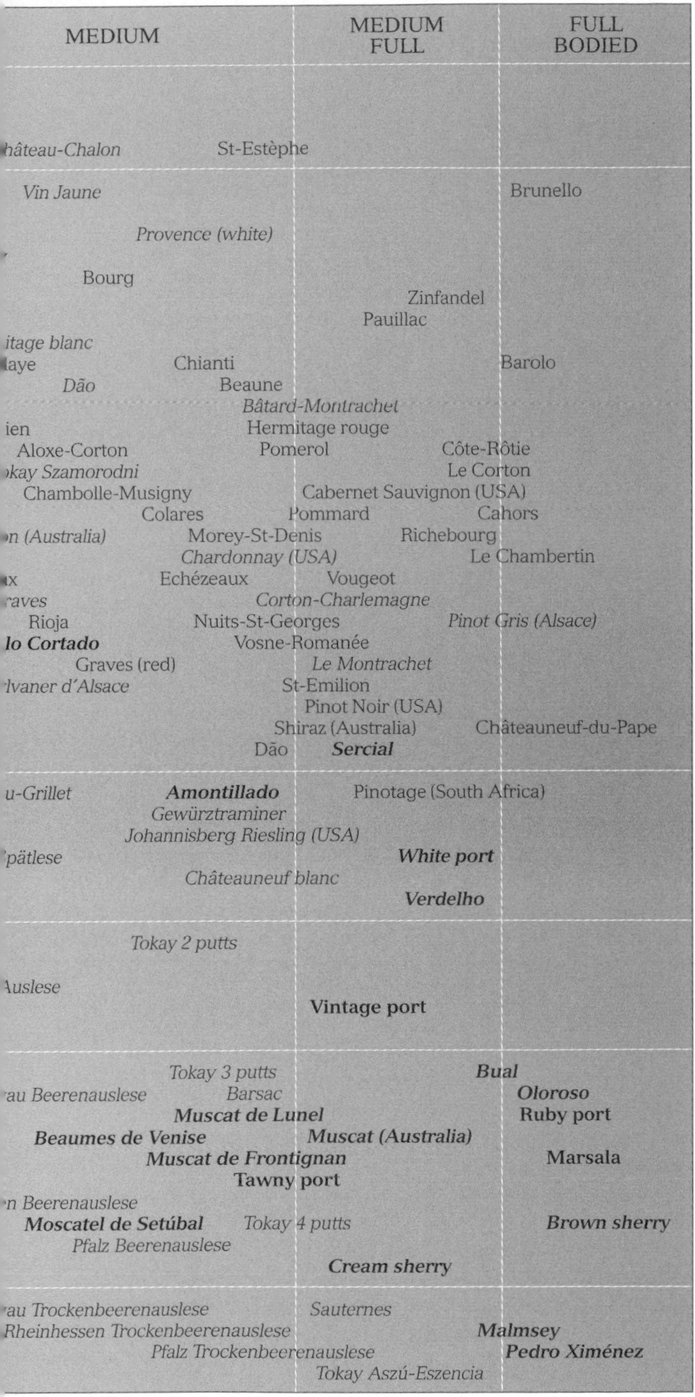

MEDIUM | MEDIUM FULL | FULL BODIED

hâteau-Chalon St-Estèphe

Vin Jaune Brunello

Provence (white)

Bourg

Zinfandel

Pauillac

itage blanc

laye Chianti Barolo

Dão Beaune

Bâtard-Montrachet

ien Hermitage rouge

Aloxe-Corton Pomerol Côte-Rôtie

okay Szamorodni Le Corton

Chambolle-Musigny Cabernet Sauvignon (USA)

Colares Pommard Cahors

n (Australia) Morey-St-Denis Richebourg

Chardonnay (USA) Le Chambertin

x Echézeaux Vougeot

raves *Corton-Charlemagne*

Rioja Nuits-St-Georges *Pinot Gris (Alsace)*

lo Cortado Vosne-Romanée

Graves (red) *Le Montrachet*

lvaner d'Alsace St-Emilion

Pinot Noir (USA)

Shiraz (Australia) Châteauneuf-du-Pape

Dão ***Sercial***

u-Grillet ***Amontillado*** Pinotage (South Africa)

Gewürztraminer

Johannisberg Riesling (USA)

pätlese ***White port***

Châteauneuf blanc

Verdelho

Tokay 2 putts

Auslese

Vintage port

Tokay 3 putts ***Bual***

au Beerenauslese *Barsac* ***Oloroso***

Muscat de Lunel **Ruby port**

Beaumes de Venise ***Muscat (Australia)***

Muscat de Frontignan **Marsala**

Tawny port

n Beerenauslese

Moscatel de Setúbal *Tokay 4 putts* ***Brown sherry***

Pfalz Beerenauslese

Cream sherry

au Trockenbeerenauslese *Sauternes*

Rheinhessen Trockenbeerenauslese ***Malmsey***

Pfalz Trockenbeerenauslese ***Pedro Ximénez***

Tokay Aszú-Eszencia

and ***liqueur wine***

highly complex cells in the nose. Such substances usually enter the nose in the form of vapour. In the case of wine they are conveyed by volatile esters and aldehydes. At this stage they are taken over by the olfactory system. The first pair of cranial nerves are called olfactory nerves. They begin as specialized olfactory cells in the lining of the upper part of the nose. Fibrils from these cells pass up into the olfactory bulbs, lying in the base of the skull. From the bulbs, the olfactory tracts – thick bands of white brain matter – pass backwards to enter the brain, and the fibres contained in the tracts are brought into relationship with nerve cells in certain parts of the brain. The original stimulus at the nerve endings is, in effect, converted into a sensation for the brain to interpret.

An interesting fact is that over-prolonged exposure to one smell may reduce the effectiveness of that smell, but that other smells may be readily detected. From a practical point of view this means that it is pointless to sniff too long or too frequently at one wine. If the first impression is lost, it is probably better to move on to the next wine, then move back to the original or tackle it again after a rest (*see also* pages 101–2).

In my experience, passing one's nose over the glass and lightly inhaling will often yield virtually all the bouquet has to offer. Nevertheless, it is sensible to swirl the wine gently and smell it again more carefully. Sometimes it is necessary to sniff vigorously and inhale deeply, either to determine whether there is fruit under the unyielding exterior or, perhaps, to isolate a fault in a poor wine.

Chambré-ing red wines, or cupping the glass in one's hands, has a good practical reason. There is evidence that whatever the state of the substance one is having to smell, its appreciation depends on that substance passing into the solution with which the olfactory cells are normally bathed. But the higher the molecular weight of the wine, the greater the need to encourage the process of vaporization – this is accomplished by gently raising its temperature. When wine is warmed, convectional currents arise, moving the wine and releasing its bouquet.

A cold start accounts for the "dumbness" of a massively constituted red wine, even if it is mature. It also accounts for the remarkable aftertaste and lingering farewell that arises from the naso-pharynx as the mouth-warmed wine passes down the throat and the released volatile esters rise though the back nasal passages.

Conversely, light wines with low extract and weight do not need to be warmed. Those which are light but relatively high-toned (such as a Mosel of a moderate year) will release bouquet with an impact that is immediate but which lacks depth. They rely not on an aftertaste but on a high degree of natural acidity to give the wine a finish – to which chilling adds crispness.

Some pungent substances have a more physical impact, stimulating the nerve endings in a tactile sense. For example, sulphur dioxide can be detected as a prickle in the nose even though its presence in the wine may not be strong enough to affect the olfactory system. Certain of the higher alcohols can also have a similar effect, producing a peppery feeling rather than a smell. Acetic acid can be both felt and smelled.

Sense of taste

The sense of taste depends on the stimulation of organs known as taste-buds. These are mainly situated in the tongue, though a few are found in the soft palate, and their sensitivity varies. The nerves connected with the taste buds carry impulses to the nerve centre in the medulla (which is the name for the lowest part of the brain stem at the top of the spinal cord), whence they are carried to the parts of the brain towards the tip and inner sides of the temporal lobe – in close relation to the area of the brain which is concerned with the sense of smell.

To cause the necessary stimulus, a substance must be in solution, and the sensation it evokes relates to one, or a combination, of the four so-called primary elements of taste*: sweetness (best appreciated at the tip of the tongue), sourness† (upper edges of the tongue), bitterness (at the back), and saltiness (at the side).

If one understands which parts of the palate detect which basic tastes, this makes it quite apparent that to "peck" at wine, *i.e.* to take a very small sip or leave only the tip of the tongue in contact, will not enable the taster to appreciate more than a fraction of the wine's physical characteristics. A reasonable mouthful must be taken and it must be swirled round the mouth so that all the taste-buds can get to work on it. Some experienced tasters take a large mouthful and draw air across their palate, often with rather an off-putting guzzling noise. This distributes the wine across the whole of the palate and allows the volatile scents to ascend the back of the nose for the olfactory nerves to play their part.

A word of warning about a common problem which is rarely discussed by other tasters and yet one to which, I must confess, I am frequently susceptible. Beware of scalding the mouth with hot liquids; the wine will taste abnormally sharp due to the acidity biting the raw tongue.

Sense of touch

Tactile impressions implying the use of fingers and hands, do not, strictly speaking, apply to the tasting process. Nevertheless, wine produces reactions which have certainly nothing to do with sight, smell, or taste, and are as equally certainly tactile.

For example, the weight (body) of the wine in the mouth; the silkiness and velvety texture of certain wines; the evaluation of extract and components detected physically while in the mouth; and the prickle of carbon dioxide in the lightly sparkling or fully sparkling state. Also, certain chemical reactions occuring in the mouth and nose affect the tactile sense more than the sense of smell. Sulphur dioxide, already mentioned, is a good example of this.

**According to Dr Roland Harper, "There is relatively little evidence to support the concept of primary tastes".* (The Human Senses in Action, 1972.)

†Sourness, in a wine context, has a derogatory connotation. Acidity, an essential component, is the word English wine tasters use (see *"Full glossary"*).

Sense of hearing

The sense of hearing does not seriously enter into winetasting. There is nothing like the delightful crunchiness of a crisp biscuit – unless it be the anticipatory pop of a cork, the sound of pouring and tinkling of glasses, the fizz of Champagne, or the ministering sizzle of Alka-Seltzer the following morning! As for those audible signs of approval, considered good manners at the Chinese dinner table, they have no part, whether involuntary or voluntary, in polite wine society.

Gastric stimulation

Before leaving the physical element of winetasting, it is perhaps worth mentioning an important effect: the stimulation of the gastric juices. Quite apart from its health-giving natural properties, wine is a superlative aid to digestion. The appetite is whetted by the smell and taste of a refreshingly youthful white wine, and by the tingling dryness, the acidity and even the slight bitterness of many reds. The nerves of taste and smell are stimulated, which in turn increase the activity of the salivary glands. Also, through a reflex nervous action, the wine markedly increases the amount of digestive juice secreted in the walls of the stomach; it flows more rapidly and the movements of the stomach are speeded up. This stimulation of the muscular wall of the stomach extends to that of the bowel, which then greatly aids the digestion of the accompanying food.

But let us turn to the act of tasting...

The elements of tasting

Your true amateur sips his wine; as he lingers over each separate mouthful, he obtains from each the sum total of pleasure which he would have experienced had he emptied his glass at a single draught.

Brillat-Savarin

THE PHYSIOLOGY OF TASTE, 1825

The order in which one tastes a wine is based on the natural physical movement of the glass from table to mouth. First of all, the glass is picked up and the wine is looked at. This is stage one. As it is raised towards the mouth the nose catches the bouquet – stage two. Then the lips meets the rim of the glass and the literal tasting, stage three, commences.

But, over and above this, there is a correlation between what one sees, smells, and tastes. The last tends to confirm visual and nasal impressions. The logical conclusion is stage four, the summary of overall impressions, and the final verdict.

Before starting, make sure that the glasses are suitable and the lighting adequate.

GLASSES FOR TASTING

If you do not possess an ideal tasting glass, just use a conventional, tulip-shaped, crystal-clear wine glass, not a fancy or coloured one. An ideal tasting glass is one which conforms to a specific design laid down by an international panel for official standards organizations. Such a glass is illustrated on the following page. There are several acceptable variations on this theme, but this is the glass which has been adopted by all the major European institutions for use in recognized tasting competitions.

If tasting a range of wines, use matching glasses of a generous size and rinse them out with wine if they are at all musty or unclean, or if they have been previously washed with detergent. Pour an equal measure in each so that the relative depth and hue can be seen at a glance. Do not fill the glass more than half full, as it will be easier to tilt above a white table top, an essential manoeuvre if the informative colour at the rim of the wine is to be seen clearly. It will also enable the wine to be swirled around in the glass without spilling, collecting the volatile substances prior to nosing.

Pick up the glass by its stem or foot – not by the bowl. This makes it easier to examine the wine, particularly if held in front of a lighted candle. It also avoids the influence of body warmth and has the minor virtue of avoiding finger marks on the sides of the glass. (Handling old bottles can be a dirty business; wine itself tends to be sticky if dripping or spilt.)

LIGHTING

Daylight is best, preferably a good north light, as artificial lighting can affect both hue and tone. In particular, avoid fluorescent lighting; it makes red wine look unhealthily brown, and even blue-tinged. Candlelight enhances the appearance of wine but for a serious tasting the only benefit of a candle is to reveal the true degree of clarity of the wine; thus it is useful in a cellar when young wine is drawn from the cask, or when decanting a bottle.

The ideal tasting glass

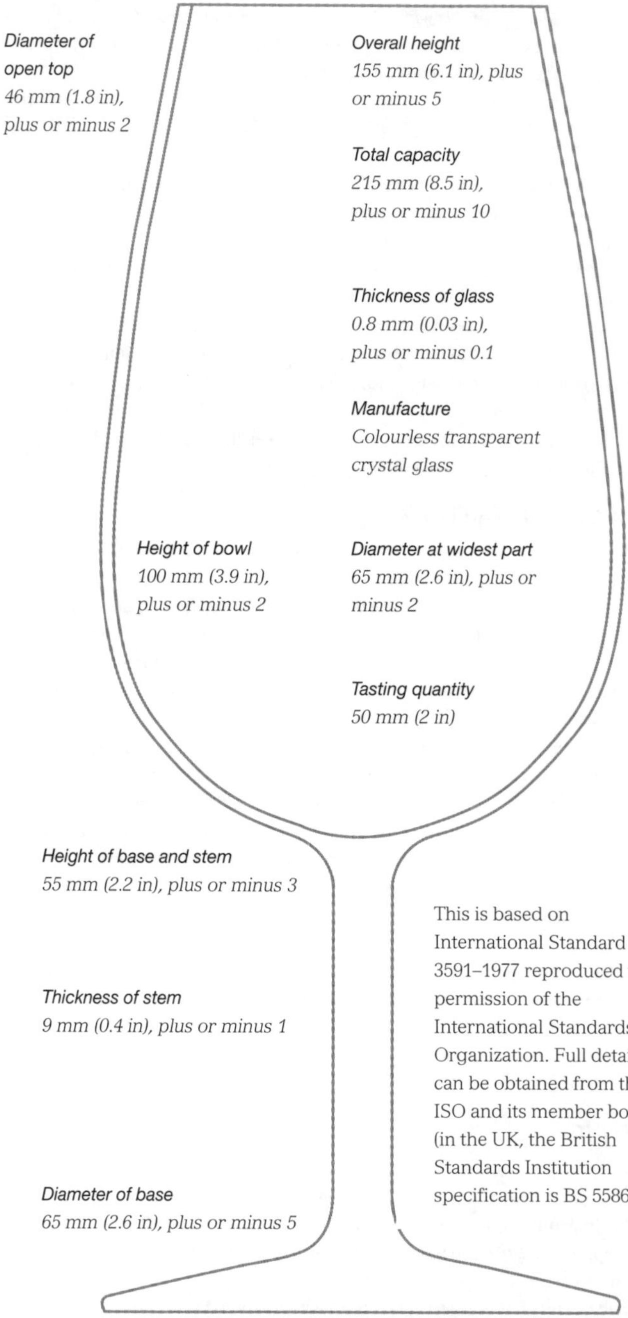

Diameter of open top
46 mm (1.8 in), plus or minus 2

Overall height
155 mm (6.1 in), plus or minus 5

Total capacity
215 mm (8.5 in), plus or minus 10

Thickness of glass
0.8 mm (0.03 in), plus or minus 0.1

Manufacture
Colourless transparent crystal glass

Height of bowl
100 mm (3.9 in), plus or minus 2

Diameter at widest part
65 mm (2.6 in), plus or minus 2

Tasting quantity
50 mm (2 in)

Height of base and stem
55 mm (2.2 in), plus or minus 3

Thickness of stem
9 mm (0.4 in), plus or minus 1

Diameter of base
65 mm (2.6 in), plus or minus 5

This is based on International Standard ISO 3591–1977 reproduced with permission of the International Standards Organization. Full details can be obtained from the ISO and its member bodies (in the UK, the British Standards Institution specification is BS 5586).

TEMPERATURE

Make sure the temperature of the wine is correct: room temperature for reds (including port), cold for rosés and whites (around 7–10°C or 45–50°F). The actual room temperature will naturally vary from place to place and with the time of year. The range could be anywhere between 16 and 18°C (60–65°F).* Make sure the glasses for red wine are at the same temperature and not brought out of a cold cupboard at the last minute.

It is worth noting that dry white wines cool more quickly than sweet: Sauternes needs more time in an ice-bucket – sprinkling sea salt on the ice can be a very effective aid to cooling. But best of all, in my experience, is to have an ice-box or refrigerator at the right temperature and then transfer the wine to an open-topped thermos flask. There is an excellent one on the market called Vinicool®.

Stage 1: appearance

Under the heading of appearance,† the taster looks at three facets: colour, depth, and clarity. As each of these is examined, the reader is advised to refer to the illustrated examples on pages 145–160.

COLOUR OR HUE

Most table wines fall into one of three basic categories: red, white, or rosé. Fortified wines vary; sherry is technically a white wine and ranges from pale straw-yellow to deep brown. Port may be red or white, the former ranging from deep purple through ruby to pale tawny. The main thing to bear in mind is that the colour should be appropriate for the type and age of wine.

Red wines

What we call a red wine will, in fact, vary in hue from deep purple through various shades of red to mahogany or even amber, depending mainly on its state of maturity, the vintage, and the type of wine. The length of fermentation and the time the grape-juice is kept on the skins have a major influence, as does the time kept in cask. The red colour comes from a group of pigments called anthocyanins extracted from the grape skins by the action of alcohol. Different grape varieties have varying types of anthocyanins. These free anthocyanins provide most of the (purple) colour of a young wine, but then, in effect, they fade or merge into larger tannin molecules which combine with the anthocyanins to change the colour to red, then red-brown as the wine ages. Oxidation speeds up this process. Dead colouring matter is precipitated and forms part of the sediment of mature wine.

Purple Indicates extreme youth and/or immaturity. Almost all young red wine in cask will have this colour. The time taken in bottle to lose its strong purple tinge depends on the initial depth of colour.

Ruby Self-descriptive. The colour of a young port or a deepish red Bordeaux or burgundy, having lost its pristine flush of purple.

**Professor Peynaud's ideal tasting room is 18°C or 65°F with sixty per cent humidity.*

†I use the term in its broadest sense: that which is perceived by the eye, and not in a limited sense like "clarity".

Red In vinous terms red is the colour approximating "claret". It indicates the transitional period between youth and the acquisition of maturity and bottle-age. The lower the pH the greater the amount of active pigments and the higher the intensity of colour. A particularly intense red is, therefore, often indicative of high acid content. Max Léglise calls cherry-red the "cruising" colour of a wine in perfect health in fruit-aroma stage.

Red-brown In a table wine this hue indicates maturity (for example, red Bordeaux with five years or more in bottle, burgundy three years or more – depending on the weight and quality of the vintage). A brown tinge can also result from baked vines after a hot summer, also from artificially heated and "cooked" wine, *i.e.* during fermentation, or from oxidation owing to overexposure to air in cask.

Mahogany A more mellow, subtle red-brown indicating maturity (red Bordeaux with ten to twenty years' bottle-age, burgundy of a moderate vintage with over ten years' bottle-age).

Tawny A term, like ruby, usually associated with port. It describes a hue tHat has been attained thvough loss of colour over a period of years in cask, a natural but expensive maturing process. Cheap commercial tawnies are made by blending white wines with red.

Amber-brown Indicates either a wine of very considerable age or one that is prematurely old and/or oxidized. Once the remaining healthy ruddy glow fades, the wine is usually dead.

White wines

Whites wines range from virtual colourlessness through the palest yellow-green and deeper shades of yellow, to gold and deep amber-brown.

Dry white wines usually start off life pale in colour and, unlike red wines, slowly gain colour with age. Sweet wines generally start off a deeper shade of yellow, turn to gold, and then take on an amber-brown tinge with age. Phenolic compounds provide the yellow pigment of young white wines, and these vary according to the grape used (for example, low in Rieslings) and winemaking methods. Higher phenolics can be produced by grape ripeness, by skins affected with botrytis producing the yellow-gold of young Sauternes and Trockenbeerenauslesen, by the length of time the young wine spends in wooden casks, and by the type of wood used.

Young natural sherry is a pale straw-yellow, the deeper shades being the result of ageing and/or blending. Practically all the dark oloroso and brown sherries gain their colour from added wine of one sort or another.

Pale yellow-green A distinct green tinge is quite common in youthful white wines due to residual chlorophyll, and is a particular, if not essential, characteristic of a Chablis or a young Mosel. It is rarely seen in the white wines made in hot climates.

Straw-yellow A pleasant lively colour common to the majority of white wines, particularly the drier ones. In Burgundy, Meursault tends to be more yellow than Puligny-Montrachet, and in Alsace, Gewurztraminer more yellow than Riesling.

Yellow-gold An abnormal colour for a young dry white wine but most frequently seen in the sweeter varieties, such as Sauternes and high-quality German dessert wines of Beerenauslese and TBA quality.

Gold Generally indicates either a lusciously sweet wine, or one with considerable bottle-age (for example, a white burgundy, usually pale straw when young, will develop a slight golden sheen after about six years in bottle).

Yellow-brown or old gold The colour of many dessert wines, fortified ones in particular. However, a brown or orange tinge in a white table wine indicates considerable bottle-age, overmaturity, and other degrees of oxidation. Many white burgundies will take on an unhealthy brown tinge after about twelve years in bottle; yet a fine Sauternes may not develop it for thirty years or more.

Maderized This word is used to describe the appearance and condition of overmaturity and oxidation. A maderized white wine presents a dull, drab appearance, with pallid yellow-brown colour.

Brown Probably well past drinking (unless it is a sherry of that name or the tawny-brown of a very old port).

Rosé wines

Wines described as rosé can vary considerably in colour and depth. Each district has its own style, depending on the type of grape used and on the method of making. The better rosés are made from black grapes, the skins being left in contact with the fermenting grape juice just long enough for red pigment to be extracted. Cheap rosés are sometimes a blend of red and white wines. Some commercial blends of pink Champagne are made by adding red wine from the Montagne de Reims.

The colour of a rosé is half its charm. A rosé wine is usually drunk young, for if allowed to age it would lose its freshness of colour and taste. Some rosés begin life the colour of onion skin, a characteristic of those wines appropriately termed *pélure d'oignon* and *vin gris*.

Rosé The perfect rosé should not look like a watered-down red wine, nor should it support an excess of orange or purple. It should be positive, bright, and appealing.

Orange Some grape varieties produce a distinct orange tint. Pure orange is not a desirable hue although a pleasant orange-pink is quite normal and characteristic of many rosés from the Loire. Orange is often more marked in Provence and the hot south.

Pink A self-descriptive hue, suggestive of artificiality. Any suspicion of a blue tinge is indicative of unhealthiness, probably from bad fining or some contamination.

DEPTH OF COLOUR

Although the basic deepness or paleness of a wine depends to a certain extent on its origin, the relative depth of colour will give a good indication of its physical content.

It is sometimes difficult to judge the comparative depth of colour of two wines. One method is to fill each of the glasses to the same height, place them side by side and look at each from a position vertically above. Alternatively, arrange a light behind the glasses and compare the relative depth of colour of the shadow cast by each wine on a white table top, a little-known but very effective way for all colours of wine.

Red wines

Depth, in association with the actual colour or hue, will also give an indication of the age and maturity of a red wine. For example, a very deep, nearly opaque, red-purple wine will almost certainly have more than its fair share of tannins and other natural components. A colour like this will only be seen in a well-made wine of a fine vintage, its properties being derived from rich, fully ripe grapes with sun-thickened skins. The converse applies equally: a pale-red wine results from too high a yield per hectare, from hasty vinification, or a poor year in which the grapes have failed to mature and whose skins are thin and deficient in pigment. As red wine matures, colouring matter is deposited. The wine becomes less deep, eventually pale, and faded.

White wines

Depth of colour is relatively unimportant in young dry white wines. The variations are comparatively small and connotations usually inconclusive. A very pale Mosel, for example, is likely to be neither better nor worse than one which is medium-pale. White wines tend to deepen with bottle-age. This is due to phenolic molecules joining together, the larger molecules having deeper amber-gold and brown colours. Oxidation will effectively speed up the process.

The depth of colour of sweet wines is more meaningful. Care must be taken not to confuse the deep gold of an old Sauternes of a great vintage with maderization. Château d'Yquem of the 1921 and 1929 vintages is very deep – deep gold, not deep brown – indicative of the extraordinarily high initial sugar content and extract. The point is that these vintages were deep in colour when young. Beware also of drawing a wrong conclusion from a pale old Sauternes. This is indicative of either a lesser vintage and/or over-sulphuring prior to bottling. The latter acts as a preservative, inhibiting development and colour change. The use of steel vats rather than wood also tends to reduce the colour.

Other aspects of appearance

CLARITY

This is of prime importance in the various stages of development of all wines from the time of fermentation, during cask life, through to the time of bottling. Thereafter, white wines should be star-bright and trouble-free. Red wines are normally expected to throw a sediment in bottle. Fine wines often have extra lustre and luminosity. The clarity of wine is best judged by holding the glass in front of a candle or some other bright light.*

**The rather attractive silver* tastevins *which are sold in Burgundian souvenir shops (and used by tourists as ashtrays) are, in fact, traditional tasting vessels with a peculiar usefulness. The circular indentations in the shallow sides reflect candlelight across the metal base to reveal at a glance in an ill-lit cellar the clarity of the new wine drawn from the cask. A* tastevin *is also more portable and less fragile than a glass, though it is somewhat pretentious to take one to a normal tasting; a proper tasting glass is more useful. (In the Burgundy and Beaujolais regions, the* tastevin *also has symbolic guild connotations.)*

Upper surface The upper surface of the wine in the glass is worth inspection. It should, of course, be bright. If it appears dull, iridescent, or bitty, trouble may be indicated. With very old wine, I also look out for the tell-tale bead of persistent small bubbles around the meniscus, which generally gives advance warning that the wine is cracking up.

Cloudiness Hold up the glass to the light, or against a candle. A dull cloudiness or obstinate haze of suspended matter in bottled wine is a bad sign; in normal circumstances, the wine should be returned to the supplier. A permanent cloudiness or dull opacity is due to metallic contamination, usually an copper or iron casse, or yeasts. Incidentally, think carefully before condemning a cloudy red wine. Was it recently delivered or the sediment disturbed when carried up from the cellar hastily and clumsily?

Old vintage port usually has a heavy sediment, or "crust", and even when carefully decanted may still have "fliers" or "beeswing" (very descriptive) in it. The latter are normal (and tasteless) and can be ignored.

Cork, not corked Tiny pieces of floating cork are harmless; so are most forms of sediment which settle easily in the bottle. Bits of cork in the wine may be due to a bad corking machine or, more usually, to the careless use of a poor corkscrew. Wine with cork floating on it is not corked – an ignorant misunderstanding in restaurants which can lead to fatuous and unnecessary complaints. Just pick the cork out with a knife or spoon.

Crystals Flakes of tartaric acid crystals are sometimes seen in fortified wine and white table wine. They have usually been caused by a sudden fall in temperature. These flakes or crystals generally settle quickly, are quite harmless and do not impair the flavour of the wine.

Limpidity A really beautiful limpid colour is often indicative of a really fine wine, whereas an ordinary wine might have a dull, nondescript, lacklustre appearance.

Grades of clarity range from brilliant, star-bright, bright, and clear to dull, bitty, hazy, and cloudy.

Intensity Last but not least, the intensity of colour – meaning the strength of colour at the rim, as opposed to the more usual tailing off to a watery edge – is in relation to red wines and old fortified wines in particular an indication of quality, strength, and extract.

Legs or tears I have never been a "leg" man myself; indeed, there seems to be some confusion over the term in relation to wine. Full-bodied wines, those with high extract and alcohol content, form "legs" or "tears" – globules with extended tails – which fall slowly to the surface of the wine after the glass has been swirled. This can, with some justification, be considered to presage richness, but I personally prefer to rely on my palate.

Incidentally, carelessly washed and dried glasses can play havoc with the meniscus. "Legs" can also be created by the surface tension pump which is due to the evaporation of ethyl alcohol at the meniscus or rim which mysteriously draws up a small quantity of wine.

LEVEL OR ULLAGE

Although this relates to the appearance of wine in the bottle rather than in the glass, it is appropriate to refer to it here. A lower level than normal can be due to several factors.

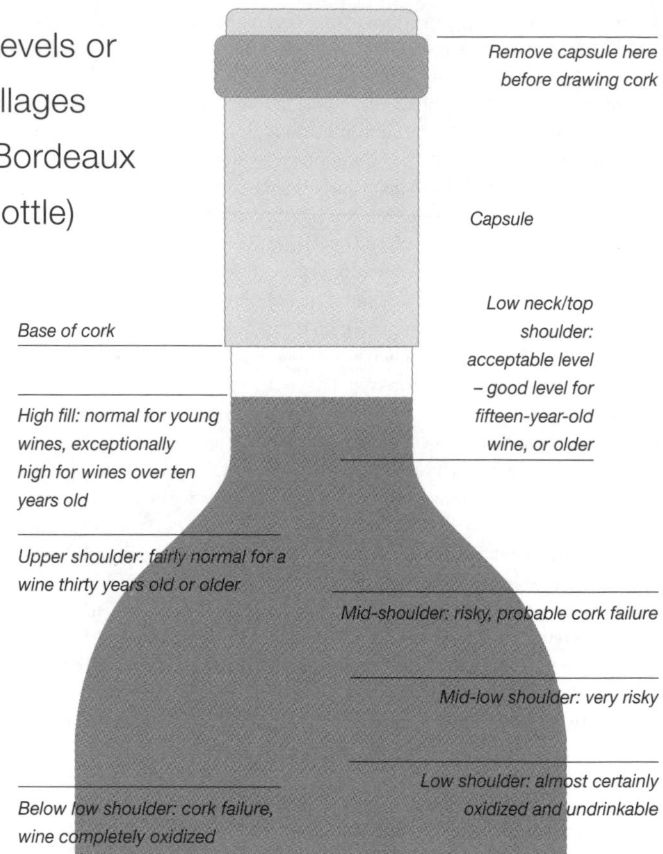

Short fill Result of sloppy bottling and careless inspection; level is at low neck or around upper shoulder. Usually little to worry about.

Reduction A natural contraction* which can occur in bottle over a period of time. In my experience mature burgundies can show a 4.5–7 cm (1.8–2.8 in) ullage without deleterious effect.

Cork failure The commonest cause of ullage is cork failure due to cork weevil, or lack of springiness due to old age. Cork weevil is not uncommon, particularly in badly maintained private cellars. It is about the only thing which will affect the condition of old vintage port, particularly if the protective wax seal has broken or worn away. The weevil will bore holes in the cork and let air in; the wine will become acetic, or at least tainted.

Corks, like human bodies, eventually lose their suppleness and firmness with age. After twenty years or so, the elasticity of cork weakens, though high-quality long claret corks can protect wine for a century.

**I understand that if a gallon of water and a gallon of alcohol are mixed, the combined total measures less than two gallons.*

Uneven ullages, quite common with very old wine, are almost always due to cork failure. Recorking – a standard practice in the great châteaux and domaine cellars – is the answer. Failing this, regular waxing of seals and capsules, while otherwise remaining unmoved in a cold, slightly damp cellar, will preserve the corks and wine. Ullaged bottles can turn out surprisingly well, as sometimes the air in the space has not harmed the wine. If the cork is not musty and the wine has a good colour, it may miraculously survive even if old and venerable. But it must be of high quality to begin with.*

Old Champagne Can look ullaged, but if the cork and foil are sound, this ullage generally turns out to be carbon dioxide out of solution. No longer sparkling, the Champagne will have turned calm and golden-sheened – much beloved of English connoisseurs, somewhat to the exasperation of the French.

Stage 2: nose or bouquet

The importance and value of nosing a wine are generally underrated, for a great deal of valuable information about any wine may be gained from the smell alone. The first impression is generally the most telling. The more mature the wine, the more important the nose becomes.

The best procedure is to take hold of the stem of the glass lightly and, keeping its base on the table, rotate it briskly. This exposes the maximum surface area of wine, encouraging the release by vaporization of its esters. It also neutralizes the smell of an unclean glass. Bring the glass to the nose and concentrate on the first fleeting impression. Is it clean and fresh? Are there any very positive characteristics: the grape aroma, high, mouth-watering acidity, etc.? Next, give the glass another swirl and give a number of short, sharp sniffs. This will reveal depths of fruit and other salient features which were not, perhaps, noticed at first. However, I do not recommend very deep inhalation, as this merely deadens the senses.†

The smell of wine can be of two types. The first is that which reminds one of another smell; the second is that which, with experience, is recognizable as a more-or-less pure chemical substance or compound. In essence, however, the winetaster has to learn to detect and recognize different grape aromas, youthfulness and maturity, pure wine scents, and, with more experience, complex overtones.

It is difficult enough to analyse and describe most common-or-garden smells, even more so the subtleties of a refined bouquet. And if it is difficult to pin down the elements of bouquet, it is almost impossible to convey them to another person. Some of the characteristics are obvious and easily describable; some can only be recognized by an experienced taster. The following aspects should be examined, preferably in this order:

**I frequently find ullaged bottles in old cellars. If ullages, in a bin of one wine, are fairly uniform, and the corks and caps appear sound, I do not worry overmuch.*

†The late Allan Sichel favoured "short, sharp sniffs with his mouth open". Frankly, I find this does not work for me with wine, although I have recently discovered that it is very effective for smelling brandy which, with nose alone, so often gives a too sharply spirity impression.

CLEANLINESS

Basically what is meant is that the wine should smell like wine, pure and unadulterated. Anything redolent of bad cabbages, old socks, vinegar, almond kernels, pear drops, or any clearly extraneous or foreign smells should be regarded as suspect, to say the least. In practice this is an automatic reflex action.

Sulphur dioxide, quite common in European white wines (it is reminiscent of burnt matchsticks or the whiff of a coke oven), is regarded as more of a nuisance than an off-smell. Aeration, decanting, and swirling in the glass all lessen the effect. If no off-odours are readily apparent, one passes on to the more positive wine smells.

GRAPE VARIETY

The experienced taster will next look out for the first major clue to the origin of the wine: the characteristic "varietal" (grape) aroma.* The classic noble vines, Cabernet Sauvignon, Pinot Noir, Riesling, Gewurztraminer, Sauvignon Blanc, and so on, produce their own individual aromas. However, even these are not always easy to detect, and the only way to memorize them is to smell first-rate examples until their characteristics are firmly lodged in the mind (*see* pages 15–20 and "Full glossary").

Wines made from lesser grape varieties and from minor districts often have a less distinct and recognizable aroma. More often it will be just vaguely varietal and, if indistinguishable but pleasant, will merely be described as "vinous".

YOUTH, AGE, AND MATURITY

The age of a wine can be accurately judged on the nose by an experienced taster. It is not as difficult as it might appear at first and, as always, the comparison of good specimens of different vintages is the best way to learn.

The physical components of young wine tend to be pronounced and raw, as they have had little time to settle down and blend together. Acidity in young wine has a mouth-watering effect. A raw cooking-apple smell indicates excess malic acid and is frequently found in young, immature white wines, particularly from poorer vintage years in northerly climes.

As the wine mellows with age, its bouquet becomes noticeably softer and more harmonious. It will also develop what is known as "bottle-age". It is almost impossible to describe bottle-age; in most white wines this shows up as a honeyed quality; red wines become richer and deeper with bottle-age. Complex and harmonious are perhaps the operative words. A wine with too much bottle-age will show deterioration by taking on a flat, dull, toffee-like smell (maderized) or what is known as bottle-stink (oxidation, which can produce a smell like bad cabbages). The point is that bottle-age is all part of the maturing process that is revealed to the taster.

FRUIT

Fruit is a desirable quality, but it should be noted that a wine can be described as fruity without having any trace of grapeyness. A distinctly

**The expressions "aroma" and "bouquet" are used in the senses defined in the "Full glossary". However, both are frequently muddled in usage.*

grapey bouquet is only found in wines made from certain unmistakable grape varieties. High tannin content in a young red wine tends to mask the fruit.

DEPTH AND INTENSITY

A bouquet can be described as light or deep, intense, nondescript, superficial, full, or rounded, depending on the development of the wine. However, care must be taken not to be misled by the "full", *i.e.* fully developed bouquet of a mature but poor-quality wine or, conversely, by the "dumb" or undeveloped bouquet of a high-quality but immature wine.

It is hard to define quality. What one is looking for is an unfolding, an exposure of bouquet that is rich, many-faceted, but soft; forthcoming yet harmonious. And the bouquet of a great wine is not only overwhelmingly beautiful but tends to linger in the glass even when it has been drained to the last drop.

There are many conventional terms used to describe the bouquet of wine. The principal ones are defined in the chapter "How to record tasting notes".

Stage 3: taste

For the beginner, for the analytical drinker, the taste of wine is all-important and probably gives the most pleasure. However, at a serious tasting, the taste, or gustatory stage, should first and foremost confirm conclusions drawn from the appearance and bouquet. The palate is a fairly basic evaluator. In fact, it provides the taster with rather less information than the eye and nose, unless the wine is new in cask. The younger the wine, the more important the palate element becomes. In any case a factor, excess acidity for example, not spotted by the nose may be detected on the palate: a sort of long-stop situation.

As indicated in the previous chapter, there are several points of oral contact which will reveal different taste characteristics. For this reason, one tiny sip is usually inadequate. Do not peck at the wine; take a reasonable mouthful, swirl it round the mouth; then, if at a tasting, spit it out and repeat the process if necessary.

ELEMENTS OF TASTE

I recommend tasting in an orderly way to avoid overlooking vital elements.

Dryness and sweetness A basic and easily judged constituent, particularly important in white wines. Do not be misled by thinness or excessive acidity, which tend to make one underestimate the actual sugar content. There is also an apparent sweetness noticeable in hot-country wines and in the wines of particularly good vintages in northern Europe: in each case, the sweetness derives from fully ripe grapes and from ethyl alcohol, which has a slight sweetening effect.

Acidity Acidity is a major element in the make-up of all wine. It gives a wine purpose, life, zest, and finish. I tend to think of acidity as the nervous system of a wine. Extremes of acidity are, however, undesirable. Excess sugar and glycerol – natural or otherwise – tend to mask the true degree of acidity.

The principal and desirable grape acidity in wine is tartaric. The most undesirable is acetic, which, when present in excess, makes the wine taste vinegary.

Body The weight of wine in the mouth is basically the result of its extract and alcoholic content. This is the "bone structure". Body is an important factor and varies according to the district, vintage, vinification, etc.

Tannins Although disagreeable on the palate (harsh, dry, and mouth-puckering), tannins form an essential element of any young red wine. Tannin is extracted during fermentation from pips and skins, the thickness of the skins of red grapes and length of fermentation having a major bearing. Tannin is also derived from the wood of casks, new oak having the strongest effect. Tannins, hard and soft, are infinitely variable. Tannins precipitate proteins and, as antioxidants, help preserve wine. They are essential for long life.

Tactile Stimuli. Smooth, creamy, velvety qualities can be felt in the mouth; so can astringent elements and the burning sensation of alcohol.

Flavour This is all-important. Even if it is impossible to describe, at least record whether agreeable. The word "typical" should be used sparingly. The intensity and length of flavour are indications of quality.

Balance This is basically what the winemaker, the merchant, and the connoisseur seek. What is meant by balance is that all the components are in harmony with, for example, no excess of acids or tannins at the time when the wine is ready for drinking. The point is that, individually, the components are useless; it is in combination that they become wine and, when complete and in perfect balance, fine wine. Two things have to be borne in mind: one is that the intrinsic components will vary from district to district, from style to style; and that over a period of time in cask, then in bottle, the balance will change subtly.

Take a red Bordeaux: when young, its tannin and acidity will be exposed and raw. It takes time – say five to ten years – for the components of a fine wine to simmer down and marry to become a well-knit, harmonious drink. (It is the job of the merchant and duty of the wine critic to be able to judge the future development of what, to the layperson, is merely a raw, young, red wine.)

In the case of a fine German wine, the grower strives to achieve, almost from the start, a desirable balance of acidity, residual sugar, and alcohol so that it can be early-bottled to capture, for his particular market, the delectable fruity acidity which, with fragrant aroma and bouquet, is the touchstone of fine Rhine and Mosel wines.

Finish A clean, crisp finish is the mark of a well-made wine. Poor-quality wines finish short or tail off to a weak, insubstantial end.

Persistence Top-quality wines have a measurable length of taste, often extending to an aftertaste or "lingering farewell" – a beautiful flavour that remains in the mouth after the wine has been swallowed. The French refer to it as persistence, and measure it with a stopwatch!

Quality, finesse, elegance, breed The elements of quality are represented by the completeness and balance of the various components in the wine. Quality can be assessed by the length of time the flavour lingers in the mouth, by its richness and subtlety, and by its aftertaste. A variety of expressive abstract terms can be used to express the degrees of quality.

They do tend to be subjective and should be chosen with care. *See* "How to taste" and the "Full glossary".

Stage 4: conclusions

It should hardly be surprising that there is a relationship between the appearance, bouquet, and taste of individual wines. Yet, in my experience, even competent tasters tend to examine each stage in isolation. Others, myself included, see each stage as a revelation leading naturally to the next, and, irrevocably, to a logical conclusion.

Notes The experienced taster might not need to make notes. Indeed, equipped with his wonderful built-in computer, a look, a sniff, and a mouthful can – if correctly programmed – give him an instant summary equivalent to, for example, "a magnificent, soft, supple wine of great breed, intensity, full, mature" or "raw, harsh, immature, and poor quality – not worth buying or keeping".

However, for the student, the beginner, or the conscientious connoisseur, detailed tasting notes arriving at a considered conclusion provide a useful exercise. They gather the thoughts and tie up the loose ends.

The conclusion, therefore, should summarize compactly all the salient points and add comments regarding the overall quality of the wine, its maturity, possibly its value and certainly its rating in the context of the tasting. (*See* pages 80–9 on how to make notes.)

Scoring If you happen to be a judge in a wine competition, then almost certainly your notes and conclusions will have to be made in a precise form, usually tabulated with numerical values. Scoring is dealt with briefly on page 81, but for exhaustive details I must refer readers to Amerine or Vedel (*see* Appendix).

Descriptions Lastly, I would again draw attention to the chapters "The use of words" and the glossary. These give a wide range of both commonly and less frequently used terms, and the definitions – which are on occasion subject to slightly different interpretations – strive to give readers not only a clear indication of their meaning but, in the case of terms like "tannin", explain something of the physical or chemical background.

Price

Price is a factor that cannot often be ignored. It is certainly the common denominator of all wine-trade tastings except those concerned solely with the wine's physical development or condition.

Only a real wine snob or hypocrite (often the same person) and perhaps the carelessly rich, need not heed the price factor, though this does not mean that "pure" or abstract tastings, comparing one wine with another, are not desirable and valuable. But for most purchasers and consumers of wine, price is the final arbiter, in the sense that value for money is sought and appreciated, as much as, if not more than, pure quality.

Recent years have witnessed an escalation of fine wine prices that appears to be out of all proportion. There is a simple supply-and-demand situation – surging world demand for wines in geographically limited supply. Unhappily, the speculator adds pressure to the naturally increasing demands of more and more wine consumers. There is one consolation: the previously often impoverished wine-grower at last receives a return on capital, using this new-found wealth to replant vineyards, to replace old vines, and renew equipment.

Increased production and competition from New World wines have taken some of the strain off the French classics. What is needed is a healthy balance between consumer, merchant, and producer. If an appreciative consumer is prepared to pay a respectable merchant or restaurateur a reasonable price, this will in turn yield the vineyard owner and winemaker a fair return for their labours, the risks, and vicissitudes. It should be remembered however, that historically, the finest wines have never been cheap. They were originally the sole province of the aristocratic, wealthy, and privileged classes, and I dare say that quite a few did not really appreciate them to the full – then as now!

At least by increasing our awareness and appreciation we will not waste the opportunities of tasting fine and rare wines when, as they surely will, they present themselves for our delectation.

Interlude

This might be an appropriate moment, between tasting and tastings, to remind ourselves – and I know only too well how easily one can lose sight of this – that wine is for drinking. Indeed, the study of wine is all rather pointless unless one actually consumes it, preferably regularly, and with enjoyment.

Wine as a drink has so many facets. At a fairly basic level it provides a simple yet ideal accompaniment to a meal. Even the most mundane wine, and at an unconscious level, will whet the appetite and aid the digestion. The mere sight of a young dry white wine, and certainly its aroma, will make the mouth water; saliva is essential to digestion. And why is red wine so appropriate with rich meat dishes? Because sipping it between mouthfuls leaves the mouth clean and dry. This is the work of these very tannins which, without food, often make a red wine taste bitter when tasted by itself. Tannin is an antioxidant. It not only preserves red wine but, with that other more recently discovered derivative from the skins of wine, resveratrol, it helps preserve us by keeping our arteries clear. Wine is seriously good for us – if taken in moderation.

Wine is a warming, friendly beverage. As mentioned in my Foreword, it loosens tongues, promotes feelings of well being, cements friendships. In short it has a beneficial, civilizing influence, and in the higher realms of fine wine, appeals not only to the senses but to the intellect.

Summary

I should like to end by making four points: first, that wine-lovers should deliberately broaden their sights. Second, in doing so, they should make allowances for strange styles and flavours, and appreciate the context – for example, rich food and hot climate that certain wines were made for and taste best in. Third, as witnessed positively by Australia and California, that wine is as good, and as fine, as the wine drinker requires it to be and will pay for. It is positive, active, articulate connoisseurship and enthusiasm, allied to thriving economies (the begetter of healthy discretionary incomes) which encourage the winemaker to make the best possible wine within the natural limitations beyond his control. For, and this is the fourth point, with all the will in the world, really good wines cannot be made in unsuitable areas, which is why one usually settles down to the enjoyment of the best of the New World and the well-tried and long established European classics.

How to organize a tasting

The only way to appreciate wine is when a few men, who understand and enjoy it meet together, feeling free to luxuriate in the delight imparted...

T. G. Shaw

WINE, THE VINE AND THE CELLAR, 1863

Experienced wine importers and merchants know perfectly well how to run their own tastings. The aim of this chapter is to advise younger members of the wine trade, amateur wine societies, and tasting groups as to what preparations are necessary and what pitfalls to avoid.

It is assumed that the purpose of a tasting is to present a range of wines in the most favourable light either to induce sales, or simply to learn more about wine.

The first thing is to decide what type of tasting it is to be, what and how many wines are to be shown, and how many people are to participate. Very often, consideration of the latter point will dictate the number of wines and almost certainly the type of tasting, so this factor will be dealt with first.

HOW MANY TASTERS?

Generally speaking, the seriousness and the effectiveness of a tasting is inversely proportional to the number who attend. A large promotional tasting, attended by anything from sixty to 300 people, will require a large hall or cellar, a large staff and very careful organization. The consumption per capita is bound to be greater than at a small tasting; even if, as is wise, the range of wines is strictly limited, the expense may be out of all proportion to the ultimate benefit.

Between forty and seventy guests may be considered the maximum manageable number at a standard stand-up and free-roaming tasting, somewhat fewer if a lecture-tasting or tutorial is envisaged.

THE AIM OF THE TASTING

If the tasting is planned to launch a range of new branded wines, it ought really to be limited to this alone. Rather like the press review of a new model at a motor show, the aim will be to demonstrate the wines' desirable selling points: their drinkability; price; the weight of supporting advertising, and the attractions of the point-of-sale material. The gathering will generally be confined to the promoters, their customers, and members of the press, who will be expected to extol the product's virtues. This is hardly a tasting in the wine-lover's sense, but is not infrequent in these days of sophisticated wine marketing.

More traditional are the tastings organized by the wine importer or merchant for customers, presenting wines of the latest vintage or current seasonal stock-in-trade. These are vital and informative tastings that benefit trade and consumer alike. Proper organization is essential and the principles involved are discussed overleaf.

Wine society or informal group tastings, usually aimed at the education and enlightenment of the members (who share the cost) can be similar in style to trade tastings, and most of the same problems arise.

But if the object is to learn something about wine, then by far the best type of tasting is the controlled and seated variety in the form of a lecture, with carefully selected wines used as illustrations. An event of this type will stand or fall on the knowledge and skill of the lecturer, and is probably best conducted by an experienced professional. The financial advantage of this type of tasting is that it is the most economical in terms of the amount of wine consumed.

HOW MANY WINES?

At big trade tastings there may well be from thirty to over one hundred different wines on show. It goes without saying that when there are a vast number of samples, the host expects his guests to discriminate, and also to spit out. After all, trade buyers are usually in the market for wines of a suitable type and price and need not waste time and clutter their minds – and note books – by tasting wines beyond their requirements except, of course, out of curiosity.

The minute the public is let in, however, there is often less discrimination. Whereas the wiser and more experienced will concentrate on those wines which interest them most, others might be tempted to treat the event as a sort of cocktail party and try to drink round the room – in the long run, wasting their time and their host's money.

It is more prudent for the organizers to be selective and show a more limited range of say ten to twenty wines as outstanding representatives of their type and price. However, if the types of wine are mixed, do make sure that they are grouped clearly and arranged on tables so that they are tasted in the right order, dry before sweet, heavy and sweet wines last.

HORIZONTAL AND VERTICAL TASTINGS

For a small wine club tasting or a tutored tasting, six to ten different wines will usually be enough. They must be well chosen, however, and worthy of study in depth. The most useful are horizontal and vertical tastings. Horizontal tastings are wines from different châteaux or different districts but all of the same vintage; vertical tastings compare different vintages ofthe same wine, *i.e.* of the same château, or of the same type or district. I have successfully combined a horizontal and vertical tasting on several occasions, with the same vintage of six different châteaux and six different vintages of one of those châteaux. The point of all this is not to make the tasting impossibly complicated but, through the comparisons, to learn more.

HOW MUCH WINE?

For drinking one allows approximately six to eight glasses per bottle, depending on the size of the glasses. For tasting, the number of glasses or "tastes" per bottle doubles, even trebles.

Allowing twelve to fifteen tasting measures per bottle, the next thing is to estimate the number of glasses to be provided per person. At a "tutored tasting" the answer is quite simple: one per person per wine. At a serious tasting where there is a big range of wines on show one can plan for a fairly small consumption on the basis that most tasters will try and taste a little of most of the wines, but one should allow extra for the more popular types of wine and provide adequate supporting stock.

However large or small the range of wines on show, one thing can be banked on: the bigger the crowd, the more will be consumed *per capita*. The hour of the day and duration of the tasting will also have a bearing.

Summing up: with a large range of wines and a small number of tasters, allow one bottle to eight or nine people; for a small range and large attendance, one bottle will not go far. If it is just a casual tasting party, allow at least half-a-bottle a head. But at a tutored tasting, one bottle will serve fifteen or more tasters.

WHAT TIME OF DAY?

The organizer has to bear in mind not only the appropriate times to taste, from the freshness of palate point of view, but the convenience of the guests. Indeed, the latter is usually of paramount importance. There are, in fact, just two practical alternatives: before lunch or early evening.*

DURATION

The timing of an evening function will depend a great deal upon social conventions. The main thing to remember when planning the programme is to leave ample time for the tasting. Twenty minutes or half-an-hour is simply not enough. Half-an-hour may be sufficient if the tasting merely consists of a glass of something prior to a meal, for it then merely comes into the "7 for 7.30"pm category of invitation.

The length of time that is allowed for the tasting must be proportional to the number of wines on show and the number of guests invited. For ten to twenty wines and thirty to fifty people the time allowed should extend somewhere between one-and-a-half and two hours.

The point is, that although one solid hour of tasting is more than enough for even the hardiest taster, sufficient allowance has to be made for late-comers, early leavers, and social chit-chat.

The more structred tutored tasting is probably best held in the evening. The length of time required will depend partly upon the speaker. Two hours just sitting, sipping, and listening is the absolute maximum. On the other hand, it is surprising how long it can take to taste and talk about only half-a-dozen wines. One should aim at about one-and-a-quarter to one-and-a-half hours. Incidentally, it is most important that everyone arrives on time, so invitations should be explicit: 7 for 7.15 pm prompt, or words to this effect.

Big trade tastings are usually organized in appropriately large premises (in firms' cellars, the town hall, or some appealingly attractive and well-lit venue) by experienced professionals, so we will confine our attentions to two moderate-sized types of tasting.

**I used to think that serious tastings could not take place during a meal, but I have been privileged to attend a quite remarkable series of dinner tastings. The earliest were organized by Joseph Berkmann, then one of London's most enterprising restaurateurs. It surprised me how effective – as well as interesting – tasting a large range at the table could be.*

A free-ranging tasting (twenty to sixty guests)

SPACE AND FLOW

Ideally, the organizer removes everything that will interfere with table layout and customer-flow. At all costs, clutter and potential hazards must be avoided. There will be little enough room for assistants and paraphernalia.

Crowds will undoubtedly bring their own problems and one of the first, too often overlooked, is hats, coats, and bags. If there is not a cloakroom or spare room available nearby, then set aside a large table for coats, etc.

The most important considerations after this are spatial. There must be enough room for tasters to circulate without obstruction; there must be enough space between the different wines to allow tasters adequate elbow room; and also enough space, preferably barred to tasters, for staff and assistants to service tasting tables.

TASTING LAYOUT

The key to success is table layout. This will depend on the shape of the room, but basically there are two approaches: to have a series of tables round the room (continuous or spaced) with the tasters circulating in the middle, or to have a "square" of tables in the centre, enclosing staff and stock. The virtues of the latter are that fewer assistants are needed to supervise the tasting – opening bottles, keeping them in order, removing empty bottles and used glasses – and that the service and stock areas are safely isolated (but bear in mind that assistants have to push through tasters to get to the central reservation).

If a large number of wines are on display it is probably better to arrange the tables around the perimeter of the room; they can be spaced better and tasters can move from one area to another more easily. But avoid corners, as these can become congested.

Staff must be stationed at each table section, so at a big tasting this will mean one assistant per two- or three-metre (per 6.6 or 9.8 ft) section or per six wines.

Space requirements are often underestimated by people organizing tastings, particularly the space between different wines. Apart from the discomfort caused by nudgers, wines get mixed up and out of order if set out too closely. To avoid this, allow only four to six bottles to a three-metre (9.8 ft) trestle table, depending on the number of tasters expected. The more tasters, the wider the spacing.

SEQUENCE

The wines should be laid out in the correct order of tasting and, most important but not always easy, incoming guests must be made aware of the sequence of wines and encouraged to taste in that order. This is where a clearly laid-out tasting sheet comes in handy: list order and table layout should coincide. One very important point: do not place table number one too near the entrance, as a queue of early tasters may form and impede the passage of other guests and assistants.

If the room is small it is usually better to start the tasting on the far side to avoid congestion. If there are sweet or fortified wines in a mixed tasting, place them at the end of the natural tasting sequence and traffic flow to discourage guests from tasting them first.

SIDE TABLES

Still on the subject of how to lay out the room, and ignoring for the moment decoration and other incidentals, it is better to have quite separate tables for glasses, food, and literature. Ideally, the table for glasses and tasting sheets should be placed somewhere between the entrance and the first wine to be tasted. Clipboards are very useful. Informative literature of the take-home variety should be handed out from a table by the exit. No purpose whatsoever is served by burdening guests with supplementary reading matter at the start or part-way through the tasting: there is seldom time to read it during the tasting and the odds are that it will be discarded before the tasting is over.

PLACING OF SPITTOONS

Spittoons are not easy to place. They should not be on the tasting tables but on the floor, either just in front of the tables (if the wines are well spaced and there is ample room for tasters' feet) or sufficiently away from the tables not to trip people up. They are probably best placed two or three metres (9.8 ft) from the tables, more if large crowds are expected, to allow an appropriate width of passage for circulation and to encourage tasters to retreat from the table with their tasting samples, permitting other tasters a chance to get to the tables. There is nothing more irritating at a tasting than "clinging vines" who station themselves semi-permanently by a bottle, helping themselves, making notes, and spitting, all without moving their feet. Out-of-reach spittoons help to dislodge the blockers.

A tutored tasting

The room size required must be directly related to the numbers attending: each taster, as well as the lecturer, will need a chair and table space.

TABLES ARE ESSENTIAL

Make no mistake about it, tables are vital. It is impossible to conduct this sort of tasting session with tasting sheets, pencils, glasses, and possibly maps and other literature on one's lap.

Ideally either individual small tables or desks should be used, allocating one per taster. Larger tables may, of course, be shared. In any case, the spacing per person must be wider than a chair's width. Allow at least a metre (3.3 ft) per taster so that there is room on each section of the table for several glasses in either one or two rows, and the tasting sheet.

It is much more comfortable for all tasters to face the lecturer, so only one side of the table should be used. If the tables are in continuous rows then there must be sufficient space between those rows for the assistants to pour or hand out glasses. It is a mistake to assume that fewer helpers are required for lecture-tastings, for although there may be just one lecturer, the timing of the service of the wines is very important and sufficient serving staff or willing volunteers must be available.

WINE SERVICE

There are two ways of serving the wine: either pouring into glasses already on the table, or pre-pouring and handing out glasses. I favour the former. Assuming that a tasting quantity will range from about ten to fifteen glasses per bottle, it is desirable to have one assistant per bottle, *i.e.* per ten to fifteen tasters; otherwise the time taken pouring is apt to disturb the lecturer and fragment the session. It is difficult for tasters to concentrate while assistants move around with the wine. If the service is protracted there is always the danger that those who get the wine first will be tempted to taste the wine "solo" instead of waiting to be guided through the elements of colour, bouquet, and taste by the lecturer. The quickest and fairest way is to pour careful measures into glasses on trays in an adjacent room and hand them out at precisely the moment they are called for by the lecturer.

The problem of spittoons is even more acute with a seated audience. By far the best solution is to provide each taster with a plastic cup (preferably not transparent).

Details to bear in mind

TABLES

It may seem silly to say this, but the essential thing is that tables should be of normal dinner-table height, and firm. In other words, do not use tiny coffee tables or flimsy, unstable trestle tables.The tables used should not be too high or too wide, as it can be awkward to serve across them.

TABLE COVERINGS

There are several factors to consider: red wine stains; bottles can scratch; and a white background is essential to show off the colour of the wine. Cover the table, whether it is plain deal or polished mahogany. If the latter, use a large white cloth with newspaper or other lining underneath. If an ordinary trestle table is used, a white table cloth or rolls of plain white paper can be pinned to it.

LIGHTING

This is extremely important, and yet often the least-considered factor. A natural north light is best; failing that, normal tungsten lights or down lighters. Fluorescent tube lighting, even so-called "warm white", distorts the colour, giving red wine an unhealthy dark, blue-black tinge which makes it appear far younger and less mature than it really is.

Candles add appropriate glamour to the occasion but, truthfully, although a myriad of candles may look pretty, they really do not produce enough of the sort of light in which the colour of the wine can be effectively judged. Mind you, there is no reason why candles, either in proper candelabra or stuck in the top of empty bottles, should not be used in conjunction with artificial light. One or two per table look attractive, and they are useful for observing the clarity of the wine. But do remember: candles consume oxygen and add to the heat of the room.

SERVICE OR SELF-SERVICE?

At an ordinary, largish tasting, is it better for the hosts to pour out the wine, or should guests be allowed to help themselves? In practice, whatever is decided, there is usually a bit of both. At a well-attended tasting, the staff will be busy doing several jobs at once and it is fairly certain they they will not be able to spend all their time helping the guests to wine, even if this is supposed to be their main job. On the other hand, if tasters help themselves too liberally at a free-for-all tasting, then a bit of judicious and tactful pouring will be called for. This will prevent the host's stocks being depleted too rapidly and will encourage guests to taste a wider range more effectively. One practical solution is to insert pourer-stoppers or the very effective rolled metal discs into the necks of bottles.

ASSISTANTS AND STAFF

Do not underestimate the number of people required to help, from supervisor to cloakroom attendant. Numbers and calibre of staff will, of course, depend on the nature of the event, its size, and the place.

Small club tastings are usually no problem. Just make sure there are members prepared to lend a hand. Many small and medium-sized trade tastings will be manned by members of the firm, usually principals and sales staff who know their subject and are identifiable by lapel badges bearing their name and/or that of their company.

When tastings are held in catering establishments – hotels, restaurants, or clubs – staff will generally be employed. Even if supervised by a head waiter or captain, it should never be assumed that they will know exactly what is required. So a cardinal rule is to brief all staff before the tasting commences: where to station themselves, how many bottles to open, how much to pour, to clear glasses, and avoid clutter, etc.

Insist on rigorous stock control, with a complete complement of bottles, full or empty, after the tasting; otherwise bottles simply disappear. Another tip is to provide a supply of inexpensive wine or beer for the staff to refresh themselves – preferably afterwards.

Let one person be in overall charge. Have enough "front of house" personnel to host and advise; enough staff or assistants to serve. Do not forget to man the cloakroom and reception table. Make sure everyone knows precisely what he or she is to do. Even if an experienced public relations companY is employed it is worth the howt checking the details.

SPITTOONS, BOTTLES, AND FUNNELS

Properly equipped tasting rooms have permanent Spittoons of a basin, fountain or flushing variety. At the sort of tasting we have just been discussing, however, mobile spittoons are the order of the day and they run to three types: the pedestal-funnel variety, rather like a fat version of one of the nastier types of road-house ashtray; the sawdust box or bucket; and the table-top bowl or cup.

Quite the simplest to prepare and most satisfactory to use is the sawdust box. This type of spittoon is just a wooden wine case with the top removed and the inside two-thirds filled with sawdust. It is commodious and fairly absorbent; to be on the safe side, line it with oil-cloth or polythene. The disadvantage is that it is easy to trip over a box in a crowded room.

If you cannot find enough boxes, buckets of sand or sawdust will do. They present a small target, however, and knock over more easily. Never use glass jugs as table-top spittoons: wine spittal looks horrible. Polystyrene vessels or ice-buckets are best. Incidentally, empty bottles, with glass or plastic funnels stuck in the neck, seen on tables at many trade tastings, are not spittoons. They are receptacles for the taster to empty his glass in before moving to the next wine. Take care that they do not overflow: magnums are the most suitable for this purpose.

GLASSES FOR TASTINGS

Clear, tulip-shaped, stemmed glasses are desirable. Naturally, at a large tasting quantity and not quality of glassware must prevail. Standard goblets can be hired at a reasonable price from any reputable catering firm. The 170-ml (6-oz) size tends to be too big for tasting; 140-ml (5-oz) glasses are more economical, or even, at a pinch, large port glasses. More suitable types are sherry *copitas* and "dock" glasses. However, the ideal tasting glass, the "ISO", is illustrated on page 54.

The number of glasses required needs careful consideration. All depends on the range of wines on show and attendance expected. Except at a seated tasting, it is rarely a practical proposition to provide one glass per person per wine. At a large tasting one glass is normally provided on arrival and the taster is expected to use it throughout the tasting, though a clean glass is usually obtainable if by chance the first is abandoned or if a fresh one is really required. If wines of contrasting colour and style are shown at the same tasting, a change of glasses is expected. Even if the basis is one glass per taster, allowance must be made for wastage: breakages, abandoned glasses, etc., so order double the number first thought of.

Nothing looks worse than a litter of partially filled glasses abandoned on tasting tables, so staff should continually remove them. If they are left on the tables they just get in the way and encourage other people to follow suit.

If there are insufficient glasses, or if proper washing-up facilities are not available, it may be necessary to put rinsing bowls in the tasting room. They can look unsightly, however, and might be objected to on the grounds of hygiene. If assistants are expected to wash glasses on the spot, washing-up bowls should be either behind the table out of sight or on a rear service table. Far better to have an adequate supply to begin with.

HOW MANY BOTTLES?

Even at a big and busy tasting it is better to have only one bottle of each wine open at a time. This is not just for the sake of economy; its main purpose is to avoid clutter and to prevent the bottles from getting out of order. It also discourages guests from picking up an open bottle and wandering off with it, ostensibly to assist their friends. It sometimes stays with the group until it is consumed!

Nor should the entire tasting stock of bottles of each wine be put on the table in serried ranks. They may look impressive, but they soon get in the way of the serving staff. Bottles are picked up for a close look at the label – and usually put back in the wrong place, all of which adds to the disorganization and clutter. However, it is not a bad idea to have one other bottle, opened but stoppered, alongside the tasting bottle. It acts as an immediate reserve and enables waiting tasters to look at the label and the general presentation of the bottle. The point is, it is difficult to see the label of a wine being poured; it is usually obscured by hand or napkin. Last, but not least, the number of wines open for tasting may be dictated by the heat of the room. A cold white wine can gain 5°C (10°F) in as many minutes.*

CORKS AND CAPSULES

The presentation of sample bottles is important. The capsules should be cut just below the top of the neck and the top removed. Do not remove the entire capsule. Next wipe the top of the bottle with a damp cloth and finally with a clean dry cloth.

After removing the cork, preferably in one piece – not so easy with older wines – it should be tied to the neck, wet-side up, with a rubber band. Lastly a wedge-shaped stopper cork is inserted until it is time to serve.

Older red wines should, of course, be decanted. Make sure the decanter is identified by name or number. The empty bottle is then placed alongside, with cork, for inspection. (*See* page 118.)

FOOD

Except at press receptions and the more social type of tasting, food should be kept to a minimum. It merely distracts and provides counter-flavours and smells. Nevertheless, it must be accepted that some people need something to cleanse their palates between wines. Cheese squares and dry biscuits are the conventional answer to this problem. Better still, jugs or bottles of still, not sparkling, water. Avoid ice which stuns the palate.

It is perhaps important also to bear in mind that virtually all red wines and most whites have been devised by nature and man as an accompaniment to food. In fact, wine tastes different with food and, if it is to be judged in a food context, it is often easier to do so at a asting with an appropriate nibble.

The old saying "buy a wine over apples and sell it over cheese" has much more than a grain of truth in it. Cheese makes wine taste softer, mellower, and sweeter. Mild cheeses only; avoid riper and "smelly" cheeses as they are offensive and tend to spoil the taste of delicate wines. An overripe Brie will kill a mature burgundy stone dead. So small squares of a mild cheese of the cheddar variety are safe and satisfactory: allow for one generous plateful per tasting table. Dutch Gouda complements red Bordeaux.

**An ideal solution is the use of Vinicool® transparent plastic, open-topped vacuum flasks (see page 124).*

Reverting to apples for a moment, one English wine merchant, renowned for his port, used to clean his palate with a bite of apple between tasting samples of young vintage port. A noted taster in Oporto consumes charcoal before his morning tasting of young ports. I confess I have not tried these, though sorely tempted; there are few wines more palate-numbing than immature port.

NO SMOKING – OR STRONG SCENTS

One would have thought that the "no smoking" rule at tastings was sufficiently known and understood. But it seems that smokers are a law unto themselves; they do not even consider the spent matches and cigarette ends as litter, but unthinkingly discard them anywhere. A man who reaches automatically for his pipe and pouch at home will do so with equal unconcern when he has reached the contemplative end of a tasting.

So, beware. At a big public tasting put NO SMOKING signs up. Catch smokers politely at the door and advise all assistants to watch out for the tell-tale wreaths of blue smoke, particularly among the groups who are chatting in a relaxed fashion, their tasting completed.

Everyone attending a tasting should also refrain from using strong scent, powder, aftershave lotion, etc. The delicate bouquet of wine simply cannot compete with a host of foreign smells; it is difficult enough as it is without one's nostrils being assaulted by smoke and perfume at the same time.

TASTING SHEETS

There is no surer way of wasting one's efforts than to invite guests to taste without providing some form of tasting sheet. This can take the form of a printed list, a folder, or a simple, lined sheet allowing the tasters to write down their comments. There are three essential requirements:

- The sheet should list in order of tasting the name and vintage of each wine. Prices should be quoted if it is a trade tasting.
- There should be space for comments either alongside or underneath each wine, or on a blank page opposite. At least as much space should be allowed for notes as the name of the wine occupies.
- The tasting sheet should be printed on card or stiff paper. Flimsy paper is hopeless. Alternatively, provide clipboards.

Embellishments such as wine maps and descriptions of wine districts, etc., can be included. Occasionally price list and tasting sheet are combined. The scope for variety is immense, but whatever form it takes, a tasting sheet is basically an *aide-mémoire*; with wine, as with many other things, it is a matter of "in at one ear and out of the other".

SUMMARY

Plan the tasting well in advance. Consider all the vital factors: date, time, place; number of guests, and assistants; the type and number of wines. Do not leave important details until the last minute. The following check-list might be helpful.

Check-list for tastings

IN ADVANCE

Guest-list
Room booking
Wine selection and stock reservation
Printing: invitations, tasting sheets
Order tables, cloths, glasses, and other accessories
Forewarn assistants; book staff

PRE-TASTING CHECKS

Cloakroom facilities
Tasting-room layout
Tables: number, size, arrangement
Table-cloths or rolls of white paper
Wine (preferably delivered in advance, to settle); temperature of wine; room
Two bottles of each wine at each tasting position; supporting stock handy but not on view
Corkscrews: one per assistant, or table (there are never enough)
Stopper corks, wedge-shaped
Pourer-stoppers or patent metal pourers inserted in bottle necks
Rubber bands for securing original corks to bottle necks
Lapel badges to identify hosts and assistants
Lapel badges or self adhesive name tapes for guests
Glasses: quantity, shape, and size (polished and clean-smelling)
Lighting: correct intensity, type, and position
Spittoons, sawdust boxes, or plastic cups
Cloths or napkins for glasses and wiping bottle necks
Empty bottles (magnums) with funnels for dregs
Candles, candelabra, or empty bottles, and matches
Rinsing bowls, if necessary
Plain cheese cubes, and plates
Dry biscuits or dry bread, and plates
Jugs of water (without ice) or bottled still water unchilled
Trays for removal of glasses
Tasting sheets
Price lists, supporting literature, hand-outs, press kits
Sharpened pencils or ball-point pens
Maps, posters, drawing pins, and adhesive tape
Visitors book or check list of guests invited
NO SMOKING signs (remove ashtrays to discourage smokers)
Lock-up room for wine storage, particularly on strange premises

STAFF, ASSISTANTS

Brief all staff carefully before tasting commences
Allocate stands, tables, duties
Number of bottles to be opened, timing
Keep tables uncluttered, staff to remove empty glasses
Boozers, free-loaders, and smokers – refer to organizer

AFTER THE TASTING

Separation of unopened, opened, and empty bottles
Stock check

DRINKING, TASTING, AND DRIVING

Arrange for a taxi or driver (or obliging wife/husband) to take you home or back to the office, because however much you have been tasting and spitting, and not drinking, some wine invariably slips down the throat, and after an extensive tasting the effects will be noticeable – particularly if breathalyzed.

How to record tasting notes

...add a little to the literature of one of the three great joys in life.

George Saintsbury

NOTES ON A CELLAR-BOOK, 1920

Only two kinds of person can do without tasting notes: the rare and fortunate individual with a phenomenally freak memory, and the less rare who chooses not to complicate matters by ever tasting more than the firm favourites he knows and likes. (There is, in fact, a third: the really experienced specialist who spends every day tasting wines in his own particular field. For example, the sherry, port, or whisky blender. His highly developed palate for a comparatively limited range of smells and tastes may not require the support of the written word, save to record the names and proportions of the constituent parts selected for the blend.)

So, make notes. They will be useful, and referring to them can be very evocative and enjoyable.

ESSENTIAL INFORMATION

Frankly, any system is adequate that stores sufficient information for an individual's purpose in a speedy and accessible manner.

The following information is more or less essential:

- the date of tasting (too often omitted in the heat of the moment)
- the name of the wine (district, vineyard)
- the vintage year
- if in bottle, the name of the bottler (if estate-bottled the name of the estate. Château-bottlings merely require the qualifying initials CB); if from the cask, "ex-cask"
- the price (per bottle, dozen, or as appropriate)
- a description of the wine's appearance: depth, colour, clarity
- a description of its nose: aroma, bouquet
- a description of its taste: components, length, finish
- general conclusions: maturity, quality, value

One important point should be made. That is, just because there are myriads of descriptive terms available it is not essential or desirable to overdo it: indeed, the experienced taster will tend to note only the outstanding and most meaningful characteristics, the faults, and the exceptions.

A typical page of entries from my own tasting notebooks is given on page 91. I note the occasion, the host, the place, and, if it is a special dinner, the food. I also index each wine by country and district, but frankly these details are up to the individual.

TASTING BOOK

Notes are entered as the wines are tasted, in chronological order. The advantage of this system is that a series of pocket-sized books instead of boxes of cards can be used. The pages can be ruled vertically to save rewriting main headings.

The disadvantages are the amount of work required (details of each wine have to be entered every time) and the need for an accurate and up-to-date index for quick reference. Nevertheless, this is the system I have always used for my tasting books; they are my tasting diary.*

CARD SYSTEM

Of the various methods of collating tasting notes, the card system has many virtues. A separate card for each wine is stored in district, vintage, or alphabetical order. This system is handy for quick-reference. Appropriate sections can be extracted and taken to the tasting room, thus saving considerable time as headings are already prepared. The main disadvantages are that it is a bulky system and individual cards can get misplaced.

RING BINDERS

Another system combines the virtues of card and book. It consists of ruled or printed leaves, arranged horizontally, and set into a ring or spiral binder. It is used like a book, but leaves can be inserted as and where necessary. This, as a matter of interest, is the sort I use for the Bordeaux and port notes I extract from my books to index in vintage order.

Like the card system, the wines can be kept in any order: district, vintage or alphabetical. (But the system tends to be bulky unless several wines can be written up on one page.)

COMPUTER, LAPTOP

For the increasingly computer-literate – alas, not I – there is no question but that putting one's notes directly onto a laptop computer is extremely convenient. If efficiently programmed, the notes can be stored and retrieved by date, type of wine, place and host, by vintage – the permutations are endless. Many professional tasters and wine journalists use laptops, though the clattering noise some of the machines make can be off-putting in a tasting room.

ANALYTICAL SCORE CARDS

Wines submitted to a panel of judges for comparative and competitive tasting have to be tasted methodically. Almost invariably a printed tasting card is supplied, indicating the factors to be noted and assessed and giving each factor, or each group, a numerical value. Points are awarded for positive features; negative points for faults. The maximum possible can be seven points, more often twenty, sometimes one hundred.

The points weighting depends on the type and class of wine to be tasted, and the purpose of the tasting. For commercial entries judges might be allowed up to four points for colour, six for bouquet, and ten for taste; possibly four, five, and ten.

There are a variety of highly sophisticated and elaborate score cards used for equally varied types of tasting. But the vast majority are employed for either assessing and evaluating fairly closely related commercial wines, either at the academic level, producer or serious trade-buying levels, or

**Volume 1 of my little red tasting books dates from 17 September 1952; the 135th identical book was completed before this edition of* Winetasting *went to print. All are indexed.*

at the various competitions which take place regularly in wine-producing countries: for example, in Mâcon, France, Orange County, California, and in the wine-producing states of Australia. In addition, meticulous tastings along fairly rigid lines are conducted by professionals in their own regions – for example, in the major German wine areas to award seals of quality and issue proof numbers.

When dealing with wines of a similar type, perhaps lacking the marked varietal characteristics, shades of colour, nose, and taste of fine vintage wines, verbal descriptions tend to be inadequate and numerical ratings take their place. But just because some of these tastes and smells are so similar and hard to rate, and because all human beings are fallible – and most wine tasters impressionable – double-checks are required. Hence the importance of statistical procedures, triangular tests, and so forth in strictly academic and commercial tastings. To accomplish this, the same wines are presented blind, in very clinical conditions, in varying orders. The object of these exercises is to eliminate bias and to establish, as objectively as possible, the validity of the tastings, the taste preferences, and relative suitability of wines in a given context. It is also important to test the tasters. One taster's susceptibility to sulphur dioxide, to volatile acidity, even to sweetness will be different from another's. The level at which smells and tastes can be perceived by even experienced tasters is not necessarily the same for tannins, the various types of acidity, and sugars.

Members of professional tasting panels should be trained, and those selected for competition judging must not only have proven ability but be given a clear idea of the parameters of such tastings: what to look for, what to take note of, and, most important of all, on what basis points should be awarded. In Australia, for example, tasters begin as assistants to the State or area judging panel, arranging the tastings, helping out, studying procedures. They then graduate to the tasting panel itself, the senior members of which eventually "graduate" as national show judges.

EXAMPLES OF NUMERICAL RATINGS

Systems abound, all awarding plus or minus points to aspects of appearance, nose, and taste. A brief summary of some of the better known follow. The Davis score-card was evolved at the famous Department of Enology at the University of California, Davis, whose graduates fill many, probably most, of the major technical positions at wineries throughout that state, and further afield.

THE ORIGINAL DAVIS SCORE-CARD WAS AS FOLLOWS:

appearance	2 points
color	2 points
aroma and bouquet	4 points
volatile acidity	2 points
total acidity	2 points
sweetness	1 point
body	1 point
flavor	2 points
bitterness	2 points
general quality	2 points

A "superior" wine would rate 17–20, standard 13–16, below standard 9–12, unacceptable or spoiled 1–8. It will quickly be noticed that a taster, however gifted, cannot be pulled off the street and be expected to rate a wine with even a superficially simple point system such as this without an explanation of both the terms and the weighting. In fact, problems arose and a modified score-card was introduced:

appearance	2 points
color	2 points
aroma and bouquet	6 points
total acidity	2 points
sweetness	1 point
body	1 point
flavor	2 points
bitterness	1 point
astringency	1 point
general quality	2 points

An amateur would have difficulty in differentiating "bitterness" and "astringency". Indeed, this sort of tasting rating is very much one for professionals or well-trained panels.

Another 20-point system roughly following the modified Davis scale seems simpler:

clarity	2 points
colour	2 points
aroma	2 points
bouquet	2 points
acidity	1 point
balance	2 points
body	2 points
taste	3 points
finish	2 points
overall quality	2 points

Even so, each member of the panel has to have a clear idea of precisely what aspect scores what. Finally, to test the significance of scores, an elaborate series of statistical procedures has been devised at Davis. These are exhaustively dealt with by Amerine and Roessler (*see* Appendix). My view is that these numerical scoring systems are doubtless valid and useful for the more humdrum wines, but do not begin to aid the taster to form a meaningful assessment of fine wines. The system used in Germany for their seals of quality is far more explicit. The following relates to German white wines:

1. Colour:	colourless	0 points
	onion skin	0 points
	pale	1 point
	typical	2 points

2.	Clarity:	cloudy	0 points
		brilliant	2 points
3.	Bouquet:	faulty	0 points
		mute	1 point
		clean	2 points
		fine	3 points
		fragrant and flavoury	4 points
4.	Flavour:	faulty	0 points
		acceptable	1–3 points
		thin but characteristic	4–6 points
		balanced	7–9 points
		ripe and noble	10–12 points

The minimum points for an award are, respectively, 2, 2, 2 and 6 points; for Kabinett quality a minimum total of 13, for Auslese 15, Beerenauslese 16 and Trockenbeerenauslese 17.

The Italian National Order of Winetasters uses the Buxbaum system, which has a maximum of 20 positive points for the best, and 10 for the worst, *demerito*.

The French, as can be expected, have perhaps the most complete and sophisticated scoring systems and tasting cards. The OIV (*Office International de la Vigne et du Vin*) has a most ingenious and Gallically complicated style of score-card which I originally witnessed in use at an international wine competition in Budapest. Contrarily, the perfect score for a wine is zero, with the judges noting defects which are then multiplied to arrive at the qualifying score. The card used for each wine is as follows:

		Defects multiplied by				
Element	**Weighting**	**x0**	**x1**	**x4**	**x9**	**x16**
Appearance	1					
Colour	1					
Intensity of odour	1					
Quality of odour	2					
Intensity of taste	2					
Quality of taste	3					
Harmony/balance	2					

Outstanding features qualify for the 0 column, very good in column 1, good 4, acceptable 9 and unacceptable 16. Once again, judges using such a score-card must have explained to them precisely what is meant by the various terms and relative weightings.

THE 20-, 100-POINT, AND 5-STAR SYSTEM

No question about it: the 100-point system, famously employed by Robert Parker, Jr., the single most influential wine critic, and *The Wine Spectator*, a major American wine journal, is an object of both admiration and, in certain English and French quarters, of criticism. On the one hand, it dramatically consolidates the quality rating of one individual, or a panel of tasters; yet is flawed because the context in which a wine is tasted, even if "clinical", has a bearing – as do personal likes, dislikes, and prejudices, however objective the aim. Moreover, the 100-point scale is false as, based on the American examination systems, 50 is the starting point. The principal objection, as expressed by experienced tasters, is that there can be no such thing as, for example, a 97-point wine when, in different circumstances, in a different context it might only achieve 91.

The other worrying thing about these well-publicized scores is that they sweep the ground from under the feet of the reader and, in practice, emasculate the trade. The retailer, particularly in the USA, tries to buy wines that are rated 90 or over, for these are the wines the consumer will believe to be best.

The 20-point scoring is simpler but can be equally misleading. Though I occasionally employ a 20-point system, it is only in the context of a range of wines in a particular category at one tasting, and my scores are never published. They merely help me, looking back at my notes, to recall which wines seemed to be superior at the time. The 20 points are divided as follows:

Appearance *(depth, colour, clarity, viscosity)*	3
Nose *(grape aroma, bouquet, condition, development)*	6
Taste *(dryness, body, tannin, acidity, flavour, length)*	6
Overall quality *(balance, finish, complexity, finesse)*	5

A similar system (3, 7, 10) is used by the British Airways tasting panel, of which I was a long-serving member, at blind tastings of wines to be selected for various "classes" and destinations.

For the record, Hugh Johnson and I put our heads together to devise a tasting scorecard for The Sunday Times Wine Club. It is reproduced on page 87.

DESCRIPTIVE RATING CARDS

A variety of purely descriptive, as opposed to numerical, tasting cards have been published, but outstandingly the most interesting (again not surprisingly) is French. Steven Spurrier has kindly given me permission to reprint his English adaptation of the card devised by Castell and published by the INAO (*see* pages 88–9).

The only problem with this elaborate card is that it is bulky, and perhaps, for the advanced taster, somewhat inhibits the imagination and development of one's own vocabulary.

RATINGS AND MEDALS

Most professionals are wary of medals awarded at wine competitions and, every so often, the organizers of such competitions have something of a purge, determining to give medals sparingly to avoid their devaluation and subsequent loss of credibility resulting from overmarking. Many competitions are organized in wine-producing areas and open mainly to wine from those areas.

In Australia, where annual wine competitions not only thrive but are taken very seriously by the producers, high awards can lead to big sales. There, to qualify for a gold medal a wine has to score 18.5 or more out of 20; for a silver 17–18.4, and for a bronze 15.5–16.9. California has a number of similar events.

In France, the highest award is generally the *Grande Médaille d'Or,* next comes the *Médaille d'Or,* then *Médaille d'Argent* followed by *2me Diplôme d'Honneur* and *3me Diplôme d'Honneur*.

England has only one competition for local wine producers, awarding gold, silver, and bronze medals. The outright winner is presented with the Gore-Browne Trophy, donated by a redoubtable lady wine-growing pioneer in memory of her husband. However, not to be outdone, England also boasts two major wine competitions, the International Wine challenge and The International Wine & Spirit Competition Ltd, in which wines of different types and origins are judged in their respective classes. Medals are awarded annually, "double-golds" being not uncommon.

There is no doubt that competition is healthy, and if the possibility of winning a medal will induce wine producers to strive for even better quality, so much the better for the eventual consumer. Another benefit is the opportunity to compare; to see what one's rivals are up to and with what success. If the judges are fair and representative, the producer can perhaps gain a clearer idea of what style of wine has the greatest appeal. And of course, the attendant publicity is good.

The one major snag is that some really top-class producers care not to enter their wine. They have an established reputation which does not need the endorsement of a medal. For Château Lafite or the Domaine de la Romanée-Conti, entering such competitions would be demeaning, and any subsequent award superfluous. And there is always the nagging worry that they might not come top!

THE SUNDAY TIMES WINE Club — THE CHRISTIE'S – SUNDAY TIMES WINE CLUB TASTING CHART — CHRISTIE'S

Name of Wine District/type Merchant/bottler	Vintage Date purchased Price	
SIGHT Score (Maximum 4) ☐ CLARITY cloudy, bitty, dull, clear, brilliant DEPTH OF COLOUR watery, pale, medium, deep, dark COLOUR (White wines) green tinge, pale yellow, yellow, gold, brown (Red wines) purple, purple/red, red, red/brown VISCOSITY slight sparkle, water, normal, heavy, oily	starbright, tuilé straw, amber, tawny, ruby, gardne, oeil de perdrix, hazy, opaque	Comments
SMELL Score (Maximum 4) ☐ GENERAL APPEAL neutral, clean, attractive, outstanding off (eg. yeasty, acetic, oxidized, woody, etc.) FRUIT AROMA none, slight, positive, identifiable eg. riesling BOUQUET none, pleasant, complex, powerful	cedarwood, corky, woody, dumb, flowery, smoky, honeyed, lemony, spicy. mouldy, peardrops, sulphury	
TASTE Score (Maximum 9) ☐ SWEETNESS (white wines) bone dry, dry, medium dry, medium, sweet, very sweet TANNIN (red wines) astringent, hard, dry, soft ACIDITY flat, refreshing, marked, tart BODY very light and thin, light, medium, full bodied, heavy LENGTH short, acceptable, extended, lingering BALANCE unbalanced, good, very well balanced, perfect	appely, bitter, burning, blackcurrants, caramel, dumb earthy, fat flinty, green, heady, inky, flabby, mellow, metallic, mouldy, nutty, salty, sappy, silky, spicy, fleshy, woody, watery	
OVERALL QUALITY Score (Maximum 3) ☐ Coarse, poor, acceptable, fine, outstanding	supple, finesse, breed, elegance harmonious, rich delicate	**HOW TO USE THIS CHART** Wine appeals to three senses: sight, smell and taste. This card is a guide to analyzing its appeal and an aide-memoire on each wine you taste. Tick one word for each factor in the left hand column and any of the descriptive terms which fit your impressions. then award points according to the pleasure the wine gives you. Use the right-hand column for your comments.
SCORING Total score (out of 20)	DATE OF TASTING	

Compiled by Hugh Johnson and Michael Broadbent MW © 1975

WINE TYPE (WHITE/ROSE/RED)

Appellation:	*Type:*
Laboratory observations and conclusion	**Date of analysis**
Specific Gravity Alcohol Residual Sugar Potential Alcohol Total SO_2 pH Free SO_2 colour index P/x Index of permanganate	Total Acidity Fixed Acidity Volatile Acidity (corrected for sulphuric acid)

METHOD OF VINIFICATION

Visual examination

Surface of the liquid *Brilliant – dull. Clean – iridescent – oily*

Colour

White Wine	*Pale with green or yellow tints – pale yellow – straw yellow – canary yellow – gold – amber*
Rosé Wine	*Pale with violet or rose tints – grey – light rose – deep rose – partridge eye – onion skin*
Red Wine	*Red with crimson or violet tints – cherry red – ruby – garnet red – red brown – tile red – mahogany – tawny*
Hue	*Frank – oxidized – cloudy*

Aspect

Crystalline – brilliant – limpid – hazy – cloudy – turgid – lead – grey/white – opaque, with or without deposit

Legs/Tears

Quick or slow to form – non-existent – slight – heavy

Temperature of the wine	**Any factor hindering the tasting**

OLFACTORY EXAMINATION

First impression *Pleasant – ordinary – unpleasant*

Aroma

Intensity	*Powerful – adequate – feeble – non-existent*
Quality	*Very fine – racy – distinguished – fine – ordinary – common – not very pleasant – unpleasant*
Character	*Primary – secondary – tertiary – floral – fruity – vegetal – spicy – animal – oxidized*
Length	*Long – average – short*

Abnormal odours

CO_2 – SO_2 – H_2S – mercaptan – strongly oxidized – woody –lactic acid acescence – phenolic – corky

flaw	*temporary – permanent* *slight – serious*

Details

Any factor hindering or stopping the tasting

The INAO tasting card (see page 85)

GUSTATORY EXAMINATION

First impression

Flavours and sensations

Sweetness	
Sugar	*Heavy – very sweet – sweet – dry – brut*
Glycerine and alcohol	*Soft – unctuous – velvety – smooth – rough –dried-out*
Acidity	
Excessive	*Acid – green – tart – nervy – acidulous*
Balanced	*Fresh – lively – supple – smooth*
Insufficient	*Flat – flabby*
Body	
Alcoholic strength	*Light – sufficient – generous – heady – hot*
Flesh	*Fat – round – full – thin – meagre*
Tannin	*Rich – balanced – insufficient – astringent – bitter*
Aromas in the mouth	
Intensity	*Powerful – average – weak – long – short*
Quality	*Very fine – elegant – pleasant – common – faded*
Nature	*Floral – fruity – vegetable – spicy – wood – chemical – animal – other* *young – developed – complex*

Inherent or abnormal flavours

"Terroir"	*Marked – noticeable – faint – non-existent*
Sickness	*Grease – turned – aldehydes – sweet – sour – rancid – acetic acid – lactic acid*
Accident	*Stagnant – mould – lees – woody – cork – metallic – H_2S – herbaceous – acrid*

Final Impression

Balance	*Harmonious – bold – correct – unbalanced xs acid, xs sugar, xs tannin, xs alcohol*
Aftertaste	*Straightforward – unpleasant*
Resistance of taste and aroma	*> 8 sec 5–7 sec 4–5 sec <3 sec* *Very long – long – medium – short*

CONCLUSIONS

Conformity to appellation or type

Score out of 20

Summary of tasting

(character of wine – future, readiness for drinking)

The use of words

"When I use a word," Humpty Dumpty said in a rather scornful tone, "it means just what I choose it to mean – neither more nor less."

Lewis Carroll

ALICE'S ADVENTURES IN WONDERLAND

Put quite bluntly, most people simply do not know how and where to start describing a wine, and many are reluctant even to express an opinion. Some, knowing more, are less shy; but do they really mean what they say, or is a familiar-sounding wine word being used just because it is familiar-sounding, perhaps impressive? The odds are that it will not convey the speaker's intention.

Renewed thoughts on the use of words in relation to wine were stimulated by an interesting paper by Adrienne Lehrer.* However, I was really shaken into action by contradictory statements about identical wines made by fellow Masters of Wine on a visit to the winelands of the Cape. It seemed to me that if experienced professionals, as well as untrained amateurs, could disagree on whether a wine was full, light, or dry, or whatever, it was less likely to be a sensory problem than a semantic one: either carelessness in the use of words or alarming imprecision.

Clearly some guidance is needed.

ARE WORDS NECESSARY?

At this stage, it might be justifiably asked whether it is necessary to use words at all. Surely wine can be consumed, enjoyed, and appreciated to the full without a word being said or written? There are several reasons for talking or writing about wine, basically:

- to express a simple preference for one wine over another
- to communicate the style, quality, condition, etc. of a wine to someone else
- to increase the awareness of other tasters

ON WHAT SORT OF OCCASION?

Tastings The context in which wine is tasted is all-important. In the first chapter, I mentioned different circumstances for this, from the cask to the table. On each of these occasions a written or mental note might be made, possibly after some discussion.

At the sort of tastings described in the earlier chapter, one would normally make notes, ranging from an abbreviated preferential tick or dismissive cross to more detailed descriptions.

Lectures A lecturer on wine has several responsibilities:

- to stimulate interest and enthusiasm
- to open the eyes of the audience by drawing attention to features they might not have noticed
- to select words which are evocative and meaningful
- to use words which can be clearly related to the wine being tasted by the audience

**"Talking about Wine" in the journal* Language, *Volume 51, Number 4 (1975), Committee of Linguistics, College of Liberal Arts, University of Arizona.*

14/12/99 Dinner at 88 Rosebank: Jancis and Nick, Janet and Freddie, Spencer and Bart.

xx x (x)	'95	Ca' del Bosco Brut Zero magnum	fairly pale lively mousse	crisp, refined, elegant mouthwatering	bone dry, in fact austere but good flavour, balance and acidity
xx x	'49	Château-Chalon (Henri Maire)	amber-gold sl. sediment	characteristic, meaty, like old amontillado	fairly dry – an acquired taste! idiosyncratic. Ex. with D's pâté.
xx xx	'92	Echézeaux (Henri Jayer)	not deep translucent ruby	immediately attractive fresh varietal character good, not great.	a chance buy at trade tasting and a great success. Sweet, charming, ready now
xx (xxx)	'82	Barbaresco Sori San Lorenzo (Gaja) magnum	(double decanted at 6.45) still deep intense youthful	packed with glorious fruit crisp. great depth touch of blackcurrant	Clearly a great classic, but still in the making. Magnificent. Swingeing tannic, immature Needs another 10–15 years
	'55	Fonseca London-bottled 1957 by C. Buswell.	(fully branded cork. Unlabelled) mellow and mature	lovely, soft, sweet bouquet with hint of liquorice	Still sweet, lovely texture what port is all about. Perfection.

• when lecturing wine-trade students, to guide them in the use of words, particularly those long-tried and conventional terms which, when written, will be understood by an examiner or, equally, by a customer

Selling wine It is fairly common practice for wine merchants to annotate their lists, describing the qualities of different types of wine, of vintages, even of individual wines. Similar eulogies will be conveyed by the salesman to the potential customer. It is easier to use words in a selling context, possibly because the descriptions are qualitative and general, not analytical: pleasure-invoking adjectives, and opinions regarding readiness to drink, rather than specific descriptions. Perhaps, for white wines, these constitute merely whether they are sweet or dry; reds, whether full-bodied or light.

At dinner parties There are indeed many reasons for giving, or attending, a dinner party. If it is mainly a social event, grand, or less formal, the purpose will be to impress or to entertain: the occasion and the guests will take precedence over the fare. The food and the wine are likely to be relegated to a supporting role. The choice of wine will depend on appropriateness and price. It is not a subject for discussion. Even so, if you are keen on wine there is no harm in making a discreet note.

If it is a food-and-wine occasion, the host will expect comments, even a discussion, though the level and intensity will depend as much on the knowledge and enthusiasm of the people present as on the quality of fare.

The point is: whether wines are discussed considerably or not at all will depend on the type of dinner, the guests, and the intention. To pontificate on wine in a non-wine context is tactless; not to comment intelligently on a wine in a wine-orientated context is a failure to rise to the occasion.

GREAT WINE – FOR WHOM?

From my travels over the past few years, it has become abundantly clear that the vast majority of owners of fine and rare wines have one major concern: on what occasion, and for whom, shall their vinous treasures be opened? It is less a matter of expense than sheer waste, and the knowledge that once a cork is drawn, that is it.

A fine picture can be looked at scores of times and resold; a piece of silver can be admired for its beauty of craftsmanship and still retain its intrinsic value. Apart from haute cuisine, great wine is the only work of art which has to be consumed in order to be appreciated. Thereafter its only value is a treasured memory.

It seems sensible, therefore, to keep the finest wines for dinner parties or tastings which will be attended by people who really appreciate them – or at the very least for like-minded convivial souls. Having gathered together fine wine and appreciative palates, host and guests alike are unlikely to be satisfied with grunts, nods, and a mere smacking of lips.

CHOICE OF WORDS

Fine wine demands to be talked about. Words are needed. There is a wide spectrum of words, but they more or less boil down to two categories: factual and fanciful. There is, I believe, a place for both.

When it comes to wine, facts very often turn out to be opinions – but let us not be put off by academic pedants. Better to fumble and stumble than not to try to express ourselves at all.

Terminology The arts and sciences, gardening, and snooker all have their own specialized words, often far more obscure than those used by wine tasters, so why all the fuss, why the occasional snigger? It is extremely difficult to find words to describe taste, even more so bouquet, but perhaps one ought to try. The most brilliant taster will be able to conjure up words which happen, at that moment, to fit, to illuminate the wine being tasted. The experienced taster harnesses his imagination.

Basic words At the end of this chapter I have extracted a short list of words which, if carefully (I avoid the word "correctly") used, are meaningful to British tasters who have had a modicum of training and experience.

Fanciful words By all means let us indulge in flights of poetic expression, similes, flower analogies, and so forth, but be careful about the context.

Unqualified and ambiguous words One taster will loosely describe a wine as "full", another taster might disagree totally. The point here is that "full", unqualified, can conjure up several meanings in other tasters' minds: full-coloured (deep), full-bodied (high alcohol and extract), full bouquet (well-developed, very forthcoming), full-flavoured (positive, mouth-filling).

So adjectives like "full" or "light" should either be qualified or used in a distinctly recognizable context: colour, bouquet, weight in the mouth, style, flavour, etc. Words such as "hot" and"round" can have several meanings. A list of ambiguous words appears on pages 98–99.

Use of similes and analogies The French themselves, in writing and in speech, tend to be far more poetic than the English, their descriptions often roaming up a romantic path, associating wine with flowers, scents, exotic foods, and the more delicate aspects of lovemaking. The English are generally more reticent, more terse, and, let us be honest, often less imaginative.

I cannot generalize about Americans. Their writing and talking depend on so many factors, from ethnic background to type of reader and audience. There is a tendency, in some quarters, to verbosity and polysyllables, many Americans preferring to use long words rather than simple expressions, but this is not confined to those who write, or speak, about wine.

One could argue that likening a bouquet to violets or saying a taste is reminiscent of truffles is not very meaningful if the listener or reader is unfamiliar with the smell of one and the flavour of the other. Yet I believe it is quite defensible to do so; analogies add extra dimensions and help other tasters to identify and memorize aspects. There are instances where, at a dinner party of like-minded individuals, the sheer compatibility of guests, food, and wines will spark off conversation of a high order. It doesn't matter that a profusion of abstract similes, analogies, evocations, richly enlightening at the time, would, if recorded, sound pretty flat the next morning.

A fine example of evocative writing, neatly bridging the gap between the French and English approaches to wine, was demonstrated by the late André Simon. In the first issue of the *Quarterly Journal of the Wine and Food Society*, he recorded what was to be the first of a series of "memorable" meals. It took place at the Hind's Head at Bray in 1934. At the end of the dinner the host, Barry Neame, asked André for his initial reaction to the wines. He answered that his "first thoughts evoked memories of Berkshire". A 1926 Chablis reminded him of "the grace of the silver willow", the 1919 Montrachet "of the stateliness of the Italian poplar", the 1920 Cheval Blanc "of the magnificence of the purple beech" and the 1870 Lafite "of the majesty of the royal oak". But as to the brandy (an 1842 Roullet et Delamain), "There was no tree with its roots in common clay to be mentioned in the same breath..."!

THE WINE SNOB

Out of a lesser man's mouth, with inappropriate wines, without the touch of real poetry and, above all, without imagination and understanding, André Simon's words would represent the quintessence of wine snobbery. "Snob" is a term I try to avoid – but, alas, it is only too frequently used, equally by the ignorant and by the academic. As I believe the snob's main armoury is language, it is appropriate to raise the subject at this point.

If there is such a thing as a wine snob, he or she will have all the attributes of any other sort of snob: affectation and pretentiousness covering up the lack of everything that makes a person worthy of serious attention. The aristocrat of the table, the nature's gentleman of the cellar, the true amateur, the deeply knowledgeable, are rarely, if ever, snobs.

Those who are modest, undogmatic, who listen to others' views, and are honest in their own opinions, should be safe from the brickbats of the envious and ignorant. Those who are knowledgeable about wine should merely be careful on what occasion and in whose company they air their opinions and display their scholarship.

THE WINE BORE

People who say little or nothing are not bores, just boring. It is the man of words (woman equally) who is at risk. A great expert can be a bore, particularly if speaking out of context, being repetitive, pedantic, opinionated, never listening to others or merely intoning in a tedious, grinding, long-winded way.

The wine bore is the person who speaks about wine when no one is inclined to listen, or to the exclusion of all else. The answer is to try, which is not always easy, to talk about one's enthusiasm or business only in the presence of those who are interested, and, if possible, to anticipate the level of that interest.

CONTEXT OF TASTING

The trouble is, those of us who talk about wine lay ourselves wide open. If we talk of what we know not, to impress, we are wine snobs; if we talk of what we know, wine bores. Let us therefore forget these pejorative terms and concentrate on building up our knowledge, and on the correct use of words. "Context" has cropped up several times in this book. It happens to be the crux of the problem. The context in which wine is tasted, and talked about, is of the greatest importance.

The occasion As stated earlier, tasting occasions, opportunities, and settings vary. The same wine may be viewed in a different light, and one's impressions and notes can differ.

Time and timing Tiredness or a rushed tasting will affect one's judgement and reduce the value of the tasting notes.

Lighting and colour The effects of natural and artificial lighting were discussed in the earlier chapter.*

Service of wine Wine served too warm, too cold, or tasted in too warm or too cold a room, will not taste the same. Wines served in one order might taste slightly different from the same wines served in another order.

Personal influences A dominant personality, or a dogmatic one, can make one's judgement waver. Try not to be diverted: rely on your own opinion.

I could go on. The point is that the senses, being delicate, are swayed by a multiplicity of outside factors. The impressions and the notes will reflect these; we must be conscious of influences, and counter or allow for them. After all, we are only human!

SUBJECTIVE OR OBJECTIVE TASTING

This brings me to a point which, I am sure, will be contentious. After over fifty years of tasting and teaching I am convinced that to talk about, let alone claim, total objectivity – "relating entirely to the external object" – in tasting is nonsense.

Moreover, to be a subjective taster is nothing to be ashamed of. One can even argue that a subjective approach – "arising out of the senses" – is the most enriching approach to fine wine. The problem is, as usual, to note or convey both subjective and objective impressions using words which can be understood. The sole object of one's concentration should be the wine, but in the ultimate analysis, "I, the taster", am the final arbiter.

JUDGEMENT AND TASTE THRESHOLDS

There are two areas in which judgment is required: at the commercial level and at the amateur (in the French sense). At the commercial level, a merchant (with or without formal training) will taste and use his judgment, and note and convey information about the wine to his customers. At wine festivals and shows, where wine is tasted competitively, the judges must work to a common approach and system of assessing wines. The more similar in quality and style the wines are, the more precisely the basis of judgment must be defined. When it comes to detecting small differences, particularly in wines of neutral character, the sensory thresholds (the level at which elements of smell and taste can be detected) of the judges are important. It would be sensible to test these, and it is possible to do so.†

QUANTIFYING TASTE

I cannot subscribe to the dictum that, in effect, nothing is worth knowing unless it can be expressed numerically; in respect of fine wine I cannot help feeling that a preoccupation with numbers merely serves to divert the taster from the true appreciation of the many facets of quality and style.◊

**Professor Jacques Puisais (Directeur du Laboratoire Départemental et Régional d'Analyses et des Recherches, Tours) has conducted experiments leading him to conclude that certain wall colours will make a wine taste sweeter or more acid.*

†Refer to the several Amerine and Roessler works in the Appendix.

◊Emile Peynaud stated, I note with satisfaction, "that which cannot be measured is often of greater significance than that which can".

Having said this, I can see little harm in allocating marks to a wine, so long as it is realized that a simple "out-of-ten" (twenty or one hundred) score is only one taster's judgment of one wine, or one in a range of wines, in a particular context at one moment of time. At best it is an approximation, supporting one's notes. However, I find it helpful in two other respects: at a comparative tasting it enables me to make up my mind and, afterwards, helps me recall which wines I preferred.

AVERAGING SCORES

Beware: to take the average of the scores or marks of a number of tasters – particularly if they are many and varied in experience and ability – can be highly misleading. It can reduce to a blurred, middle-of-the-road sector both outstandingly good and below average, even faulty, wines. An overgenerous scorer, therefore, will neutralize a highly critical one. One solution is not to take into account exceptionally high or exceptionally low ratings.

STATISTICAL PROCEDURES

The French and American academics' partiality to algebra is altogether another thing. The object of the statistician is to reduce the chance element. In effect, one eliminates as far as possible all the conditions that induce the varying subjective impressions already referred to, and, after testing the tasters, analyses the results mathematically. I concede that with certain types of wine and in certain circumstances there is a case to be made, but it is generally beyond the level of knowledge and out of the area of interest of most wine-lovers, professional, or amateur.

SUMMING UP

Be honest with yourself. Try to express your own impressions and opinions, but be careful in your use of words – particularly if you need to convey them to a third person or even to be meaningful to yourself at a later date.

Frankly, the subdivisions are infinite. One can argue endlessly about what words should be used. What might be acceptable to, and perfectly understood by, one person, may sound fatuous to another. There are no hard-and-fast rules. Words will vary from person to person, group to group; they will depend on usage, on teaching. Some will come into favour, some will fall out of favour.

In a social context, with good wines and like-minded people, loosen up: don't be afraid to express an opinion or a preference; let your imagination roam. Evocative comments help open up new vistas for others, and aid the overall appreciation and mental digestion of the wine. It is not so much precision that is required as a vital exchange of reactions and ideas, enabling so much more to be revealed, so much more to be gained.

In the final analysis, words should be used to illuminate and to enlighten; and they must be used as meaningfully as possible. If in doubt, refer to the following glossary. Check what you think you mean by what – let me be honest – *I* think I mean. You might not agree with all the definitions. At least they will provide food for thought. Lastly, try to use words in the correct context, and qualify them when necessary.

Some descriptive words

Below are listed basic words and expressions in the order of tasting of any red or white wine. Refer to the "Full glossary" (*see* pages 126–44 for full definitions).

RED WINES

Appearance

depth	very pale, pale, medium-pale, medium-deep, deep, very deep, opaque
colour/hue	purple, mauve, ruby, red, tile-red, brown-tinged, red-brown, mahogany
clarity	bright, dull, bitty, hazy, cloudy; light or heavy sediment

Nose or bouquet

condition	clean, unclean (sulphury, oxidized, vinegary, etc.)
fruit	fruity, lacking fruit, vinous, varietal, named variety
development	dumb, immature, undeveloped, well-developed, forthcoming, very mature, over-mature
quality	poor, ordinary, good, fine, great, magnificent

Palate

apparent dryness	(noticeably) dry, slightly or unusually sweet (for a red wine), tannic
body	very light (VL)*, light (L), medium-light (ML), medium (M), medium-full (MF), full-bodied (F), heavy
tannin	astringent, noticeably drying, soft tannins, mellow
acid	soft, lacking acidity, refreshing, perfect acidity, over-acid, tart, acetic
fruit, flavour	fruity, lacking fruit, vinous, flavoursome, lacking flavour (describe flavour – use analogies when appropriate)
development	well-developed, very mature, mature, beginning to mature, undeveloped, "green"
overall balance	well-balanced, unbalanced
length and finish	long, short, lingering, fine aftertaste

**I use abbreviations in my own notes. The possible confusion between initials is avoided by tasting, and using words, in a regular order and under appropriate headings. For example, under "Palate", "D, MF" indicates "dry, medium-full-bodied". Other abbreviations I use: fl (flavour), bal (balance), Y (youthful/ immature), V/A (volatile acidity), B/A (bottle-age), mat (mature), ex (excellent),t & a (tannin and acidity), etc.*

WHITE WINES

Slight difference of emphasis, particularly regarding colour and sweetness:

Appearance

depth	colourless, very pale, medium, deep
colour/hue	green-tinged, yellow-green, yellow, straw, yellow-gold, gold, amber, deep gold, brown
clarity	star-bright, bright, dull, cloudy, hazy, bitty

Nose or Bouquet

more or less as for red wines

Palate

dry/sweet	bone-dry, dry, medium-dry, medium-sweet, sweet, very sweet
body, acidity	more or less as for red wines (tannin is not normally a factor in white wines); acidity is important, balancing sugar content
in addition	fruit, development, balance, finish are other factors to consider

Words used in the description of wine by category

For ease of reference, I have listed here those words in common use, those which need qualifying, those to use with care and additional qualitative adjectives. For a full list of tasting terms and their definitions, refer to the "Full glossary".

Words in common use

acid/acidity
aroma
balance/well-balanced
bouquet
clean
dry/medium-dry, etc.
fruity
grapey
hard
harsh
poor
refreshing
soft
sweet
tannin, tannic
tough
vinegary
watery

Words in common use which should be used in a qualified context

aftertaste
big
bland
body
bright
character
coarse
dull
fat
fine
finish
flat
full
heavy
light
little
long
mature/maturity
meaty
medium
neutral
ordinary
peppery
positive
rich
round
sour
strong
varietal
weak
youthful

Words to use precisely and with care

astringent
baked
bite
bitter
corked
dumb
earthy
extract
feminine
flabby
flinty
forthcoming
green
hot
iron
maderized
mouldy
nutty
oxidized
penetrating
piquant
pungent
robust
rough
sharp
smoky
stalky
tang/tangy
tart
vinous
woody
zesty/zestful

Additional qualitative descriptions

aromatic
breed, well-bred
complex
distinguished
elegant
finesse
flowery
fragrant
insipid
luscious
mellow
metallic
musty
noble
perfumed
powerful
raw
ripe
scented
sensuous
silky
smooth
spicy
subtle
supple
unripe
velvety
vinosity
well-developed
yeasty

How to taste – a practical recapitulation

I am tempted to believe that smell and taste are in fact but a single composite sense, whose laboratory is the mouth and its chimney the nose.

Brillat-Savarin

THE PHYSIOLOGY OF TASTE, 1825

So far I have given the reader a good deal of background detail: how the senses work, the elements which make up the tasting process, and the characteristics of the regions, grapes, etc. The organization of tastings and the use of words have also been dealt with. What I propose to do now is to summarize the act of tasting: what precisely to look for, how to smell and taste effectively, and what factors to bear in mind. To start with, white wines tend to be less complex than reds, reflected in the fact that the colour variations are narrower and less significant; the aroma of a young white wine has immediacy which is more readily detectable, whereas the bouquet of a red evolves more slowly and subtly. On the palate, whites tend to have a simpler counterpoint of sweetness and acidity, fruit, and measurable length; reds are less of an open book – alcohol and tannins add to their complexity.

Appearance

The two main elements are depth and the actual hue or colour. Secondary factors are clarity and viscosity. Here is how to set about spotting them.

DEPTH

Assuming we have an appropriate tasting glass, a white-topped table, and suitable lighting (previously described) the depth of colour is observed by leaving the glass on the table and looking down at an angle of 45° or from immediately above.

The variations in the depth of white wine are slight and relatively unimportant. The depth of red wine is important and significant: a pale colour usually indicates lightness of body and extract (though some fine burgundies with fairly high alcohol content can be misleadingly pale), a deep colour foreshadows a fuller-bodied wine, and a very deep, virtually opaque appearance will be indicative of high alcohol content and extract and probably substantial tannin and fruit.

The depth of colour can be controlled by vinification, but in classic districts like Bordeaux, a deep colour generally indicates a good vintage, and conversely, a weak, feeble colour a poor vintage. Hot sun thickens the skins which provide this red pigment; warmth creates, through the leaves, the grape sugar which, during fermentation, is converted into alcohol. So, in a good year, after a hot, sunny summer and early autumn, the wine produced will have a deep, intense colour and high alcohol content. Lack of both sun and warmth – cloudy, cold, and wet weather – results in thin skins and low sugar levels, resulting in low degrees of alcohol and pale colour.

COLOUR OR HUE

Pick up the glass by the stem, tilt it over the white table top, and, from above, observe the colour at the deepest part of the bowl and its graduation to the rim. The actual colour is partly dependent on the grape variety.

White wine Notice the hint of green in young dry whites, particularly from northerly wine districts like the Mosel and Sancerre; the more positive yellow pigment of a ripe Chardonnay from Meursault or the Hunter Valley, or the already yellow-gold shades of young dessert wines and the deeper yellows, golds, and ambers which result from mature bottle-age.

Red wine A bright purple rim indicates immaturity, a plummy red the transition stage, and, before the red-brown of maturity sets in, there is a no man's land which I describe as "on the turn". Note the rich mahogany rim of an old red Bordeaux and watch out for the tell-tale drab brown of one that is too old and oxidized. Colour, incidentally, is often the most accurate measure of the maturity of red wine.

CLARITY, BRIGHTNESS, LIMPIDITY

Pick up the glass by the stem and hold it up to a light. A fine wine in a healthy condition seems to have that extra sheen, whereas a lacklustre appearance will usually indicate a lacklustre wine. Slight bittiness is usually of little importance, as are pieces of cork, usually the result of careless cork pulling. Cloudiness, a slightly milky, blue, or orange hue indicate a fault.

VISCOSITY, LEGS, TEARS, AND BEADS

Keep the base of the glass on the table and rotate it, swirling the wine up the sides of the glass. Observe the way the ring of liquid slips down and forms legs or tears. There are two good and one minor reason for swirling the wine: most importantly, it helps coat as much of the inside of the glass as possible, maximizing the surface area. I also believe it helps to rouse the wine, sometimes to shake out odd smells (particularly old wines). And if the glass itself is not clean and polished, the swirl does the trick! (For significance *see* page 59.) At the same time, see if there are any tell-tale beads round the rim of the wine, tiny bubbles which, in a young white wine and some young reds, indicate the presence of carbon dioxide which will give a *spritzig* prickle or *pétillance* in the mouth; in an old red wine it is more likely a sign of cracking up.

Nose or bouquet

Having swirled and aroused the wine, helping it to release its volatile ethers, pick the glass up by the stem and just waft it under the nose. It is essential to give one's fullest concentration to this in order not to miss the vital first impression. Just note whether the wine is clean and fresh, has a distinctive varietal (grape) aroma, shows youthful acidity, or mellow age. Not all that a wine has to reveal is conveyed by the first impression, but it sometimes triggers an immediate recognition. It is certainly the most evocative stage. And it is the first impression which, hopefully, will capture the fleeting volatile elements of the wine's make-up. Emile Peynaud, with refreshing simplicity, describes volatile substances as "those capable of escaping from the glass or disappearing in the mouth". They are easy, superficially, to spot but very difficult to analyse, extremely important in relation to quality; quoting Peynaud again, "give the wine its personality".

Next, give another gentle swirl, hold the wine to the nose, and this time inhale gently. While doing this, try to sort out each element: the fruit, perhaps a noticeable grape variety, the acidity – mouth-puckering malic, the cooking-apple smell of unripe green grapes; the pleasant mouth-watering tartaric acid; the high-toned, vinegary whiff indicating excess volatile acidity.

Beware: if you inhale too protractedly the nose will become almost anaesthetized. The same applies to really deep, long sniffs. Both will result in a diminution of smell.

Sometimes a very young red wine yields little on the nose. A leathery smell indicates the presence of considerable tannin; a pepperiness, high alcohol content. Persist gently and patiently to detect and draw out latent richness and fruit.

A mature white wine of a good vintage will have a soft, fragrant, honey-like bouquet. A fine mature red Bordeaux will show a well-knit mellow, warm-brick smell which will develop in the glass to a rich, wholemeal-biscuity fragrance. But a magnificently opulent bouquet sometimes serves to disguise the structure of an old wine which may be falling apart.

Young wines have raw component parts which can, in effect, be separated, *i.e.* individually detected. As wines mature, those component parts blend together, losing their individual identities, becoming a harmonious, homogeneous fragrance – but not by any means the same: for example Bordeaux and burgundy, Rhine wine and Loire, New Zealand Chardonnay – each will have its own character, weight, and style.

Palate or taste

For the experienced taster, the wine in the mouth will largely confirm what has been detected by the eye and nose. Take a sip, a reasonable mouthful.

Notice the entry: at this stage sweetness will be detected. Draw in air as the wine crosses the tongue. This will help the aromatic elements of taste to fill the mouth. If at a tasting, spit out; otherwise swallow, noting various facets of flavour as it crosses the palate, its component parts, length, and finish. Note the elements in a logical order:

SWEETNESS

Perhaps the most important feature of a white wine, and certainly the first to be noticed. Is it dry, *i.e.* totally lacking sweetness, slightly sweet, or very sweet? Virtually all red wines are fully fermented out, leaving little or no residual sugar. So the dryness/sweetness factor is not important: red wines are basically dry. However, a certain softness and slight sweetness is noted when a red wine has been made from fully ripe grapes, of a particularly good vintage, or from a hot, sunny wine area. This is due partly to a minute amount of residual sugar but also from the unusually high level of ethyl alcohol, which gives an impression of sweetness.

Sweetness should be judged on entry not at the back of the mouth, as the acid content of the wine can have a masking effect or, conversely, may exaggerate the dryness. Wines with naturally high acidity, like madeira and some German dessert wines, need sweetness as raspberries need sugar.

ACIDITY

Acidity makes one cluck one's tongue. An agreeable degree of tartaric acid will give the wine a pleasant, refreshing quality. For me, acidity is the nervous system of a wine; it is one of the essential structural elements, a cornerstone which sustains the wine and without which it will be flabby and dull. Acidity gives the wine finish. It also counterbalances the naturally high sugar content of sweet wines.

Too much acidity – raw, unripe acidity – upsets the balance, tastes tart, and is mouth-puckering. There are, however, various different sorts of acidity and many words used to describe their degrees and effects – such as acetic, sharp, tart, green, sour – listed in the "Full glossary".

BODY, WEIGHT, ALCOHOL

Is the wine light and insubstantial in the mouth or is it heavy, massive, mouth-filling? The dominating factor is alcohol. An alcoholic strength of 11°G L (*see* Glossary) or eleven per cent by weight or volume (the same thing) is considered light: for example a wine from the Mosel. A medium-weight wine will probably be between twelve and 12.5 per cent, say a moderately good red Bordeaux of an average vintage. A "full-bodied" wine's alcohol strength such as Corton or Côte-Rôtie will be in the thirteen to fourteen per cent range whereas "fortified" wine like port, madeira, will average twenty per cent.

However, alcohol does not travel alone. A full-bodied, young red wine might also be laden with tannin; it will have extract and, in short, substance. But, in the end, alcohol is recognized as the wine's backbone.

TANNIN

Tannin is a highly important element in red wine. It is an antioxidant and acts as a preservative. It is derived mainly from skins during fermentation, and is also leached from new-oak casks during maturation.

Hard tannins are astringent and can be distinctly bitter; soft, ripe tannins less so. Both, as the wine matures, soften and precipitate colouring matter. Tannin also performs other useful functions; each sip leaves the mouth clean and dry in readiness for the next mouthful. It is also good for the digestion and helps keep one's arteries clear!

FRUIT, OAK, AND OTHER FLAVOURS

The sugars, acids, alcohols, and tannins are, perhaps, the basic structural elements. The flavour of wine is supplemented by a myriad of other trace elements. These are volatile or fixed derived from the fruit itself, from the minerals taken from the soil, from the process of fermentation, the yeast, the wood... even from the air.

A lot of the spicy and aromatic flavours (and smells, for they are both linked) are directly attributable to a particular cause. Vanilla is derived from ethyl vanilline, the principal odour of oak wood, and leather from tannin. But by far the most smells and tastes are described by analogy, the closest resemblance to the wine in the mouth. Yet all are there for a particular physical or chemical reason.

That is why the taster should first of all try hard to recognize smells and tastes such as tobacco, pine or petroleum, caramel, crusty bread, liquorice, pepper, cinnamon. Also note the wine, its origin, age, grape variety, so that one can link a smell and a place, a soil, a method of winemaking, a hot year. The combination of these smells and tastes often results in something indefinable. Add an element, try to take it away, and the whole ensemble crumbles. This is the mystery and the challenge of wine.

The taster should not be afraid to try and put into words the immediate impact of the smell and taste of a wine – no matter how fanciful these may sound. Let the wine do the speaking, just do your best to translate.

BALANCE, FINESSE – THE ASPECTS OF QUALITY

By balance we mean that the interwoven component parts are in equilibrium. Not just the fruit, tannin, acidity, and alcohol, but also the subtler, volatile, and often elusive elements which add to the sum total.

A young wine can be considered balanced despite lack of development, but only a fully mature wine will have softness yet firmness, delicacy with strength, length without attenuation, unfolding and revealing the more one smells and tastes.

Length is a measure of quality: the time the flavour takes to cross the mouth. The aftertaste is the persistence of flavour and fragrance after the wine has been swallowed. Intensity and fragrance are important aspects of quality.

A poor wine might well have a raw, coarse texture, lack of positive flavour, and a grubby, unclean end-taste. An ordinary wine comes into the mouth with no particular impact, has a neutral, faintly wine-related flavour which disappears via a short, insipid end. A good wine will have a positive entry and positive flavour – a beginning, a middle, and an end. A fine wine has length, possibly a silky texture, a mouth-filling yet delicate flavour, good length, a crisp finish, and a lingering aftertaste. A great wine is a fine wine with extra dimensions and, like a kaleidoscope, will present the taster's nose and palate with a myriad of extraordinary changing patterns.

MAKING YOUR OWN TASTING NOTES

Try different ways of expressing in words the elements and qualities of the wine in your glass, first noting the basics for example: "deep purple; low-keyed nose; dry, full, tannic, unready". Then expand: "deep, opaque at the core, immature purple rim. Nose: bouquet undeveloped but with distinctive aroma, Merlot dominating. Will develop. Palate: hint of ripeness on entry but overall dry with substantial tannin and acidity. Full-bodied, high alcoholic content, rich extract, good length. Conclude: drinkable in five years, possibly fully developed in ten, sound, mature life span up to twenty years from the date of tasting". And what about a numerical rating, say 17/20 for intrinsic quality and future promise? If all this is too much, then at the very least: "deep, young, will be good".

A last word of advice: try and gear your notes to match the type and quality of wine. It is fatuous to dream up an elaborate description of a wine whose sole virtue is a bargain price allied to modest drinkability. Conversely it is a tragic waste not to notice, and note, the beautiful appearance, fragrant nose, and lovely taste of something really special.

Tasting expertise

The palate, like the eye, the ear, or touch, acquires with practice various degrees of sensitiveness that would be incredible were it not a well ascertained fact.

T. G. Shaw

WINE, THE VINE AND THE CELLAR, 1863

There are, I believe, two general but little-understood points concerning tasting ability, and they are related. First the more one has tasted, the less clear-cut may be one's reactions and the less dogmatic one's pronouncements. This is because the experienced taster, almost always a professional, will have been exposed to such a wide range of closely related smells and tastes, and have met with many exceptions to the rules. The corollary is an easily noted one: that the beginner and amateur, having fresh perception and an uncluttered vinous memory, is frequently more certain of him or herself and sometimes more accurate in identification.

Second, a point which may probably be widely accepted but that is rarely admitted: successful "guessing-game" experts almost always perform in the comparatively limited field of very fine wines and good vintages, the characteristics of which stand out in sharp black and white compared with the half-tones of middle-quality wines or the bleak wash of the *ordinaires*. It is not at all uncommon for the highest scorers to be amateurs, for their greatest performances are usually set in an even more limited (however excellent) context: that of their own and their friends' cellars. I do not wish to belittle the seasoned and discerning amateur palates, or spoil their fun. On the contrary, without such enthusiastic and enquiring attitudes, without their scholarship, the incentive to produce such wines would diminish – to everyone's loss. I merely make these points to keep things in perspective. Having cleared the ground, I would like to pursue the subject of tasting "blind".

TASTING BLIND

It is my firm opinion (one of the few these days unwhittled by doubts!) that to assess the qualities of a wine by tasting it completely blind, without any hint of what it might be, is the most useful and salutary discipline that any self-respecting taster can be given. It is not infrequently the most humiliating. The first thing it does is to concentrate the thoughts, exposing fresh and unprejudiced senses to the problems of analysing the appearance, bouquet, and flavour. To know what the wine is before one starts to taste is like reading the end of a detective novel first: it satisfies the curiosity but dampens the interest.

The occasion... Should blind tastings and guessing games be conducted at the dinner table? This is perhaps the most vexed question of all. I am sure that my colleagues in the British wine trade, particularly fellow Masters of Wine, will be the first to agree that it is one of the hazards of their occupation to be expected to perform before an anonymous-looking glass of wine and under the expectant gaze of only too un-anonymous hosts and fellow guests; to pronounce vineyard, vintage, and the name of the cellar-master in ten seconds flat. It is not that it cannot be done, even in this time.

It can, but only in rare and exceptional circumstances (and I exclude all known methods of cheating, like bribing the butler!). The point is that unless there is an immediate and quite positive click of recognition, the only alternative is an extremely elaborate round-the-houses process of elimination, an intellectual exercise that takes time and may well be acutely boring for those waiting and watching. At a dinner party, particularly, the surest way of offending one's hostess is to undergo these mental contortions, letting one's meal go cold, and possibly even delaying subsequent courses.

...and the company Broad-minded professionals do not mind making fools of themselves in the company of others in the business. At least, they reassure themselves, their friends in the trade know how really difficult it is to identify wines, and they all have the comforting knowledge of their common manifold blunders. It is another thing to be exposed before, and caught out by, amateurs – perhaps their own customers or readers – who simply do not understand the complexity and problems involved.

DINNER PARTY TASTINGS

I personally subscribe to blind tastings, at least of the principal wines, at a dinner party, but only on the following conditions:

- that the occasion is an appropriate one – good and carefully planned wines with appropriate food
- that the company is like-minded; otherwise the whole thing becomes a bit tedious and unbalanced, off-putting for expert and nonexpert alike
- that reasonable time is allowed for thinking about the wine; the service of wine and food must be timed carefully to accommodate this. Nothing is more irritating and fatuous, in my opinion, than for a host to say, "What is it?" and then blurt out the answer before anyone has had a chance to taste the wine properly
- that the length of time is not dragged out and that no one is forced to a complete and final answer if it is not naturally forthcoming. Indeed, in mixed company (not just of "genders" but professional and amateur) I think it probably tactless of the host to try to extract nearest answers in a competitive manner. If people want to be sporting, let them have a go. (This can be a good thing, for one is stimulated by hearing other people's reactions and points of view.) On the other hand, it should be remembered that some people can no more guess wines in public than they can stand on a table and sing

The dinner-party host has peculiarly difficult responsibilities. There is a danger of two extremes that, respectively, can be disheartening and deadly: if beautiful wines are produced and not noticed or commented on at all; if too much of a rigmarole is made of the occasion. Even variations in the middle range can be unsatisfactory. It is of little satisfaction for a wine-loving guest to enjoy the wine but not to know what it is. The very least that should be provided is a small menu card with the wines listed, which can be taken away by the interested guest. Quite frankly, I carry a little note card and make notes furtively or blatantly depending on how well I know the host.

MENU AND WINE CARDS

How does one provide the guests with a menu card without revealing in advance the names of the wines? There are at least two ways. One is to provide a small folded card with a seal. When the seal is broken, the list of wines is revealed inside. (I first came across this, charmingly done, by that most articulate of wine-lovers, the late Tony Alment, one of that excellent breed of civilized medical men who seem to be the universal backbone of wine-loving fraternities.)

The other is a variation I use occasionally, slightly more elaborate in that it reveals the identity of each wine in turn. I write the menu on the left-hand side of a stiff card, and the matching list of wines, well-spaced, on the right. Each wine name is covered with a finger of paper held in place by a paper clip. Those who cannot wait can quietly remove the covers. Those who want to rise to the challenge and persist until they have exhausted their memory banks can do so without keeping everyone in suspense. It is nice to be able to arrive, by deduction, at a district or vintage. But I believe the main benefit of not knowing the wine in advance, even at a dinner party, is concentration of thought and judgment; for the professional, this is a good discipline and, for the amateur, part of the learning process. Before leaving tasting mystique and expertise, I would like to comment on two interesting aspects of blind tasting.

FIRST IMPRESSIONS

It is the subconscious, evocative memory that enables a taster, presumably highly sensitive to smells and tastes, to reach a perfect, or at least remarkably accurate, assessment of a wine tasted blind. The value of first impressions is well-known to experienced tasters, but their true significance is less well understood. As we have seen from the earlier chapter covering the physical aspects of tasting, the sense of smell, though often a Cinderella in development, is primitive and primal, and has the capability of almost instantly recalling a total experience from the memory, seemingly without the intervention of intellect.

What is most frequently not understood is that if the memory-brain does not instinctively and immediately produce an intelligible reaction, the reliance on this for the wine in question might as well be abandoned straight away, and conscious reasoning must begin.

WORKING IT OUT

This second approach is totally opposite to the reflex action of the first impression; it requires the exercise of thoughtful reasoning; the use of eyes, nose, and palate to deduce the answer that the nerve cells and memory failed to conjure up at first go. I personally, at this stage, try to detect the grape used, the regional characteristics, and work out a rough age-bracket; then, by the process of elimination, arrive backwards at the answer, or, at any rate, at an approximation of district and vintage, with a definite opinion of quality. This takes time and patience. The results are rarely as spectacular as those produced by one's evocative memory. These methods and techniques are dealt with below in greater detail.

NO CHEATING!

The very last word on this subject is an appeal for honesty, tempered with consideration. Cheating and short cuts in the tasting game are self-defeating. The concientious taster puts his blinkers on, is honest with himself, and is not influenced and led astray by others. On the other hand, the pursuit of zealous tasting expertise is best pursued in appropriate company, and then only with discretion; otherwise the whole thing becomes a bore.

Appreciation, recognition, and deduction

Having covered first principles, the senses, the approach to tasting and, broadly, those elements which give rise to taste, the time has come to dig a little deeper.

Tasting is not just an isolated theoretical exercise. It is usually an assessment of physical attributes in relation to a particular wine or wines, with a specific end in view (*see* pages 8–9). It may well have one of the following purposes:

- to assess the quality, state of development, and possibly the value of a known wine
- to assess the relative quality and value of a known type of wine – possibly one of a range of similar or identically named wines
- to identify, from its taste characteristics, the style, region, quality, and maturity of an unknown wine

We might even reduce the taster's problem to a basic two:

- knowing the name and full details of the wine, to judge its true qualities, etc.; this boils down to assessment and appreciation
- knowing little or nothing about the wine, to find what it is, from an accurate assessment of its characteristics, by tasting alone

This is encompassed by two words: recognition and deduction

Before embarking, however, I must stress that what follows next must be seen in the context of a relaxed and informal group of like-minded amateurs (in the French sense) concentrating their attentions upon the merits of vintage wines. I am not, for example, writing about clinical laboratory tests to measure tasting thresholds, to isolate elements, to detect and quantify small differences in new wines made from experimental vines – those worthy endeavours we can leave to schools of viticulture and oenology. Equally out of court are those formally, often excellently, organized tasting competitions, inter-district and international, where judges sit in splendid isolation to award medals to the best commercial entries.

I am not trying to belittle either approach, though I confess I am confused and bored with some of the scientific approaches to sensory evaluation, with their emphasis on methodology, triangular tests, random numbers, and abstruse mathematical formulae. Awarding gold medals can take on nationalistic or political overtones; some are like beauty contests, when it appears to the impartial onlooker that the really lovely girls have stayed at home. The fact of the matter is that well established fine and great wines are not entered for such competitions.

APPRECIATION AND ASSESSMENT

At its most elementary level, appreciation manifests itself in a positive liking (or dislike) for a wine, whether at a tasting or at a dinner party.

At the same level, discrimination is expressed by a preference for one wine among a group of wines. This is the hedonistic approach.

Wine merchants often find that even people fairly new to wine can be quite discriminating. Given two or three wines to taste, the customer will often express a marked preference for the best-quality wine of a group, price notwithstanding. However, the beginner falters when trying to express the degree of quality, and in sifting and describing the individual characteristics which, in combination, have affected his natural taste instincts.

Without wishing to be condescending, what I am trying to say is that appreciation and simple discrimination are relatively easy. The next stage, assessment, is more complex and requires some background knowledge and tasting experience. Take one very important element: quality, for example. Quality is always relative. Even the best Balkan Riesling will be on a lower quality plane than a Rheingau of *Prädikat* level from a good estate; the best sparkling Loire wine beneath a leading Grande Marque Champagne; and the best single-vineyard Beaujolais will be below the peak of a *grand cru* Côte de Nuits. One has to know the relative quality strata before one begins.

There is a whole kaleidoscope of tastes (and smells) that emanate from the physical characteristics of grape varieties, soil and climatic influences, winemaking techniques and effects of age (*see* "Origins of taste characteristics"). They reveal style, region, and maturity as well as quality. The greater one's understanding of all these factors, the more accurate and rapid will be one's overall assessment and final pronouncement.

RECOGNITION AND DEDUCTION

Imagine that you are in the position where you are confronted with a glass containing an unknown wine. The steps which follow – the process of recognition and deduction – are perhaps the most difficult a taster has to contend with. He will have to bring to bear all his critical tasting faculties and knowledge. Guessing is not allowed. Or is it? Let's not be too dogmatic, for there is surely only a fine dividing line between the inspired guess and split-second recognition: both may stem from a subconscious signal from the evocative memory. However, what usually happens is that we are baffled and taunted by a half-familiar smell or taste that evades recognition. It remains on the tip of the tongue – literally in this case – and the harder we try, the less is revealed.

If there is failure of recognition at this stage, the only solution is to back out, start again, and attempt deduction by a systematic examination of taste characteristics. This requires a good palate, a detailed knowledge of regions and vintages, and the ability to link the reactions of the former with the recollections of the latter. This, sadly, is as difficult as it sounds. There are, however, two useful techniques to consider: elimination and bracketing.

DEDUCTION BY ELIMINATION

The technique of elimination entails a mental exercise. Take the most positively identified characteristics of the wine, compare them with the known characteristics of other wines, and cross off those that do not remotely match up. In other words, first eliminate all the obvious wines it cannot be; then consider those it could be; finally, deduce what it must be. This simple and effective method can be used to arrive at the grape variety, style, and geographical area; even the district and vineyard. It is also useful to confirm or strengthen previously half-held opinions.

Method What happens in practice is this: one picks up the glass of unknown wine and examines first its appearance, bouquet, and flavour, sifting the normal, straightforward, or classic from the unusual or "foreign".

Take its appearance first of all. Is it unusually deep (this applies to either red or white) or abnormally pale (red mainly)? Is it strikingly young and purple or "sear and yellow"? Is it star-bright or hazy or slightly *pétillant*? The important thing is not just to notice these factors but to work out what might cause them. For example, unusual depth of colour in a red wine might be due to a fine, hot vintage year in a temperate region like Bordeaux, or might indicate its origin in a sun-baked section of the Rhône Valley, or from warmer regions like California, the Cape, or the irrigation areas of Australia.

It could also arise from the vinification – a long fermentation which extracts a good deal of colour from the skins. With unusually pale-coloured wines the reverse might apply. All these will be clues, pointers. It is vital in the early stages not to jump to conclusions, but to leave the tracks open, passing on to the nose and then to the taste for a further crystallization of impressions, and then on to the final confirmation.

So, I repeat: get as many clues and leads from the appearance as possible; leave doubts hanging in the air and then pass on to the nose of the wine. Once again, one looks for any unusual or outstanding characteristics: first of all, whether there is a distinctive grape aroma and whether it is from a classic European region or "New World". If you can recognize the grape variety, the areas where this grape is never grown can be eliminated. Incidentally, strength of aroma, in the sense of fullness and forthcomingness, is not the sole criterion: a fine classic grape aroma can be subdued, even scarcely noticeable, particularly when the wine is young and undeveloped. What one is really looking for is clarity and purity of character. The more indeterminate and neutral the smell, the poorer the quality.

The most important thing of all is to realize that the combination of appearance and nose can provide many, if not all, of the clues to a wine's identity. By spotting the main characteristics and eliminating what the wine cannot be, one's conclusions can then be confirmed on the palate; or, at least, one is left with likely alternatives to consider.

Confirmation In what way can the palate aid and confirm? Firstly, note the major taste factors on the palate: sweetness (in white wine, mainly); the levels of tannin, acidity, and alcohol; the extract, its richness; the continuity of varietal characteristics (*i.e.* flavour to match the grape aroma); finesse, breed, and, above all, length and intensity of flavour and finish – in short, quality. It is the linking of these taste factors to the appearance and smell which should firmly anchor the total impression and lead one straight – or more cautiously by elimination – to a logical conclusion.

By now it should be obvious that one can only eliminate on a broad "taste front" by having a wide knowledge to match, or on a narrow front with a detailed knowledge. Take heart, however; though considerable tasting experience is desirable, it is surprising how much can be achieved by limited experience aided by a basic knowledge of grape, district, and age characteristics.

By constantly reading wine books and articles, one can, over a period, gain knowledge of what certain types of wine should taste like, and link the recollection of these characteristics to the actual taste of the wine in the glass. Indeed, I shall go one stage further and say that it is perfectly possible to deduce what a wine is even though one has never before tasted it, simply by recognizing taste characteristics one has read or heard about. It would be rash for the taster in such circumstances to say that the wine definitely is from such-and-such vineyard; better to conclude that it might well be. Indeed, to be dogmatic at all in the field of tasting is both risky and tiresome.

What to expect Now, one of the difficulties facing the keen wine-lover is finding out what a wine ought to taste like. By no means all of the many otherwise excellent books on wine actually help. Nevertheless, if you read widely, an impression of the characteristics of the wines of various areas and districts should eventually be conveyed.

A combination of reading and visits (with tastings, of course) to various wine areas is the best way of learning the salient characteristics. The chapter "Main regional characteristics" should point the beginner in the right direction. Over a period of time, one's memory will be furnished with a library of names and tastes – together with the inevitable exceptions to the rules that ensure that one never has a dull moment.

DEDUCTION BY BRACKETING

To round off this section, here is a short exposition upon the useful method of bracketing, followed by two examples of the blind-tasting technique. Bracketing also involves elimination. It is most useful when trying to assess the age of a wine.

Once again, some knowledge is required, this time of the vintage characteristics of the area that one assumes, or knows, the wine to have come from. At one end of the bracket will be the oldest vintage it could possibly be; at the other, the youngest. The bracket may extend over ten or twenty years, or even longer in the case of really old wines.

The next stage is to jot down the most appropriate intervening vintages, eliminating the off-years if the wine is robust, well-made, and classic (and vice versa if the wine is light and feeble) until one is left with three or four possible vintage years. The final piece of elimination follows a thoughtful examination of the wine, comparing it against the known features of those singled-out vintages until, hopefully, one is left with just one inevitable choice of year. Incidentally, it is not sufficient merely to know that 1990, for example, was a classic year in Bordeaux. It must also be borne in mind that not all the wines of the Bordelais are made in the same way, and that the varieties of grapes grown and blended can have different effects on the colour, bouquet, and taste.

One must know how the wines – at any rate the key wines – have developed in different districts, and be aware of the fact that the wines of St-Emilion, for example, and certain red Graves, develop more quickly than the firmer wines of the Médoc. Once again, this sort of information is "bracketed" in one's mind and a conclusion often reached by the process of elimination described.

Examples

The trouble about trying to explain in words techniques that are second nature to the experienced taster is that the whole exercise is made to sound impossibly difficult. This is certainly not the intention. There is nothing I dislike more than the academic use of long words where short ones would do, as if one had to surround oneself with an off-putting protective layer of super-professionalism. My aim all along has been to try and break down the barriers of the unknown into logical and progressive steps. If words are used that sound curious and stultified (or even pure "winesmanship") to the amateur, let him or her remember that all specialists have their own peculiar vocabularies, whether they are musicians, lawyers, gardeners, or judges of dogs at Cruft's.

To help explain how elimination techniques work in practice, here are two examples of wines tasted blind. The approach, train of thought, and notes made were precisely as follows:

WINE NO 1 (WHITE)

Served "blind", no sight of the bottle or label! – in a standard ISO tasting glass (*see* page 54), cool but not cold.

Appearance Pale yellow – frankly the sort of colour common to many dry white wines – but star bright with the sort of extra sheen of good winemaking.

Nose Clearly of good quality but hard to define, and still youthful. A touch of honey. Ripe grapes. As the varietal character is not – to me, at any rate – salient, I proceed to eliminate: it does not have the often raw, sometimes floral, usually acidic aroma of Sauvignon Blanc nor, equally certainly, Chardonnay in any of its forms: buttery, smoky-oaky, vanillin. Of the other distinctive grape varieties, certainly not a spicy, rose scented, lychee-like Gewurztraminer, nor any of the grapey-smelling Muscats. Sémillon, possibly, Chenin Blanc, perhaps, but if it came from the Loire it would be more acidic, as would a classic Riesling. Not sure. I shall taste it and see.

Palate Although I expected a dry wine it is distinctly sweet when it enters the mouth, the natural sweetness of very ripe, possibly late-picked grapes and highish alcohol. When combined with the strength of the wine, considerable body and extract, an undefinable richness. This absolutely rules out a Riesling from the Rhine or Mosel which is far lower in alcohol (sometimes as low as 7°; for a dry wine 11° or 12°), lighter in style, and with very noticeable acidity. The flavour is delicious but, like the nose, baffling and unlike the more obvious varietals. So I thrash around, thinking of other areas, other white wines – north Italy, Condrieu, something from south California, Santa Barbara?

What I do notice is the texture, fleshy without being fat, wonderful length, clearly one of the rare white wines which has the constitution to wear well. Which classic region produces white wines with this sort of class and level of alcohol? I turn to Alsace, but having ruled out Riesling and Gewurztraminer, both of which, in Alsace, can have highish to very high (by table wine standards) alcoholic levels, I conclude that it must be a Pinot Gris.

It turns out to be just that, a Pinot Gris from the Heimburg vineyard, vintage 1998, and from the renowned Zind-Humbrecht estate. It turns out that the wine does indeed have a fairly substantial alcoholic content,

13.5 per cent – though not dissimilar to many white burgundies. (Some Alsace wines hover around fourteen per cent, and I later tasted a 1998 Zind-Humbrecht Gewurztraminer from a *grand cru* vineyard (Hengst) at an astonishing sixteen per cent, slightly over that of a fino sherry and half way to port's twenty per cent!). The richness of the Heimburg Pinot Gris is due to very ripe grapes with a high natural sugar content, picked at 118° Oechsle, leaving forty-nine grams per litre of residual sugar.

Conclusion A wonderful wine. But when or with what does one drink it? Perhaps with a rich chicken dish, or halibut. Best of all, with this sort of semi-sweetness – perfect with cheese.

WINE NO 2 (RED)

Appearance Impressively deep, its core or heart almost opaque and intense at the rim; a rich, once ruby colour still fairly youthful though showing some tawny maturity at the edges. After swirling the wine in the glass, I also notice long and fairly thick legs (or tears) clinging to the sides of the glass. Definitely not a weak and watery wine made in a cool climate from indifferent grapes. The trouble is, it could be almost any "gold medal" New World wine, or possibly a Barolo or Barbaresco, or... Well, an impressive colour. Good wine. Good vintage. So what?

Nose Remarkably forthcoming, arises to meet the nose halfway well-knit and harmonious. A distinctive varietal aroma, yet no question of the blackberry, soft-fruit character of Cabernet Sauvignon. A red Bordeaux, certainly a good-class Médoc, might be less forthcoming, possibly lower-keyed.

In any case it doesn't smell like claret; none of the cedary element, often a touch of iron, oyster shells, for example, in a Pauillac. Distinctive, delicious, but not Bordeaux. Not even European. South Africa? With due respect, no. California possible but not a recognizable Napa style. For this richness and quality, a good-quality Australian. Not Hunter Valley, best for Shiraz; not Victoria – I like their vibrant Pinot Noirs. Coonawarra, the Bordeaux of Australia, possibly. But surely not one of those Cabernet/ Shiraz blends?

Palate Noticeably dry and on the lean side, unlike many opulent, over-fleshy New World reds. A classic, of its sort. Very good flavour, good length but very tannic.

Conclusion With Australia in mind, but having half eliminated several districts I shall plump for South Australia, probably a top Barossa Valley vineyard and major producer, of a good vintage. The wine turned out to be Penfold's Bin 707, their top one hundred per cent Cabernet Sauvignon, Kalimna Vineyard, Barossa, and of the excellent 1996 vintage.

THE ULTIMATE TEST

After all this, it need hardly be restated that tasting blind – deducing a wine's precise origin and age – is the most severe test of a taster's true knowledge and ability. Happily, however, it is not necessary to strive to reach, let alone to have reached, this stage in order to appreciate the taste of wine, and to enjoy drinking it. But if achievement in the higher realms of winetasting is sought, it will now be apparent that a sensitive and trained palate alone is not enough: it has to be supported by a good knowledge of areas and districts, of grape varieties, of styles and winemaking methods, and of vintage characteristics. And a good technique is helpful.

From cellar to table

Claret and Burgundy should be drank [sic] moderately warm. A gentle warmth brings out an appreciation of body, diminishes the astringency, and develops all the finer qualities prominently including that of bouquet.

Arpad Haraszthy

WINES AND VINES OF CALIFORNIA, 1889

The information in this chapter is a little off the subject of tasting. Nevertheless, during the course of my travels – and lectures – the questions of decanting, airing time, and temperatures (of storage and service) regularly arise. The following is, therefore, a summary of my answers to these questions, and I hope that this practical advice will be found helpful.

Cellars and "cellars"

There is no doubt about it: the traditional cold and slightly damp cellar beneath the ground floor of the English and Scottish country mansion was, still is, ideal for storage of wine of all types.

But even I, as an old-fashioned romantic, readily concede that an above-ground, temperature- and humidity-controlled wine "cellar" will protect and preserve wine in the most demanding of climates. During my frequent travels in the United States I have witnessed the efficacy of air-conditioning, the only possible drawbacks being the exposure to heat *en route* from supplier to final destination, and failure of the electricity supply*.

TEMPERATURE

Assuming that one has a single storage unit and wants to set the air-conditioning unit at a steady year-round temperature, I would suggest 13°C (55°F). This, in my experience, is the average temperature of the traditional country-house cellar. I say average advisedly, for I have found it to vary from a fairly rare, unvarying 9°C (48°F) – this was in the famous cellar at Fasque, a house in Scotland belonging to the Gladstone family: the whole house was cold; the cellar, a smallish (roughly seven metres square/twenty-three feet square) three-section area with stone floor, walls, and ceiling, beneath the centre rear of the house – to temperatures well above 16°C (60°F) and, even worse, those near to recently installed boilers or with central-heating pipes traversing the cellar.

By and large, the best traditional cellars have been in the basement area, but with air bricks or vents just above the outside ground level. Ventilation is important, and a slight current of air is considered essential to prevent stale air and dank conditions which encourage the formation of mould and rot. I will just mention one remarkable modern cellar, built in

**With an eighth floor apartment in London and a weekend house in the country without a cellar, I have solved the problem of wine storage by using two patent systems: a humidity and temperature-controlled "Eurocave®" the size of a wardrobe in the flat, and a French-designed "spiral cellar" – concrete steps with "bins" round the walls – dropped into the foundations of the house.*

California with three sections. The main area, in which cases of youngish vintage wine are stacked, is maintained at a steady 13°C (55°F); beyond it, through double glass doors, is the old-wine section where pre-phylloxera claret, ancient Sauternes, Rhine wine, and other rarities are stored in metal racks at a temperature of 10°C (50°F). The outer cellar area is held at 16°C (60°F) or perhaps even a little warmer. Here are stored the very young vintage ports, to encourage their development, and wines for everyday drinking.

HUMIDITY

This is rarely a problem in country-house cellars but it is important to control in artificially maintained modern cellars. The ideal appears to be around sixty per cent. Without adequate humidity there is the risk of corks drying out and shrinking.

The other extreme, damp, will not harm the wine, but, if excessive, it will soon cause labels to disintegrate, cartons to collapse, and the base of wooden cases to rot. "Bin-soiled" labels are not really worrying but become a problem when the labels become unreadable. The longer the bottles are stored in a damp cellar, the more the labels are likely to deteriorate, which is why vintage port was always traditionally binned away unlabelled, identification being by means of bin labels, bottles having wax seals embossed with the vintage year and either the bottler's name or that of the shipper or his brand name. As the final line of defence, the long port corks are branded with the name of the port and its vintage.

The effect of a damp cellar can sometimes be catastrophic. I recently came across one in which a stack of cardboard wine cartons had collapsed and the contents, red Bordeaux and burgundy of different châteaux, domaines and vintages, were very hard to sort out. Not only were the labels badly damaged but, to make matters worse, the weight of the collapsed boxes resulted in breakages which, in turn, stained the remaining labels.

For the unsophisticated I can define the ideal, which is based on the late Lord Rosebery's cellar at Dalmeny House, near Edinburgh. When entering the cellar there is a distinct chill: one needs warm clothing. And as for humidity, a gummed label will start to curl in seconds after it is put on a flat surface.

SHELVES AND BINS

Without becoming too technical or complicated, the type of shelves or bins will depend greatly on the space available and partly on the needs of the owner. Assuming that storage is to be as versatile as possible, I recommend:

For long-term storage:

- an open space for stacking red Bordeaux and any other wines in original wooden cases
- sturdy shelves one or two cases deep, one to three cases high, for storing cases and cartons (one end of a box/carton usually bears the name of the wine; keep this to the outer side)
- rectangular "bins" or shelves two to four bottles deep, about 75 cm (29.5 in) high and 90 cm (35.4 in) wide, the bottles being stacked in rows

on wooden laths; this is the traditional method and, for large quantities, is far and away the most economical use of space

• diamond-shaped wooden wall bins, each side measuring roughly one metre (3.3 ft); this is convenient for smallish quantities

For everyday use:

• small bins or shelves, one bottle deep

• diamond-shaped bins as mentioned above

• traditional metal and wood single-bottle racks; these are ideal for a collection of odd and old bottles but uneconomic in space for large quantities of one wine.

DECANTING TABLE

It is handy to have a small table for making notes while binning your wine, for decanting and for minor cellar equipment. I will not presume to enumerate such minutiae here, save to say that many cellars I have been in, and not just in the United States, are incredibly elaborate, with fancy lights, decorated with wall maps, and a veritable museum of vinous miscellany!

BRINGING WINE UP FROM THE CELLAR

This is not meant to be superfluous waffle but practical advice. It is given in answer to questions I am frequently asked about how far in advance one brings up, or pulls out, wine for a dinner party, its temperature, and how, in general, to handle it.

The need for looking ahead does not apply to ordinary everyday wines, nor for most white wines. The following remarks apply to most good quality red wine, red Bordeaux in particular. My practice is to bring the wine from the cellar at least twenty-four hours before the meal in question and then to stand the bottle upright on a sideboard in the dining room. This gives it reasonable time for the sediment to settle and also allows the wine to lose its cellar chill and gradually attain room temperature. Never, in any circumstances heat the bottle, either by standing it in front of a fire or in hot water. Most restaurants have a "dispense" area where a range of red wine is kept at drinking temperature. But if you are planning a dinner party in a top-class restaurant with really good wine it is sensible to order the wines at least a day before to avoid the problem of having the red wine brought to the table too cold or, worse, "just warmed a little, sir".

Opening a bottle

When to draw the cork How far in advance should one open a bottle? This is the most frequently asked question, particularly in relation to fine and/or old wines, and one to which there is, paradoxically, no firm and sure answer. (The question does not arise for most white wines, rosés, and everyday reds: just pull the cork and serve.) If your vintage wine is old enough to have thrown a deposit, then I recommend drawing the cork a couple of hours before decanting. The reason for this is that if there is a stubborn or difficult cork and one jolts the bottle and disturbs the sediment, the wine is given time to settle down again before decanting and serving. Leave the bottle upright after the cork has been drawn and either carefully balance the cork on the top of the bottle or reinsert it fractionally.

Removing the cork This might not be deemed worthy of mention in a book on tasting, but a great deal of ingenious thought, from the eighteenth century onwards, has been given to this essential operation. The object of the exercise is to remove the cork cleanly, without it breaking or dropping bits into the wine, and without shaking the bottle and disturbing the sediment. Most corks give little trouble, and most corkscrews work, after a fashion.

However, some corkscrews are decidedly better than others. The best have added refinements such as ease of insertion and maximum pull for minimum effort. The early to mid-nineteenth century patent continuous-action and ratchet types were undoubtedly the best*; the highly effective modern version is the Screwpull® which, for ease and ultimate refinement, is outstandingly the most efficient, its only slight drawback being the time taken to remove the cork from the thread of the screw when drawn. As an added bonus (not thought of by the inventor) its base can be used as a candle-holder. However, my favourite – and most effective – Screwpull® is the ring-handled pocket version.

On occasion, the long corks of very old red Bordeaux and of mature vintage port are best tackled with a broad-bladed and long-shanked corkscrew. Old red Bordeaux corks can be crumbly and a broad-flanged corkscrew will give greater support when opening, minimizing the bits of cork and cork powder dropping onto the surface of the wine. Some prefer compressed-air cork removers; the cushion of air probably does not disturb the wine, but I have never liked the implement.

Old vintages of port pose a different problem. In addition to the length and strength of the cork, the traditional port bottle was slightly bulbous between the top of the shoulder and upper neck, the lower half of the cork swelling to form a very efficient air-excluding wedge which makes it difficult to extract the cork in one piece. Also, with some older bottles, the glass top has an internal ridge which forms an obstruction. In face of these difficulties I normally partially insert the corkscrew and remove just the upper half of the cork, pushing the lower part back into the bottle. I find this is better than thrusting the corkscrew the full length of the cork and only pulling out bits. On the rare occasions when the precise name and age of the port is unknown, I break the bottle after decanting in order to retrieve the lower half of the cork and, matching it with the upper part previously removed, hope that branding will reveal the shipper's name and vintage year – impossible if a difficult cork has been removed in little pieces by just digging away with the corkscrew.

Cracking a bottle of port To "crack a bottle" is an old colloquialism for opening/sharing a bottle. But if the bottle happens to be of old vintage port, the "cracking" can be literal. One way is to use the back of a heavy knife, the other is with port tongs. Both methods have as prime aim the literal cracking of the upper part of the neck in order to remove it cleanly, with the cork still in place. The top removed, one decants the port in the normal way. If necessary, one can then break the glass of the severed neck to remove the branded cork in one piece. I frequently do this to identify otherwise

**Those who would like to delve into this fascinating sideline are recommended to read the authoritative and well-illustrated book,* Corkscrews for Collectors *by Bernard M. Watney and Homer Babbidge (Sotheby Parke Bernet, London and New York, 1981).*

anonymous old bottles. It is sensible to wrap the neck in newspaper or an old cloth to stop fragments of glass flying around. I use a hammer, but with just sufficient force to crack the glass, not to damage the cork.

Now to describe the heavy blade and port tong techniques. Perhaps I can best describe the first method by recalling a superb performance by an old friend, a retired colonel with an excellent cellar, who – quite unselfconsciously – at a great wine dinner held a bottle of old port in his left hand and, over the fireplace, with his right hand briskly swept the back of a sword upwards, more or less parallel with its neck. Catching the underside of the lop of the bottle he removed it, and the top of the neck, at one stroke. The bottle itself received a bit of a jolt but the crust was firmly formed and there was no problem decanting.

Two words of advice: the back of a light modern bread knife will not do, an old fashioned carving knife is better – unless one has a cutlass handy! Also modern, machine-made port bottles do not have a sharply jutting lip or ledge just below the top of the neck like the bottles of old, which makes it difficult to strike it effectively.

Port tongs are as traditional but, happily, in the right hands, more effective. The object is to introduce a sudden change of temperature which will crack the glass.

Take a pair of cast-iron port tongs (they can be bought from enterprising merchants of vinous artifacts) and stick the pincer end into the fire or onto a really hot stove until it is just about red hot. Clamp the tongs round the upper part of the neck of the bottle, hold them there for a few seconds to heat the glass then touch the neck with a cloth soaked in cold water. The neck will crack. Remove the whole of the top carefully so as not to disturb any shards of glass, and decant. The advantage of this method is that it works even with modern port bottles.

Decanting

More fatuous argument has been stimulated by this side issue than almost any other. The reasons for decanting are quite elementary, and the procedure is not difficult.

The principal reason for decanting is to be in a position to serve wine clear and bright, leaving any bits of sediment in the bottom of the bottle instead of pouring it into the glasses. Does it matter? Well, yes, it does. It is not only unsightly to have a hazy or bitty wine in the glass, but the sediment – mainly dead colouring matter in red wine – will affect the taste. The second – in my opinion far less-important – reason for decanting is to aerate the wine. It is in this area that there is a great deal of muddled thinking, so let me deal with this first.

AERATING WINE OR “BREATHING TIME”

By general consensus, young vintage wines can take, possibly need, plenty of breathing time, older wines less, very old wines scarcely any – just extract the cork and decant carefully.

If it were only as simple as that.

Once again I must preface my remarks by saying that the vast majority of the world’s wines can be treated in an off-hand way: just open and pour.

Virtually all commercial reds, rosés, and quite a few better-quality whites do not change with exposure to air in normal serving and drinking conditions. However, all will oxidize and "flatten" in taste if left open or ullaged for any length of time, by which I mean several days.

So we are talking here about better-class vintage wines, principally red. The important thing to bear in mind is that once exposed to air, fine red wines will change. The main problem is to anticipate how much and how quickly. The longer I deal with fine wines the more firmly convinced I am that if the wine is good – from a good producer, well-made in a fine vintage year – when it is put into the bottle, then, as long as the storage conditions have been sound and the cork has not deteriorated, the wine will also be good, stable, and drinkable when the cork is drawn, no matter what its age. A good, sound wine – five, ten, twenty-five, or fifty years old – is unlikely to crack up shortly after the cork is extracted and the wine decanted; indeed, quite the opposite: a century-old wine will catch its second breath, unfolding its bouquet, expanding, and developing over a period of two or three hours, sometimes longer.

If the wine is of an inferior vintage and lacked body and balance when young, or if the storage has been poor, allowing the cork to shrink, then the wine is likely to break down very soon after it is poured out, in perhaps a matter of minutes.

Red Bordeaux of a sturdy and more recent vintage, say a 1998, even one of the tougher 1990s, will be so full of tannin and extract, so closed up, that decanting early afternoon for drinking around 8.30pm will encourage it to "relax" and soften a little. How many times has one been told, and occasionally discovered accidentally, that a young red wine seems softer and better on the palate the next day? The same can occasionally happen to very old wine of the finest quality, though it is a brave or singularly curious person who will risk this.

It is my considered opinion that no noticeable oxidation occurs for a very considerable period after the cork is drawn, and, surprisingly, little change occurs in the decanter. The main development takes place in the glass. The greater the wine, the more revealing and complex the bouquet, and the longer it and its flavour will last. To give an example: at a recent Bordeaux Club dinner, my range of reds opened with a (my only) bottle of Lafite 1961. The problem was how to present this wine at its very best. I took the wine from my London cellar to Christie's two weeks in advance. The day before the dinner I brought it carefully up to my office, leaving it standing upright. The afternoon of the dinner, I dusted the bottle gently, removed the capsule, and wiped the top, first with a damp cloth, then with clean dry kitchen paper. The cork was drawn about 5pm and stood loose on the top, less to prevent air than dust from getting in. The wine was decanted at 6.45pm into a rather wide-mouthed carafe, without a stopper, and at 7.30 carried in, just before the first guest arrived, to the boardroom where we were to have dinner. It was actually served at 8.30pm. By 9pm the bouquet had blossomed nicely and by 9.45 it had developed fully, with a nice warm, spicy, biscuity fragrance. I kept a little in my glass, and two hours after it had first been poured it still smelled incredibly delicious.

As a matter of interest, the last of four red wines I served was an 1875 Château Desmirail. The bottle had an excellent provenance. It came from the private cellar in Paris of a noted connoisseur, had been recorked, probably in the mid-1930s, and its level was still good. In the middle of the dinner I returned to my office to draw the cork and decant the wine which was then served right away. To describe this remarkable pre-phylloxera red Bordeaux would need another chapter. Suffice to say that there was not a trace of decay on nose or palate. It seemed fatter and rounder after fifteen minutes and even an hour later the scent in the emptied glass was exquisite.

My final advice on "air" is: be bold, and try decanting well in advance. Above all, with a really fine wine (and this applies as much to a top-class white burgundy as to claret) give the wine a chance to blossom in the glass: sip it, make it last, revel in its glorious development.

WHY DECANT?

Before recommending the best method of decanting let me again mention those wines which rarely, if ever, need decanting. Basically, they are all wines without a sediment: very young red wines, ordinary commercial red table wines, young white wines, including sherry; also rosés, Champagne, ruby and tawny ports, and madeira.

White wines that benefit from decanting are old ones, whether sweet or dry, which quite frequently have a slight powdery sediment; or younger whites which, through a sudden change of temperature, might have a tartrate deposit – perfectly harmless and tasteless white crystals; and some rare old sherries and old *solera* and vintage madeiras. The latter with their glowing amber colours, and old Sauternes, usually a beautiful warm yellow-orange, shot with gold highlights, look particularly beautiful in clear glass or cut-glass decanters.

Prime candidates for decanting are mature red Bordeaux and vintage port. Even young claret, which has had little time to throw a sediment, might as well be decanted. It does give the wine a little air, which has a slight softening effect and, in any case, the colour always looks so attractive. When it comes to red burgundy, there are two schools of thought. In Burgundy itself, it is extremely rare to decant the wine. I am not at all sure of the reason for this, but I am sure that great care must be taken when pouring from the bottle and ample time given for the sediment to settle. You need a steady hand or a decanting cradle with a cranking handle and smooth action. In the latter instance, the glasses are brought to the decanting cradle, not cradle to glasses. If this contraption is not used – for most of us do not possess one – then I recommend that the glasses are all lined up alongside the bottle, the wine being poured steadily into each glass.

In either case, it is essential for the pouring to stop before the sediment reaches the upper neck. (I recently witnessed a magnum of beautiful burgundy being spoiled by my host, a noted connoisseur, who poured steadily into eight large glasses, continuing round to the bitter end, giving everyone's glass a final *coup de grâce* of sediment!) I personally consider that mature red burgundy should be decanted. It is far safer.

HOW TO DECANT

The bottle must have been left resting, preferably upright, undisturbed for an hour or two, better still, for a day, before decanting so that the sediment has had time to settle. This is, of course, particularly vital if, as I recommend, the bottle has been moved from cellar or store to the dining room, or wherever one decides to decant. The only exceptions are, perhaps, old Sauternes which are intended to be served cold and can be decanted in the cellar, and vintage port, which can be lifted carefully from the bin and decanted on the spot.

So, assuming that the bottle has been standing upright, capsule removed, and cork extracted, the following should be ready at hand:

Decanter Should be clean, dry, sweet-smelling, and also at room temperature. (It is amazing how little thought is given to the temperature of the decanter and glasses. There is no point, having nursed the wine to room temperature, in putting it into decanters and glasses which have been removed at the last minute from a cold cupboard.) Incidentally, if the stopper has been left in a decanter for any length of time, the air within can smell stale, particularly if the decanter had not been properly rinsed out and left upside down to dry before it was put away.

Candle For me, the ideal is a four-to-six-inch candle in a table top candle-holder. The base of a Screwpull® corkscrew works admirably. A tall tapering candle in an equally tall candlestick is impossible to decant over unless it is on a low table or stool. The alternative to a candle – and just as effective to decant over – is an electric light bulb or torch placed on the table and shining upwards.

Funnel A plain glass funnel is best. A plastic funnel looks nasty and I always worry about its cleanliness. Silver funnels look splendid, but when and with what were they last cleaned? Traces of metal polish will taint the wine. There is just one type of wine for which I personally use a funnel and sieve, and that is for vintage port. The reason for this is that the sediment of vintage port, known as the crust, is heavy and flaky. The wine pours bright and one merely catches the crust in the sieve.

PROCEDURE

Place the candle-holder on the edge of a table top, the decanter to the left, the bottle to the right – unless, of course, you happen to be left-handed.

Make sure that the neck, shoulder, and at least the upper half of the bottle is free of cellar dust or grime which will otherwise obscure the view through the glass.

If you have a funnel, put it into the neck of the decanter. If not, and a funnel is not absolutely essential, one just has to pour slowly and carefully.

Now, either leave the decanter where it is or pick it up by the neck with the left hand – all depends on you, and the height of the candle, the flame of which should be about four inches below the level of the top of the funnel.

Place the right hand over the lower half of the bottle, not at the upper or shoulder end, pick it up and tip it very gently over the rim of the funnel or the lip of the decanter. Start pouring slowly but steadily. Once the wine has started flowing then manoeuvre the bottle gently towards the lighted candle so that the eye, the underside of the shoulder of the bottle, and the candle are in a straight line. Do not line up vertically, *i.e.* with the bottle directly above the candle, as the flame from the candle will smoke up the glass and obscure one's view of the wine. A slight angle is much better. Do not stop pouring while this manoeuvring is going on; otherwise the sediment in the bottle might be disturbed.

By the time you have reached the right position, a little over half the contents will have been poured into the decanter and the wine should be showing clear and bright as it passes over the shoulder into the neck. Continue pouring steadily, watching carefully for the first traces of light, powdery sediment which will be easing up the underside of the bottle. I personally let the very light sediment move up towards the shoulder, and if a fair amount of wine is still in the bottle, continue until the main swirl of heavier sediment appears. Let this slide across the shoulder of the bottle but do not let it enter the neck.

This is the moment to stop. By now the base of the bottle will be higher than the neck. To stop decanting, quickly but smoothly lower the base of the bottle. It is more effective than pulling the bottle away horizontally from the funnel, as this movement results in the remaining wine welling into the neck risking sediment spilling into the decanter.

The amount and type of sediment will vary to some extent depending on the style and age of the wine, but the method described above should cope with all situations. Burgundy bottles have more gently sloping shoulders, and one has to be a little more careful than with Bordeaux or Bordeaux-type bottles, which have rounded corners to hold back the sediment.

Vintage port The bottles used traditionally by English merchants to bottle port were of extremely dark glass, often so dark that the level of the wine cannot be seen even if the bottle is held against a high-powered spotlight.

The sediment or crust of a port is also different. This forms along the lower side of the bottle. It is a continuous process. The sooner a vintage port is laid down (binned) after bottling and the longer it is left undisturbed, the more steadily and firmly the crust will form, and, consequently, the easier it will be to decant when it is fully mature.

With an old (say twenty-five years or older) vintage port, no candle is needed when decanting. Traditionally, port used to be decanted in the cellar: the bottle would be lifted gently from the bin, put into a wooden cradle (not a flimsy basket-work version), the cork extracted, and the wine poured steadily into the decanter via a funnel with a sieve. The wine would inevitably be bright, its black, flaky, filmy crust being caught by the sieve.

Muslin and filter papers The use of a strainer is very tempting. It appeals to the timid, the palsy-handed and, dare I say it, the mean-minded among us.

Frankly, if the wine has been handled properly, cellared for a decent length of time, brought from cellar to sideboard to settle, and uncorked properly, there should be no need to use a filter.

On the other hand, even the most farsighted and careful will on occasion find themselves with a rush job or that they have inadvertently disturbed the bottle, giving the wine insufficient time to settle down. This is perhaps the only good excuse for using a piece of fine clean muslin or linen cloth over the funnel to act as a filter. Filter pads – those used for coffee – are a fairly untenable last resort. My own experience is that muslin rarely does a proper job and filter pads can give the wine a slightly powdery taste and can even take the stuffing out of a wine.

As for extracting the last ounce of liquid from a bottle by filtering the remnants, sediment, and all, this, in my opinion, is shortsighted. The dregs, however well-strained, do not taste good, and if tipped into the decanter might slightly spoil the rest of the otherwise bright and sound wine.

Cloudy wine One occasionally comes across a bottle of wine which has a suspended haze of very fine particles that will not settle. If it is a young wine which has been recently purchased from the regular supplier, take it back. If it is a very old wine, there is little one can do. It is probably worth trying a filter pad, but the wine might not be up to much anyway.

Glasses Another word on the subject of glasses. The "ideal" glass for tasting is illustrated on page 54. As it happens, this is a most excellent size and shape for virtually all white and red wines. However, a table setting looks more interesting if one uses different glasses for different types of wine.

I personally like a slightly smaller tulip-shaped glass for my white wine and matching, but larger, glasses for reds. Having for years scorned "goldfish bowls", I must confess a liking for fairly large, rounded glasses for burgundy: the perfume seems to arise more exotically from them. But do remember that large glasses use up a lot of wine and, a minor phenomenon, the larger the glasses, the more one's guests drink (if you do not believe this, try a little experimenting).

Dessert wines and vintage ports are often served in small glasses, which is a mistake. A medium-sized tulip or thistle glass is better than a *copita*, ghastly schooner, or thimble. In addition to shops specializing in glasses, many wine merchants now carry a range, sometimes uniquely their own.

One man, George Riedel, has made the world of wine aware of the importance of correct glasses. His Austrian-based glassworks produce a wide range of shapes and sizes specifically designed to enhance the colour, bouquet, and taste of different types of wine. They work!

The temperature of wines at table

It may be comforting, or irritating, to be told that there is no such thing as a precise temperature at which a specific wine should be served. The season of the year and the temperature of the dining room have a bearing. One thing is certain: extremes are undesirable. Having said this, the temperature of wine is important, and lack of consideration will result in a wine performing less well than it should.

RED WINES

It is said that red wines should be served at room temperature. This is a broad generalization, for not only are some dining rooms too cold and some too hot, but the age and weight of red wines require different serving temperatures.

- young red Bordeaux, Barolo, Barbaresco, and good New World Cabernets tend to have a high level of tannin and a certain raw austerity. The bigger the wine and the younger the vintage, the warmer it should be served: say 18°C (65°F), even up to 20°C (68°F) in a warm room or on a warm day
- mature red Bordeaux: about 18°C (65°F). Once, on a hot June day, I recall a fine red Bordeaux (it was a fifteen-year-old Domaine de Chevalier) being served. The temperature seemed perfect. To my surprise, when tested with a thermometer it turned out to be 21°C (70°F)
- old red Bordeaux (1970 and older) should not be served too warm. It seems to take the stuffing out of the wine. Possibly a maximum of 17°C (63°F) depending on the natural room temperature

• red burgundy and a good New World Pinot Noir should definitely be served cooler than red Bordeaux. In Burgundy itself it is very often brought straight from the cellar. Burgundy is less tannic, usually more alcoholic, and slightly sweeter. It tastes livelier if served around 16°C (60°F)
• Rhône, New World Syrah, and other full-bodied reds: about 16°C (60°F) or, if very tannic, up to 20°C (68°F)
• Beaujolais and red wines from the Loire: serve these styles cool, say between 12° and 15°C (54°–58°F)

WHITE WINES

It is generally true to say that white wines should be served cold. But how cold? In my experience, far more care is needed to get the temperature right for white than for red. I shall just deal with recommended temperatures, then with the methods of achieving and holding those levels.
• Light wines: Muscadet and the range of light, dry, acidic white wines made with the Sauvignon Blanc grape such as Sancerre should be served cold, between 7° and 10°C (45°–50°F)
• Most Chardonnays best served cool, not cold
• Fine white burgundy: I single this out for special treatment for though it is always dry, the alcoholic content can be surprisingly high, in the thirteen to fourteen per cent range. It is therefore a big mistake to serve, say, a Bâtard-Montrachet too cold. I would suggest thirty minutes in the refrigerator. As it rises almost to room temperature in the glass the bouquet will develop miraculously
• Medium-dry German wines and others with a light, fruity-acid balance: serve chilled, about 9°–10°C (48°–50°F)

Chilling white wines The late Otto Loeb drank TBA poured at room temperature into ice-cold glasses. I tried this recently. It seemed to work, but the glasses did not stay cold for long. To chill a standard-size bottle of white wine in a refrigerator set at, say, 5°C (42°F) will take roughly thirty minutes to reach 15°C (59°F), and one hour to reach 13°C (55°F). In two hours it will have dropped below 10°C (50°F).

The problem with white wine is keeping it at the ideal serving temperature. Ice buckets are, in my opinion, unsatisfactory. In them wine tends to become over-chilled. Moreover, they are messy to use and labels come off. So I should recommend using ice buckets only for light dry white or sparkling wines which can endure maximum chilling. A practical tip: do not use chips or cubes of ice alone; instead, part fill the bucket with water so that the bottle can be put back into the bucket easily. A generous sprinkling of salt keeps the temperature down.

The ideal way to keep white wine at an even serving temperature after chilling is to stand the bottle in a Vinicool®* open-topped flask. The bottle will hold its temperature for the entire time needed for serving and drinking. The flasks have the added advantage of being transparent so one can see the labels on the bottles.

Glasses for white wines are, conventionally, smaller than for red. The reason for this is largely ignored, or taken for granted: there is a smaller surface area of wine and glass to transmit the warmth of the

**Obtainable from wine merchants and speciality stores.*

room. My last tip is to pour only a half-glass at a time, topping up frequently from the cool bottle.

ROSES

From anywhere, should be served cold: 7°–10°C (45°–50°F).

CHAMPAGNE

Non-vintage Champagne and sparkling wines should be served almost ice cold. But the bouquet and flavour of fine vintage Champagne, like great white burgundy, is muted and suppressed if too cold. Serve cool enough to be refreshing, not so that the glasses frost.

SHERRY

Fine finos and manzanillas should be served chilled, at 9°C (48°F). Serve fine old amontillados and olorosos at room temperature. Some suggest serving "cream" sherry on the rocks; why not?

MADEIRA

Temperature depends on the grape style:

- Sercial, the lightest and driest style, serve cool, say at 9°–10°C (48°–50°F)
- Verdelho, roughly medium-dry, also cool, but not too cold
- Bual, richer and fuller-bodied, I suggest around 13°C (55°F) or, if old, and fine, over 16°C (60°F)
- Malmsey, the sweetest and richest, at room temperature

PORT

A surprising variation of temperatures is recommended:

- White port is generally dry or medium-dry, so serve chilled
- Ordinary ruby or tawny port is generally drunk at room or "pub" temperature
- Fine old tawny (ten-, twenty-years old and older) is the favourite drink of the port shippers in Oporto, where they serve it cool
- Vintage port and LBVs at room temperature

Full glossary of tasting terms

The first difficulty that tasters encounter is to find and to translate into precise and clear language the qualities and defects of a wine....

Pierre Bréjoux
REVUE DU VIN DE FRANCE, 1977

acetic vinegary smell; sharp, over-tart on the palate. A vinegary condition resulting from the action of acetobacter, harmful ferments that attack wine left open in bottle, or fermented at too high a temperature, or carelessly bottled. Ullaged wine, whether in cask or bottle, will usually be suspect – the latter usually due to poor, wormy, or dried-out corks which let air in and wine out (weepers), the remaining wine often becoming acetic and undrinkable.

acetone a high-toned, estery aroma connected with the ester ethyl acetate, or with nail-varnish-like amyl acetate.

acid, acidity on the nose: mouth-watering, refreshing (tartaric), sometimes like raw cooking apples (malic); detectable on the tongue, giving wine essential crispness and zing. "Volatile" acids are more pronounced on the nose, "fixed" acids (tartaric, succinic, and citric) less so. Esters of both acids make an important contribution to the overall aroma and bouquet of wine. There are several types and degrees of acidity commonly found in wine, some beneficial and some detrimental. The right sort of natural acidity is an essential component of a sound wine; it acts as a preservative and provides the essential zest and finish. It also stimulates the gastric juices – one of the oft-forgotten main purposes of any table wine. Lack of acidity can be detected by a general flabbiness, lack of vitality, and a weak, watery finish; excess acidity by a sharp tart effect on the tongue. Youthful acidity tends to mellow with age. Some wines, such as Vinho Verde, Champagne, and wines from the Mosel, have a deliberately and refreshingly high acid content. Fruity acidity is perhaps the most desired characteristic of German wines (*see also* TARTARIC, MALIC, and SORBIC acids).

aftertaste the internal bouquet that sometimes remains in the throat and back nasal passages after a wine has been drunk. Unpleasant if the wine is strong-flavoured and in poor condition; at its best, however, the hallmark of a great wine and usually part of what is more poetically referred to as a "lingering farewell".

aggressive more than lively on the palate, perhaps too tannic and astringent.

alcohol an essential component, binding and preserving. In pure form, the higher alcohols – amyl and butyl – have an unpleasant, throat-catching odour; phenethyl has an intense, rose-like smell; and ethanol a burning sensation. However, diluted, as in wine, alcohol is scarcely detectable on the nose, though it can be assessed by its weight in the mouth, by a sort of burning taste and cumulatively, by its well-known effects on the head of the imbiber. Alcohol has a certain sweetness, giving richness and warmth to full-bodied wines. Although table wines may vary from light Mosels around 11° to Rhône and Sauternes in the 13° to 14° bracket, the effect on the weight, character, and strength of the wine is disproportionate.

almonds, bitter the smell of almond kernels or bitter almonds emanates from a badly fined wine, possibly, but rarely, after using illegal "blue" fining. Probably drinkable but not sound.
apples a fresh, raw smell, indicative of an immature young wine (*see also* MALIC acid). Tokay sometimes has a scent of old apples.
aroma that part of the smell of wine derived from the grape, whether distinctly varietal or merely vinous (oenologists also use the word in respect of odours resulting from fermentation), as opposed to BOUQUET, which is derived from the development of the wine itself in bottle.
aromatic fragrant; a richness of aroma and taste; spicy overtones, particularly from aromatic grape varieties, such as Muscat.
asbestos odour imparted by new filter pads or old, dirty, overused pads in bottling. The wine is flat and alkaline. (Asbestos is harmless if ingested.)
astringent a dry, mouth-puckering effect caused by a high tannin content (often accompanied by a high degree of acidity). Might well soften and mellow as the wine matures. Not bitter.
attenuated becoming thin on the palate, losing fruit and flesh, usually in respect of an old wine.
austere tough, severe, simple, uncomplex, possibly undeveloped.
backward retarded, undeveloped for its age/vintage.
baked "hot" rather earthy smell produced by sunburnt, sometimes shrivelled grapes – a result of excessive sunshine and lack of rainfall. A characteristic of some red wine produced in hot vintages in the Rhône Valley and in naturally hot wine-producing areas such as southern California, Australia, and South Africa.
balance combination and relationship of components (*see also* WELL BALANCED).
banana overtone on the bouquet of wines made from frost-bitten grapes; also a specific smell of old wine in poor condition.
beefy substantial, muscular, well-endowed with alcohol, tannin, and extract.
beery an undesirable smell and taste caused by secondary fermentation in bottle. The wine may be drinkable, just, but will be basically unsound; poor on finish.
beetroot, boiled reminiscent of, and a recognition symbol for, the Pinot Noir grape aroma.
big manly wine, well-endowed with vital components, not just high in alcohol.
bite implying a substantial degree of acidity (plus tannin). A good factor in young wine. Generally mellows with age.
bitter, bitterness detected on the palate, on the back of the tongue and finish. Mainly unpleasant. A taste, not a tactile sensation, though it can be a desirable quality in certain wines (usually an acquired taste) and vermouths. Bitterness is derived from either chemical or vegetable extracts. A certain bitterness can be imparted by colouring matter, though the depositing of this during maturation will normally reduce its pristine harshness. Polyphenols extracted from wooden casks, particularly when dirty and contaminated, will also, when oxidized, impart a bitter taste. More rarely, an unpleasant bitterness is due to amertume, a bacteriological disease.
bitters substances added to wine (for example, in the making of vermouth). They have a bitter taste and stimulate the appetite and digestion. Bitters

can be of vegetable origin, like gentian, or aromatic, containing volatile oil, like orange-peel. Quinine has a similar effect, plus additional properties such as a remote action on the nervous system.

blackcurrants the nearest fruit-smell to the Cabernet Sauvignon grape. Detectable to some degree wherever the grape is used but particularly marked on wines from Pauillac and, to a slightly lesser extent, Margaux. Perhaps the first major clue to a Médoc in a blind tasting.

bland not complimentary: mild, easy, and characterless – but not unpleasant.

body the weight of wine in the mouth due to its alcoholic content, extract, and to its other physical components. These factors stem from the quality of the vintage and geographical origin, and in turn affect the style and quality of the wine. Wines from hotter climates tend to have more body than those from the north (compare the Rhône with the Mosel, for example).

botrytis short for *botrytis cinerea* known also as "noble rot", *pourriture noble*, *edelfäule*, that is encouraged to develop on the skins of grapes in Sauternes, the Loire, and the best vineyards in Germany during the delayed autumn harvest. Botrytis shrivels the grapes, reduces the water content, and concentrates the sugar. The effect on nose and palate is akin to honey.

bottle-age extremely hard to describe but easily recognizable on the bouquet to an experienced taster and a vital factor in the judgement of a wine's age/maturity and development in bottle. With white dessert wines, it has a mellow, honeyed quality; with reds a breaking down of raw edges to reveal fully evolved character, softness, and mellowness.

bottle-sickness temporary oxidation after bottling.

bottle-stink stale-air smell on drawing the cork, usually dissipates.

bouquet in the broadest and most often-used sense, the pleasant and characteristic smell of wine. In the narrower sense, the odour created by the wine's own development: by the esters and aldehydes formed by the slow oxidation of fruit acids and alcohol (*see also* AROMA).

breed finesse arising out of the pedigree or class of a wine.

buttery self-descriptive smell and taste (not texture).

caramel a slightly burnt, toffee-like flavour which can have a literal origin in the case of certain spirits; however, it can only be reminiscent in the case of wine. A characteristic flavour of some madeira, marsala, and old Sauternes.

carbon dioxide responsible for the bubbles in Champagne and sparkling wines, also the tingle of *spritzig* and slightly effervescent, *pétillant* table wines.

cats the smell of tom cats, a strangely attractive grape smell associated with certain young white wines.

cat's pee an inelegant but appropriate description of the aroma of an acidic Sauvignon Blanc.

cedar characteristic scent of many fine clarets.

chaptalization legal addition of sugar to must: increases strength; softens tannins; improves unripe, acidic grapes in a poor vintage.

character a wine of any quality that has positive and distinctive features.

characteristic having the style and character of the grape, district, vintage, etc. Often sweepingly used to avoid a detailed description.

chocolatey a chocolate-like smell and taste: rich, thick, slightly vanilla. Not bad, not unusual (some burgundies), but inelegant and not a pure varietal characteristic.

cidery smell; a defect; early oxidation.
cinnamon smell and taste imparted by new-oak casks.
clean absence of foreign and unpleasant odour and taste.
cloves smell and taste imparted by new-oak casks.
cloying a sweet and heavy wine which palls, lacking the acidity to make it crisp and interesting.
coarse rough texture, lacking breed, and possibly indifferently made. Do not confuse coarseness with the rough rawness of a fine yet immature wine.
common lacking breed, but nonetheless can be sound and drinkable.
complex many-faceted smell and taste. The hallmark of a well-developed fine wine.
cooked a heavy, sometimes sweet but not unpleasant smell from the use of sugar, concentrated grape juice, or high temperature during vinification.
corked an "off" and thoroughly obnoxious smell. An overused and misunderstood expression; a sommelier's scourge.
corky having a distinct smell of cork, arising from a poor, soft, or disintegrating cork, or one infected by weevil. A poor cork can, of course, let air in, in which case the wine may oxidize completely and become corked. The two expressions are frequently interchanged due to lack of agreement over definition.
creaming or *crémant*. Light, slightly frothy mousse. Half-sparkling.
crisp a desirable feature in white wines: firm, refreshing, with positive acidity.
cruising mid-red colour, neither immature nor mature, on turn.
deep an adjective that needs qualification: deep-coloured; deep bouquet, depth of flavour – opposite of superficial, indicating underlying richness and layers of flavour.
delicate a light wine with charm and balance, fragile.
depth richness, subtlety – seemingly "layers" of bouquet or flavour, all interlocked and supportive.
developed in relation to wine, a stage of maturity: undeveloped, well-developed (mature, balanced, rounded); over-developed (over-mature, cracking up).
distinguished notable character and breed.
dry not sweet; absence of residual sugar; fully fermented.
dull appearance not bright; nose and taste lacking interest and zest.
dumb undeveloped, but with inherent promise of quality. Often the sign of an immature, undeveloped, adolescent stage. Aeration sometimes does the trick.
dusty an evocative, cellar-like smell; possibly high tannic content – or dirty glasses.
earthy characteristic overtone derived from certain soils, or a rustic character.
eggs, bad (hydrogen sulphide) disagreeable, but harmless. Probably due to bad cellar treatment, poor wine making.
elegant stylish balance and refined quality.
estery high-toned, acetone smell. An ester results from the reaction of an organic acid and alcohol.
eucalyptus descriptive, analogous, spicy bouquet associated with certain top-quality Cabernet Sauvignons, notably Heitz Martha's Vineyard which is surrounded by eucalyptus trees that probably do affect the grapes, but also some of the finest ripe vintages of Château Latour.

extract soluble solids (strictly speaking, excluding sugar) which add to a wine's body and substance.

farmyard a ripe, earthy, manure-like, sometimes pigsty smell probably due to the presence of butyric acid, one of the several normal volatile acids which, in excess, creates this smell. Not uncommon in even major classified red Bordeaux.

fat fullish body, high in glycerol and extract. If sweet, verging on unctuous.

feminine subjective and purely abstract term indicating a style of wine that is attractive, not heavy or severe, with charm – delightful qualities that all but a misogynist might conjure up!

filter-pads *see* ASBESTOS.

fine an all-embracing expression of superior quality. Perhaps the most overworked adjective in the vinous vocabulary.

finesse grace, delicacy, distinction. Lacking in most wines which appeal to the modern "global" taste.

finish the end-taste. A wine cannot be considered well-balanced without a good finish, by which is understood a firm, crisp, and distinctive end. The opposite – a short or poor finish – will be watery, the flavour not sustained and tailing off inconclusively. The correct degree of the right sort of acidity is a decisive factor.

firm implies a sound constitution and balance, positive in the mouth, as opposed to flabby.

flabby feeble, lacking crisp acidity, probably without FINISH.

flat dull, insipid, lacking acidity. Or merely a sparkling wine which has lost its effervescence.

fleshy good rich texture, just short of fat.

flinty an evocative overtone. Certain white-wine grapes grown on certain soils have a hint of gun-flint, often imagined in the bouquet and flavour, *e.g.* Pouilly-Fumé.

flowery fragrant, flower-like. Usually a lightness of touch.

forceful strong, assertive character; well-endowed with tannin and acidity.

forward advanced in maturity for its age or vintage.

foxy the curious and distinctive earthy tang, flavour, and finish of wine made from Concord grapes of the native north American species Vitis Labusca (not to be confused with the Italian Lambrusco). It does not imply an animal smell but relates to the wild or "fox" grapes.

fragrant attractively and naturally scented.

fresh retaining natural youthful charm, vitality, (and acidity).

fruity attractive, fleshy quality derived from good, ripe grapes – but not necessarily a grapey aroma.

full (bodied) high in alcoholic content and extract. Filling the mouth. A table wine with an alcoholic content probably over 13°.

G L (Gay Lussac), a measure of strength, by percentage of alcohol by volume or by weight.

g/l grammes per litre (of sugar, of acidity).

gamey overripe, touch of decay, often on the verge of cracking up. As with game birds, very old burgundy and red Bordeaux can be attractive, if something of an acquired taste. French: *faisandé*.

garlic, wild a faint reminiscent whiff denoting the presence of SORBIC ACID.

gentle mild, unassertive, but pleasing.

geranium not a complimentary flower simile: a geranium-like odour caused by the presence of an obscure micro-organism derived principally from esters formed during fermentation.

goaty a rich, ripe, animal-like flavour – for example, ripe, fat Pfalz wines made from the Traminer grape.

graceful abstract term: elegant, stylish.

grapey a rich, Muscat-like aroma produced by certain grape varieties, including Muscatelle and crossings such as Scheurebe, Sieggerebe, and Müller-Thurgau.

great as overworked as fine. Should be confined to wines of the highest quality – which, in practice, means top growths of good vintages. Having depth, richness, character, style, complexity, fragrance, length, and aftertaste.

green unripe, raw, and young. Youthful, mouth-watering acidity produced by immature grapes, or the unsettled acidity of an immature wine.

grip a firm and emphatic combination of physical characteristics. A desirable quality in port, for example. The opposite to flabbiness and spinelessness.

gritty coarse-textured in the mouth.

hard severity due to the overprominence of tannin and, to a lesser extent, acidity. Usually the product of a hot vintage or over-prolonged contact with skins and pips during fermentation. Usually mellowed by time.

harsh self-descriptive. Due to excess tannin and/or ethyl acetate associated with acetic acid. Close to ASTRINGENT.

heady high in alcohol. Tipsy-making.

hearty robust, zestful, warm, alcoholic (red) wine.

heavy more than just full-bodied; over-endowed with alcohol and extract. Watch out for the context in which it is used. For example, a strapping Côte-Rôtie will appear too heavy for a light summer luncheon but would be the right weight to accompany a steak-and-kidney pie in midwinter. "Heavy" is also an old British Customs official definition: a fortified wine subject to a higher rate of duty.

hedonistic a simple, subjective, personal rating. I like....

herbaceous between grass-like and flowery. Pleasant, open, fresh, appealing. Usually young white wines.

high-toned nose of assertive volatile character, often acidic.

hollow a wine with a foretaste and some finish but without sustaining middle-flavour. A failing rather than a fault.

honest a somewhat condescending term for a decent, well-made but fairly ordinary wine; true to type.

honeyed characteristic fragrance of certain fine wines such as Sauternes and Beerenauslesen; also indicative of bottle-age.

implicitly sweet apparent sweetness from sources other than sugar, *e.g.* glycerol, alcohol.

inky "red ink": an unpleasant, tinny, metallic taste due to the presence of tannate of iron produced by the action of tannin on iron – a nail in a cask will have this effect. (Tannate of iron is the chief constituent of ink.)

insipid flat, somewhat tasteless. Lacking firmness, character.

iron a faintly metallic, earthy-iron taste derived from the soil. Noticeable in some St-Emilions and in these circumstances entirely natural, adding recognizable character.

kerosene *see* PETROL.

lactic acid *see* MALIC.

lanolin a soft, sweet, harmonious, possibly slightly oily smell like lanolin, associated with classic wines made from the Chenin Blanc and Sémillon grapes in good ripe vintages.

leathery reds rich in tannin (leather is made by hides or skins being impregnated with tannin) with leathery texture.

legs the English term for globules which drip or ooze down the sides of the glass after the wine is swirled. Also known as TEARS. Generally indicative of a rich wine (*see* page 59).

lemon lemon-like overtones. For example, noticeable on some fine but immature white Hermitage wines.

length the longer the flavour, the finer the wine. The French use the word "persistence" and measure it in seconds as it crosses the palate.

light a low degree of alcohol (under 12°G L). Lack of body. A desirable characteristic of certain styles of wine, such as young Beaujolais and Mosel-Saar-Ruwer wines. Rather confusingly, "light" is an official term for a natural, unfortified table wine.

limpid clear, luminous (appearance).

limpidity colour appears to have extra sheen, outstanding brightness, and luminosity.

little scarcely any bouquet or aroma. Either a wine of no quality or character, or dumb. A minor wine.

lively fairly explicit. Usually in reference to a fresh, youthful wine, or an old wine with fresh and youthful characteristics.

long length of flavour in mouth; a sign of quality.

luscious soft, sweet, fat, fruity, and ripe – all these qualities in balance.

macération carbonique a "whole-fruit" modern method of winemaking involving fermentation of the whole grape. Results are, at best, a pleasant, fresh, quaffable style of wine; at worst, tinny, and jammy. Author's view is that this method reduces the individual character of wines, those of one district tasting much like another.

maderized the heavy, flat smell of an over-mature, somewhat oxidized white wine (sometimes accompanied by brown-tinged colour and flat taste). (*See also* OXIDIZE.)

malic acid although without smell, its presence due to unripe "green" grapes has a mouth-watering, cooking-apple effect – mouth-puckering. A "malolactic" fermentation in cask converts the raw malic acid into softer and more amenable LACTIC acid.

manly or masculine: positive, possibly assertive, even aggressive; muscular.

mature the maturity of a wine is one of its most crucial factors. Wines vary enormously in make-up, and take anything from a matter of months to many years to reach full maturity, depending mainly on their tannin, acid, and alcohol content. Maturity can be detected on nose and palate; the maturity of red wines is most easily and visibly measured by the brownness of the rim. An immature wine has raw, unknit component parts. A perfectly mature wine has all its constituent elements in harmony.

mawkish a trifle flat: drab-flavoured, sickly.

meaty heavy, rich, almost chewable quality, mellow yet tannic.

medium (body) neither light nor heavy in alcohol and extract – probably between 12°C and 13°G L, depending on style of wine.

medium-dry containing some residual sugar but dry enough to be drunk before or during a meal.

medium-sweet considerable residual sugar, but not really a dessert wine. Many German wines come into this category and are better drunk alone, without food.

mellow soft, mature. No rough edges. A desirable characteristic normally associated with maturity and age; also essentially associated with alcohol, glycerol, and fructose.

mercaptan a slightly sour, unpleasant, rubbery smell indicating deterioration due to the breakdown of sulphur dioxide originally used as a preservative.

metallic tinny – not a pleasant quality (*see also* INKY). Usually due to some metallic contamination during winemaking, storage in cask or bottling. If distinctly unpleasant and associated with a deepening of colour (of white wine) and a tawny deposit, it is usually due to copper contamination.

milky an undesirable taste, more than LACTIC.

mouldy an undesirable flavour imparted by rotten grapes or old, stale, unclean casks, etc.

mousey smell and taste, flat yet ACETIC. Sign of bacteriological disease, *tourne*, usually affecting only wine in cask.

mulberry a more opulent, succulent type of fruitiness, softer than the blackcurrant of young Cabernet Sauvignon, associated with exceptional, ripe claret, often with Merlot dominating.

mushrooms fresh-picked. A pleasant, analogous scent.

mushroomy specific smell of some very old wines.

musky a difficult term: spicy/dusty, reminiscent of musk.

must unfermented grape juice.

musty due to poor casks or a cork fault. If the latter, allow the wine to stand after pouring; the smell may wear off after a few minutes.

neutral a wine without positive flavour or marked physical characteristics. A common feature of many blended wines, from quite respectable commercial brands to litre-bottle carafe wine.

noble indicates stature and breed; a wine of towering elegance.

"noble rot" *see* BOTRYTIS

nose the broadest term for the bouquet, aroma, smell of a wine; the professional taster "noses" a wine.

nuance having components reminiscent of specific smells, *e.g.* of almonds, or struck flint.

nutty a crisp, rounded flavour associated with full-bodied, dry white wines such as Corton-Charlemagne, or a good-quality amontillado. Fine old tawny port has a distinct smell of cobnuts, hazelnuts, or Brazil nuts.

oak an important component, particularly in relation to fine wines. Oak casks impart an oaky, vanillin, spicy, cinnamon taste and smell: attractive in moderation, undesirable if exaggerated.

objective relating to the object, measurable, factual.

off-taste describes unclean, tainted, or diseased wine; though not necessarily undrinkable.

old can be a factual statement or imply a state of bouquet and taste adversely affected by overmaturity, or just lacking freshness.

olfactory to do with the sense of smell and its perception.

ordinary in wine terms, mildly derogatory: a wine of no pretensions or with little merit.

organoleptic the testing, by use of the senses, in an analytical context, of wine and food.

oxidized flat, stale off-taste due to exposure to air.

peach-like self-descriptive. Characteristic of the bouquet of certain German wines, notably ripe wines from the Ruwer.

pear-drops (amylacetate) an undesirable overtone sometimes noticeable in poorly made white wines of lesser vintages. Wine probably unstable and in dubious condition, but may be drinkable.

penetrating powerful, with almost a physical effect on the nostrils. Almost certainly high in alcohol and volatile esters.

peppery a sort of raw harshness, rather hard to define, due to immature and unsettled components which have not had time to marry. Noticeable on young ruby and vintage port and many full, young red wines. Probably higher alcohols.

perfume an agreeable scented quality of bouquet.

persistence measure of length of flavour and of bouquet.

petrol analogous smell, slightly oily, petroleum overtone. Kerosene-like; a characteristic of classic Rieslings.

pine related to turpentine. Breezy scent; quality Médocs.

piquant fresh and mouth-watering acidity. A desirable and customary feature of wines from the Mosel, Saar, and Ruwer, and other districts, like Sancerre. Less desirable but not necessarily unattractive in other youthful red and white table wines with a little more acidity than expected or warranted.

plummy a red wine colour indicating neither youth nor maturity; in between, lacking clear definition.

poor not off or bad, but of no merit, character, or quality.

positive marked, noticeable, and notable, as opposed to little and dumb.

powerful self-explanatory, but more appropriately used in the context of a big red wine.

pricked an unpleasant sharpness due to excess volatile acidity. A pricked wine will not be pleasant to drink and will be beyond treatment. It might just be drinkable unless it has reached the final vinegary stage.

prickly indicates on the nose, but particularly on the palate, a sharp-edged, raw, possibly almost effervescent quality. Only tolerable in certain circumstances: raw, young Vinho Verde and similar *pétillant* wines.

puckering, mouth- a tactile sensation induced by astringency and a high tannin content.

pungent powerful, assertive, heavily scented, spicy, often indicating a high degree of volatile acidity, as in old madeira. The equivalent on the nose to astringency on the palate.

quality quality wine, like fine wine, can be a vague and general term, often abused. In the EU, "quality" by virtue of its correctness, refinement, and clarity of colour; its pure varietal aroma or harmonious overtones of bouquet; with all its components well-balanced with rich and complex flavour, length, finish, and fragrant aftertaste.

racy an abstract term indicating zest, vivacity, breed.

raspberries a pleasant, zestful wine aroma, a feature of pure Cabernet Franc. For example, a good Bourgueil (red Loire).

refreshing pleasant, thirst-quenching acidity.

resinous literally imparted by the addition of resin, mainly to Greek table wines. A very old practice but something of an acquired taste.

rich self-explanatory. Should not automatically imply ripeness or sweetness, but rather a full ensemble of fruit, flavour, alcohol, and extract.

ripe describes a wine in full bloom, having reached its maturity plateau. A mellowness prior to its decline. Ripe grapes give a wine a natural sweetness and richness.

robust full-bodied, tough yet rounded. A good, strapping mouthful of wine. Could apply equally to a 13.5° alcohol Châteauneuf-du-Pape, Taylor 1994, or La Mission Haut-Brion 1995.

rough a coarse, edgy sort of wine, usually of ordinary quality.

round a feature of a well-balanced, usually mature wine. No raw, immature edges.

rubbery probably presence of mercaptan, a disagreeable accident of complex chemical background, not infrequently seen on old white wines due to the breakdown of sulphur. *See* MERCAPTAN.

rugged big, masculine, high in alcohol, over-tannic.

salty one of the so-called four primary tastes, but perhaps the least applicable to wine. A self-descriptive tang characteristic of good fresh manzanilla, or, occasionally, Muscadet.

sap the little-used equivalent of a French term implying the quality of inherent life that drives a fine young wine.

savoury rich, spicy – a lip-smacking, flavoursome style.

scented agreeable, positive, grapey-flowery, high-toned aroma.

sensuous rich, smooth, opulent flavour and texture.

severe hard, unyielding, and probably immature.

sharp a degree of acidity between piquant and pricked. Implies a stage beyond that of being attractively refreshing. It could, however, become mollified with bottle-age.

short refers to the length of flavour on the palate, abruptness, indicating lack of quality.

sick diseased, out of condition.

silky a firm yet distinctly soft texture on the palate. Usually a characteristic of most really fine dessert wines, also of good-quality Pomerols.

simple better than ordinary. Straightforward, uncomplex.

sinewy lean yet muscular.

smoky a subtle overtone characteristic of some grapes in certain white wine districts or derived from oak casks, *e.g.*, oak-smoky Chardonnay.

smooth soft, easy texture. No rough edges.

soft self-descriptive. Mainly in reference to red wines. Mellow; tannin and acidity fully married and absorbed.

solid full-bodied, foursquare, packed with alcohol, tannin, and acidity. Possibly somewhat undeveloped.

sorbic acid not a natural grape acid but one sometimes added as a preservative. Presence detected by a faint, garlic-like odour.

sound the first thing a wine should be: appearance clear and bright; wholesome, clean bouquet and flavour. No faults.

sour a term to be used with care. To the English, sour indicates overacidity, tart, an off-taste.

sparkling a wine containing an induced degree of effervescence – the basis and whole point of a certain class of wine, such as Champagne, the sparkle being obtained by the controlled release of carbon dioxide when the bottle is opened.

spicy a rich, herb-like aroma and flavour bestowed by certain grape varieties such as Gewürztraminer; also derived from use of new-oak casks. (*See* CINNAMON and CLOVES.)

spritz or *spritzig* a slight prickle often noted visually by small beads or bubbles at the rim and on the tongue, indicating a touch of carbonic acid gas usually induced or, in a very young, acid wine, left by the winemaker as a refreshing element in the wine. Examples abound: just a touch in some young Mosels, blatant in Vinho Verde.

stalky reminiscent of the smell of damp twigs; a damp *chai*-like smell. This stalky or stemmy aroma is detectable in young wines and can arise from overprolonged contact with grape stalks during winemaking. Undesirable.

steely a firm, lean though not thin, white wine with a fair amount of acidity. For example, a good Chablis or firm Puligny-Montrachet.

stewed a somewhat ill-defined nose, not clearly varietal, not clear-cut and not as good as it should be. Possibly heavily chaptalized.

stimulus that which provokes a sensory response.

stout substantial, fat, tannic. On the verge of coarseness.

strange atypical, having a "foreign" smell or taste.

stringy skinnier than sinewy, not very well-constructed.

strong powerful, alcoholic.

sturdy fairly tough, substantial, stolid, dependable.

suave smooth, soft, supple, and harmonious.

subjective a personal reaction which is mental rather than measurable, usually instinctive.

subtle veiled richness, unobvious complexity.

sugar grapes contain natural sugars which are converted through fermentation into alcohol. Traces of residual sugar in ripe wines are a major factor in the wine's evolution.

sugared/sugary several connotations: the sweet smell and blandness of a chaptalized wine; the high sucrose content of a rich dessert wine.

sulphury sulphur, in its various forms, not only has a very pronounced volcanic smell but its presence can be detected physically by a prickly sensation in the nostrils and the back of the throat, like a whiff from a sulphur match or coke oven. It is commonly used as an antiseptic, for cleaning casks (by burning sulphur sticks) and bottles (using a mild sulphur dioxide solution) and if carelessly used or overused, its undesirable odour will be retained. The bouquet of many young wines is masked by a whiff of sulphur which is usually quite harmless and often wears off a short while after the wine has been poured.

superficial shallow, without depth or follow-through.

supple easy to taste and sense, hard to define. A combination of sap, vigour, and amenable texture.

sweaty saddle a rudely evocative smell characteristic of certain Australian red wines made from Shiraz grapes.

sweet a wine with a high sugar content, natural or contrived. The essential characteristic of any dessert wine. There are two types of sweetness: that which is merely sweet and the other which is from the richness of fine, well-ripened grapes. The former kind will always remain sweet (*e.g.* Pedro Ximénez sherry), the latter will dry out as it ages. Fine Rhine wines and Sauternes can be recognized by the smell emanating from *pourriture noble*, but even dry wines can have a "sweet", honeyed, or grapeyness on the nose. The principal sweetening elements are fructose, sucrose, glucose; also, but less sweet, glycerol, and alcohol.

sweetness is detected on the tip of the tongue, on entry.

syrupy usually used in connection with an excessively rich, ripe Sauternes, Trockenbeerenauslese, or sweet sherry.

tactile provokes a response which can be felt physically (touched), sulphur, effervescence, velvety, creamy, burning (alcohol).

tang, tangy rich, high-toned, zestful bouquet and end-taste of an old madeira; old sherry; Tokaji.

tannin or more correctly, tannins, hard or soft: an essential preservative derived from grape skins during fermentation. Part of the maturation process consists of the breaking down of the tannin content; it is precipitated over a period by the action of proteins and becomes, with colouring matter, part of the deposit or crust left in the bottle. The presence of tannin dries the roof of the mouth, grips the teeth, and sometimes has a sweaty, leathery, dusty-cellar smell. It is a very noticeable physical component of young red wine (Bordeaux in particular) which has a practical purpose: to "cut" fatty foods and clean the palate. Tannin is less of a factor in white wines, as grape skins (main source) are removed prior to fermentation. Tannin tends to mask the fruit aroma.

tart sharp and tongue-curling due to overacidity, often with a touch too much tannin. This condition can be due to premature harvesting of grapes or a late bad harvest. The wine could recover and soften; it might, on the other hand, disintegrate. More pronounced than piquant.

tartaric acid the grape's own acidity – good and essential. Tartaric acid in the form of free acidity or acid tartrate of potassium is widely distributed in the vegetable kingdom, but its chief source is the grape. Its presence gives wine its healthy, refreshing tang and contributes greatly to its liveliness, quality, crisp finish, and ageing capacity. Occasionally it can be seen as light white flakes precipitated in white wine and sherry which have been subjected to an unusually low temperature.

taut firm, unyielding.

tears *see* LEGS.

thin deficient in natural properties; watery, lacking body.

threshold level at which a given smell or taste can be perceived. Thresholds vary from person to person, from substance to substance. It is possible with practice to lower (improve) olfactory and gustatory thresholds.

tough a full-bodied wine of overpowering immaturity (not necessarily young) with an excess of tannin. May well turn out in time to be a great wine.

twiggy like stalky and stemmy, mildly derogatory, usually relating to somewhat coarse young wines. Fine, mature red Bordeaux would never be described as twiggy; raw, young, minor red Bordeaux could.

unbalanced components are ill-matched: overtannic; overacid; lacking fruit.

unripe immature, raw, and green. Malic acidity of wine made from grapes not fully ripened.

vanilla a tannic-like compound derived from oak giving certain cask-aged wines a distinctive aroma. The principal smell of oak is derived from ethyl vanilline.
varietal a varietal aroma is one with the distinctive smell of a particular grape variety such as Cabernet Sauvignon. As a wine matures, its varietal aroma decreases as its bouquet develops.
vegetal hard to define. A flavour and character more root-like than herbaceous or flowery. Sometimes burgundy, rarely red Bordeaux.
velvety a textural connotation, related to silky and smooth, but implying more opulence; also richness of colour (red).
vigorous a lively, positive characteristic associated with healthy and youthful development.
vinegar the smell of ethyl acetate, one of the simple esters, indicative of bacteriological infection. The wine will be unfit to drink, acetic and beyond redemption. *See* ACETIC.
vinosity having firm, well-constituted, vinous character and strength.
vinous a pleasant enough, positive, winey smell or taste.
withered usually in reference to an old, dried-out wine, losing fruit and flesh with age.
wood distinct and often desirable odour derived from maturation in oak casks (*see also* VANILLA). Wood port: matured in cask or vat.
woody an undesirable taste imparted by wine kept too long in cask, or in old, unclean casks.
yeasty descriptive smell of ferments, live or dead. If detected in bottled wine, a sure indication of impending or recent secondary fermentation. *See also* BEERY.
young, youthful a positive attractive feature: fresh, with youthful acidity; or a wine that will benefit form bottle-ageing.
zest, zestful a lively, crisp, stimulating character.
zing exciting, zestful.

French tasting terms

acerbe acid; excessively sharp and bitter.
âcre harsh.
agressif raw, unripe, unharmonious.
aigre sour, vinegary, acetic-acid taste.
aimable agreeable, nicely balanced.
amateur wine-lover.
amer, amertume bitter, disagreeable.
américain, goût fairly sweet (in relation to Champagne). More vulgarly, a sugared-up blend of wine for the American market.
anglais, goût this depends on the district and context. In Champagne, dry; in Burgundy, big and smooth.
âpre rough, harsh; high tannin content.
arôme aroma, relating to the perceived qualities arising from a particular grape variety, and so forth.
arrière-goût aftertaste.
ascescence a bacteria-caused disease causing overacidity, leading to vinegar.
bois, goût de woody taste, often the result of wine stored too long in cask.

bouchonné cork-tainted; smell of cork.
bouquet scent or perfume of a developing or mature wine.
bourru, vin new wine showing cloudiness prior to falling bright.
brut very dry (in relation to Champagne, minimum liqueuring)
capiteux heady, high in alcohol.
casse showing cloudiness or darkening of colour, usually due to metallic contamination.
charnu fleshy; full-bodied but with good acidity.
chaud warm, alcoholic.
chemise coating – deposit on sides of bottle of old red wine.
chêne oaky character from the wood.
clairet light red, almost rosé.
classe wine of quality or potential.
complet balanced and harmonious.
corps body, robustness.
corsé full-bodied, well-constituted. Satisfactory but probably not mature in that state.
coulant pleasant, easy to drink.
coupé cut, *i.e.* blended or diluted.
court short, lacking balance.
crémant creaming: slight sparkle.
creux hollow; momentary thinness on palate.
cuit, goût de wine with a cooked flavour, or with a natural flavour resulting from a hot summer, or very hot soil.
cuit, vin cooked flavour; from addition of concentrated must.
dégustation tasting – the subject of this book.
délicat delicate; light consistency, usually low in alcohol.
demi-sec half-dry (in practice medium-sweet)
doux sweet.
dur hard; excess of tannin.
élégant elegant, stylish.
équilibré well-balanced, harmonious.
étoffé well-marked qualities and well-conserved.
évent, goût d' nasty, unclean smell and flat taste.
éventé wine which has been abruptly overoxidized.
faible weak, thin.
faisandé gamey, overripe.
ferme firm; the dumb unreadiness of a fine young wine.
ferment, goût de taste of a wine still fermenting; or in bottle having recently undergone a second fermentation; yeasty.
fin fine.
finesse grace, delicacy, breed, distinction.
fort strong.
frais fresh. In another context, cool.
franc natural, clean, sound.
français, goût sweet, particular in relation to Champagne.
fruité fruity.
fumet marked bouquet.
fungi at best, a not unpleasant scent of freshly picked mushrooms.
fusil, pierre à bouquet and/or taste reminiscent of gun-flint.

garde, vin de good enough to lay down, or which should be laid down to mature.
généreux forthcoming; rich in body and extract.
goudron, goût de tarry taste.
goût taste. A term always qualified.
grain character; completeness.
graisse a diseased wine which is flat, faded, and oily.
grossier big and coarse.
léger light in body and style.
liquoreux sweet and rich, implying a natural state.
long lingering flavour, intense, and aromatic.
lourd heavy, dull, unbalanced.
mâché mashed: a disturbed, tired, or unsettled wine.
maderisé maderized.
maigre meagre, thin, and feeble.
mauvais goût bad taste; unfit to drink.
moëlleux soft and rich, yet not necessarily sweet.
moisi, goût de taste of decay.
mou flabby, flat, lacking in character.
mouillé watered.
mousse froth, foam, sparkle.
mousseux sparkling (fully, like Champagne).
moût unfermented grape juice.
mûr balanced, in a mature not a youthful context.
muté muted; a must whose fermentation has been artificially arrested (leaving an unusually high unfermented sugar content).
natur, vin natural unsugared wine.
nerveux firm, vigorous, vital; fine and well-knit.
odeur smell, in the simple, direct sense: smell of cork, smell of wine, smell of yeast.
oeil de perdrix "partridge eye"; descriptive of the pale tawny-gold of certain types of wine.
onctueux full-bodied, fat, and rich. Usually applies to sweet wines but not necessarily to the exclusion of red.
paille, goût de reminiscent of damp straw.
parfum perfume; fragrance. Term for grape aroma.
passé too old; going downhill (but may be drinkable, just).
pâteux thick, pasty consistency.
pauvre poor, small.
pelure d'oignon colour of onion skin. May apply to certain *vin gris* and rosé wines; and occasionally to old and maderized white wines.
perlant slight sparkle more like a prickle (similar to the German term *spritzig*).
pétillant light, natural sparkle.
petit a little wine, probably deficient in alcohol.
piquant sharp and acid; may be an attractive tartness or purely derogatory, depending on context.
piqué pricked. Dangerous degree of volatile acidity in a wine on its death-bed.
piqûre a disease which creates a grey film on the surface of the wine, decomposing the alcohol into vinegar.
plat flat and dull.

plein full. Not just body but character.
précoce precocious; early maturing.
race breed.
rancio, goût de smell characteristic of old *vin doux*. Usually involves oxidation – and is something of an acquired taste.
riche generous.
robe colour; generally used in relation to that of a fine wine.
rond, rondeur round, harmonious.
rude astringent.
sauvage, goût foxy taste of native American vines, some hybrids.
saveur taste, in the mouth, in its broadest sense.
sec dry, fermented out.
séché dried-out; harsh and flat. Withered after lying ullaged in bottle or too long in cask.
sève sap: a combination of vigour, firmness of body, and aromatic persistence. The English have no equivalent term.
solide substantial, full-bodied but well-balanced.
souple supple: no sharp edges; elegant balance; soft and pleasant to drink.
soyeux silky texture; supple, slightly plump.
spiritueux high in alcohol.
suave soft, supple, harmonious.
sucré a sweetness mostly associated with arrested fermentation or some other less natural (added) degree of sugar.
taille, goût de raw, poor quality (after name for last pressing – the tail end).
tendre youthful delicacy. Charming: easy to drink; light; supple.
terne dull; lacking quality and interest.
terroir, goût de earthy smell, flavour derived from certain soils.
tourne a bacteriological disease that gives the wine a dull appearance, a mousey smell and makes it flat yet acetic.
troublé troubled (appearance): hazy, cloudy. Wine diseased, or temporarily out of condition.
tuilé of tile-red colour. A curious stage that a wine might reach having lost its youthful purple hue, showing a maturity which may not be long-lived.
usé worn out; past best and on decline.
velouté velvety texture.
vert green – unripe.
vif fresh, young, and lively.
vineux having vinosity; also high in alcohol.
vivace fresh and lively, implying youthful zing and possibly a certain tartness.

German tasting terms

angereichert sugared.
ansprechend appealing; attractive.
art character.
artig smooth, rounded.
beerenton taste of (ripe) grapes.
bitter bitter.
bleichert rosé rare in Germany, found in the Ahr Valley, and Schillerwein.
blume bouquet.

blumig flowery; good.
bukettreich rich bouquet.
charaktervoll characterful.
delikat delicate.
duft fragrance.
edel noble, fine.
edelwein very fine wine.
elegant elegant, stylish.
erdig earthy.
fade insipid.
faul mouldy, or rotten decayed.
fein, feine fine.
feinste finest.
fett fat, rich.
feunig high in alcohol.
firn maderized.
flüchtig little to it.
frisch fresh.
fruchtig fruity.
fülle fullness, richness.
gefällig pleasing and harmonious.
gering poorish.
gewürz spice: spiciness – of bouquet or flavour.
gezuckert sugared.
glatt smooth.
gross(e) great, big.
grün green; unripe.
gut good.
hart hard and tart.
hefegeschmack yeasty taste.
herb bitter, harsh.
hochfeine very fine.
holzgeschmack woody taste.
honigartig honeyed.
hübsch handsome, pretty; nice, at least.
jung young.
kernig firm.
körper body.
körperarm lacking body.
kräftig robust.
lebendig racy, lively.
leer empty, weak in character.
lieblich mellow, pleasant.
mager thin; lacking body.
mandelbitter bitter-almond flavour.
matt flat, feeble.
milde pleasantly soft, middle of the road.
naturrein, naturwein pure, unsugared.
nervig full-bodied.
oelig of marked viscosity; oily.

perle light natural sparkle.
pikant intriguing in tangy, spicy sense.
rafle stemmy: harsh and green.
rassig showing race; breeding.
rauh raw, rough.
reif ripe.
rein pure.
reintönig harmonious; well-balanced.
rot red.
rund round, harmonious.
saftig juicy.
sauber pure; clean.
schal musty; stale.
schaumwein sparkling wine.
schön lovely.
schwefel sulphur.
sehr fein very fine.
sekt sparkling wine.
spiel flexible, balanced.
spritzig with crisp natural prickle.
stahlig steely.
süffig tasty, not unlike *tendre* (French).
süss sweet.
trocken dry.
ungezuckert unsugared; pure.
voll full.
vornehm exquisite, elegant, distinctive.
weinig vinous, displaying vinosity.
wuchtig potent, weighty.
würzig spicy.
zukunft the future: wine capable of development.

Italian tasting terms

abboccato with some sweetness.
acerbo taste of unripe apples.
aggressivo aggressive: raw, unripe, unharmonious.
allappante unpleasant, rough, ill-tempered.
amabile gentle, slightly sweet.
ammaccato disagreeable taste, between dry and musty.
ammandorlato blend of semi-sweet and almond-bitter tastes.
ampio ample: complete and generous.
aristocratico aristocratic; wine of fine pedigree: good soil, vines, vinification, and vintage year.
armonico harmoniously blended and enhanced flavours.
asciutto dry: fermented out, clean.
aspro rough on the palate.
astringente astringent.
austero austere: a characteristic of big young wines.
carattere a wine of distinction and typical character.

caratteristico with characteristic individual traits.
carrezzevole caressing: rich, flowing.
completo complete.
con retrogusto with aftertaste.
corpo body: rich in alcohol and extracts.
costituito well-constituted.
debole a wine with little character.
deciso with decisive qualities.
decrepito old and faded.
delicato fine and harmonious.
di corpo full-bodied; with high alcoholic degree.
duro hard, excess tannin.
elegante elegant, stylish.
equilibrato well-balanced, harmonious.
erbaceo green, unripe, slightly piquant.
fiacco tired; lacking vigour.
franco blunt and straightforward. No subtleties.
fresco fresh in style, refreshing.
fruttato fruity.
generoso generous, forthcoming; rich in body and extract.
grasso unctuous.
immaturo immature.
maderizzato o marsalato maderized.
magro lean; lacking body.
marca of marked character (of grape, type, district).
morbido tender, gentle, soft, and caressing in the mouth.
nerbo literally, nerve. A wine of fibre and inner strength.
nervoso sensitive, delicate yet vivacious.
netto clean-cut; basic taste particularly marked.
neutro neutral: of little character, lacking in acidity.
oleoso oily: probably spoiled.
passabile acceptable, inoffensive.
pieno full: with richness and body.
pronta beva a quickly maturing young wine.
rotonda round: full and mellow.
ruvido rough, raw-tasting.
salato salty character.
sapido similar to the French term *sève*.
secco dry.
selvatico coarse, uncivilized character.
spogliato spoiled, through overageing.
stoffa mainly applicable to great wines with mouth-filling, many-faceted qualities.
tannico tannic.
vellutado velvety texture.
verde green, unripe.
vinoso vinous.
vuoto empty: superficial, short-flavoured.

Colour variations

The appearance of wine can be most meaningful:

- Fill a generous tasting glass about a third full
- Observe the depth of colour at a 45° angle
- Then, holding the glass by its stem, tilt it over a white background to check the actual hue of the wine at the deepest point of the bowl and the gradation of colour towards the edge
- Note the tell-tale intensity of colour at its rim
- Finally hold the glass up to a light to judge clarity and brightness

Under the heading of "Appearance" on page 55, there is a detailed description of the various points to look for when examining a wine. The following examples of actual wines, mainly from classic European wine districts, have been selected to illustrate the range of colour combinations. They will help the reader to pinpoint the most significant areas of depth and hue. The seemingly endless number of variations that can occur are due to differences of country, district, grape, vintage, and age of wine. They are not only part of the fascination, but also provide useful information for the serious taster.

For all red wines

Depth of colour, intensity, "thickness" (extract), gradation, and the actual hue, particularly at the rim

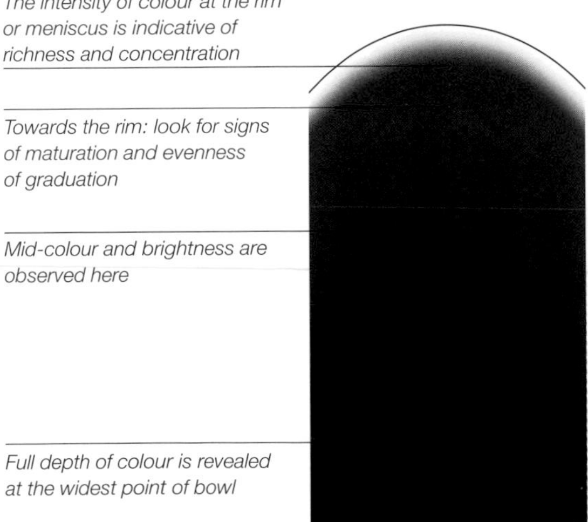
The intensity of colour at the rim or meniscus is indicative of richness and concentration
Towards the rim: look for signs of maturation and evenness of graduation
Mid-colour and brightness are observed here
Full depth of colour is revealed at the widest point of bowl

Immature red Bordeaux

A classed-growth Médoc of good vintage (sample drawn after one year in cask)

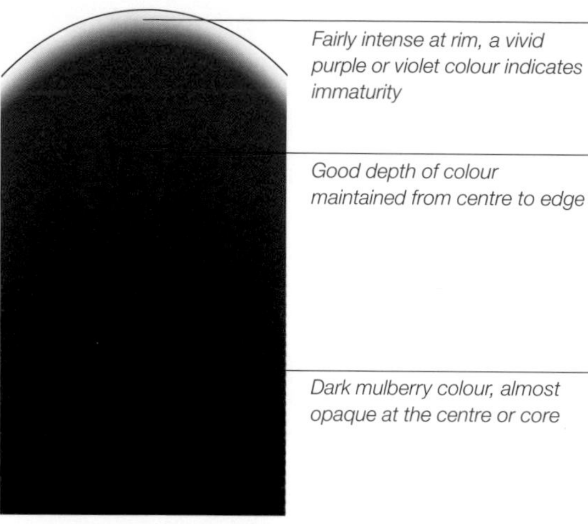

At this early stage the assemblage of wines made from the grape varieties will not be fully integrated. On the palate tannic.

Maturing red Bordeaux

Top-class château of a great vintage, maturing well after eight years in the bottle

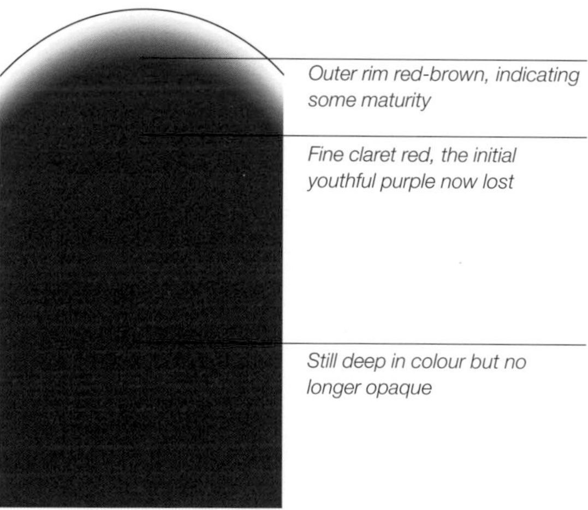

At this stage the wine's appearance will be less deep, the "nose" will be more settled and harmonious, somewhat softer, and less severely tannic on the palate.

Fine mature red Bordeaux

Perfectly mature twenty-five-year-old red Bordeaux from a top-class château of a classic vintage

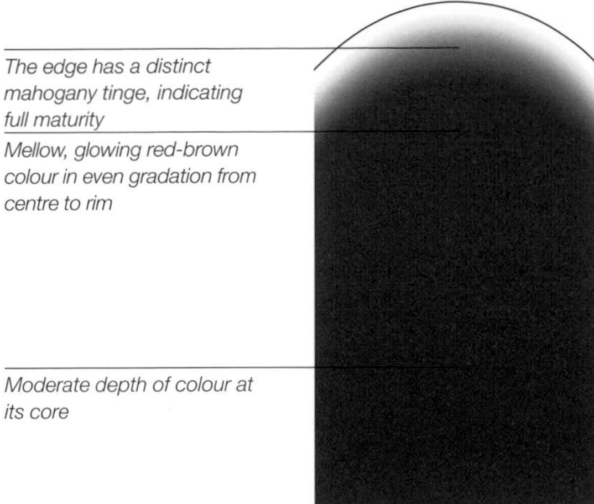

Altogether more mellow in appearance, smell, and taste. Its natural preservative, tannin, will have ameliorated and the component parts will have combined to make the perfect "food wine".

Over-mature red Bordeaux

A good château and good vintage, but after fifty years it is beginning to deteriorate

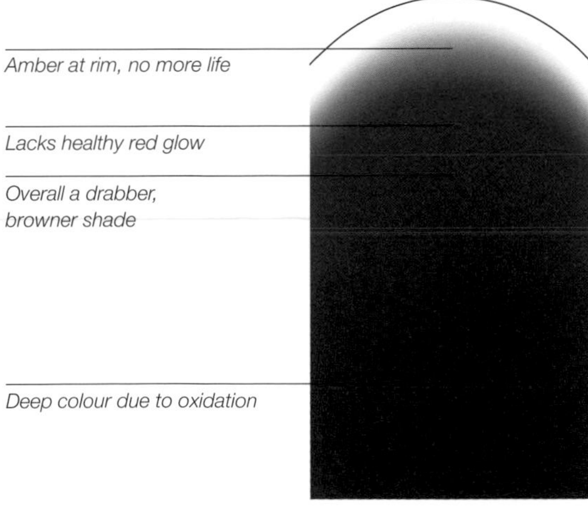

The tawny-brown tinge indicates oxidation. The wine's fruit and flavour will have diminished and it might well be flaccid with a drab "brown" finish.

Three-year-old dry white Bordeaux

Produced by a château known for both its white and red wines

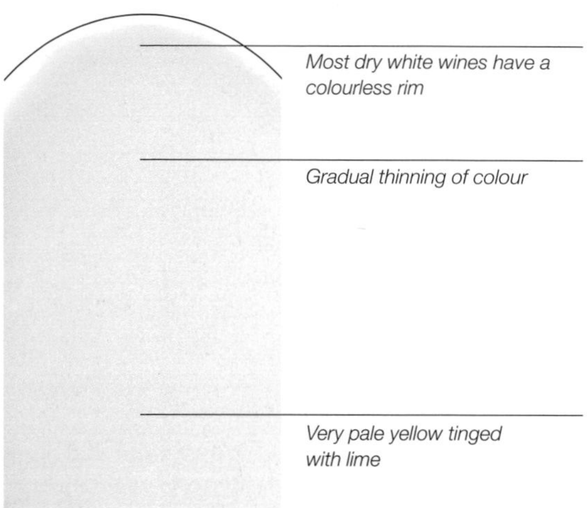

Pale and bright, mouth-watering to look at. Still with a refreshingly youthful aroma; dry, light, crisply acidic. Drink well whilst young and fresh.

Maturing eight-year-old Sauternes

From one of the top châteaux, a classic wine of a good, medium-weight vintage

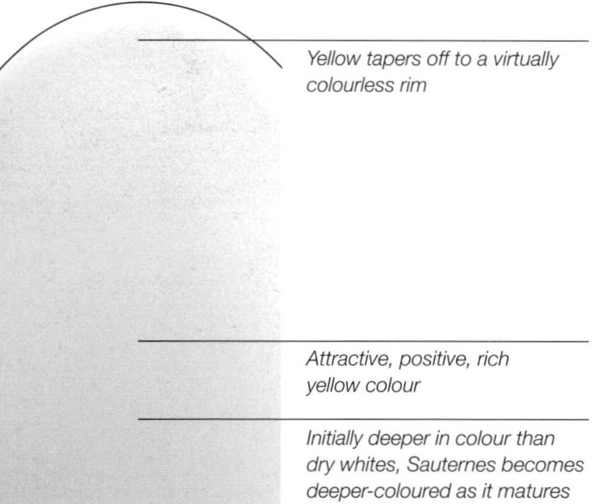

An attractive palish yellow-gold and inimitable honeyed, botrytis nose. Sweet of course, with good acidity, lovely now but will benefit from further bottle ageing. Ideal with foie gras or Roquefort cheese.

Mature great Sauternes

From a major château of a very good vintage, twelve years old, approaching its peak but capable of further development

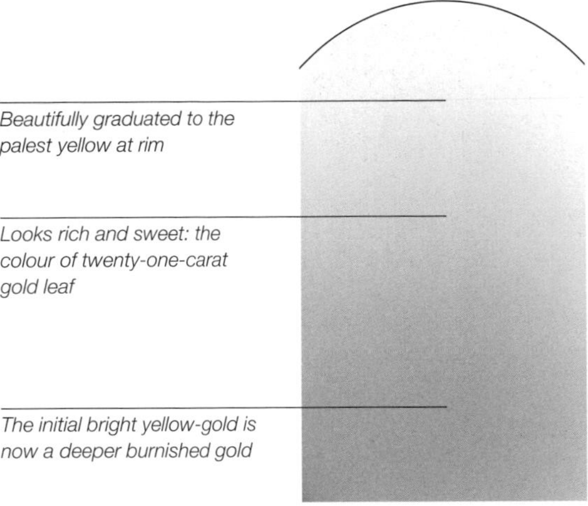
Beautifully graduated to the palest yellow at rim
Looks rich and sweet: the colour of twenty-one-carat gold leaf
The initial bright yellow-gold is now a deeper burnished gold

Gaining in colour and its rich lime blossom and honey bouquet developing well. Still sweet, its counterbalancing acidity providing stability and harmony. Perfect by itself.

Very old classic Sauternes

Just over fifty years old, a first-growth Barsac of great vintage

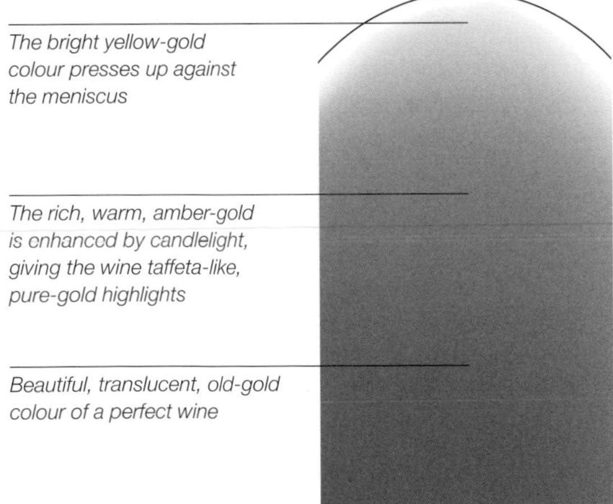
The bright yellow-gold colour presses up against the meniscus
The rich, warm, amber-gold is enhanced by candlelight, giving the wine taffeta-like, pure-gold highlights
Beautiful, translucent, old-gold colour of a perfect wine

By now a rich amber gold with a pale apple green rim, bouquet of great richness, perhaps a touch of caramel. Medium sweet, drying out a little but a revelation, with intensity, length, and delicious aftertaste.

Young Beaujolais

A year-old village wine of some quality and very good vintage; for early drinking

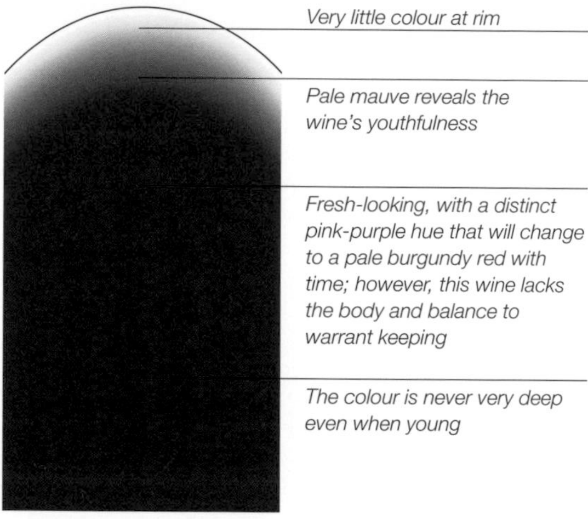
Very little colour at rim
Pale mauve reveals the wine's youthfulness
Fresh-looking, with a distinct pink-purple hue that will change to a pale burgundy red with time; however, this wine lacks the body and balance to warrant keeping
The colour is never very deep even when young

A quaffing wine, serve cool. Very distinctive "jammy Gamay" varietal aroma; dry, lightish in style with a refreshing dry tannic end.

Maturing burgundy

A three-year-old Côte de Nuits, of good vintage, starting to mature

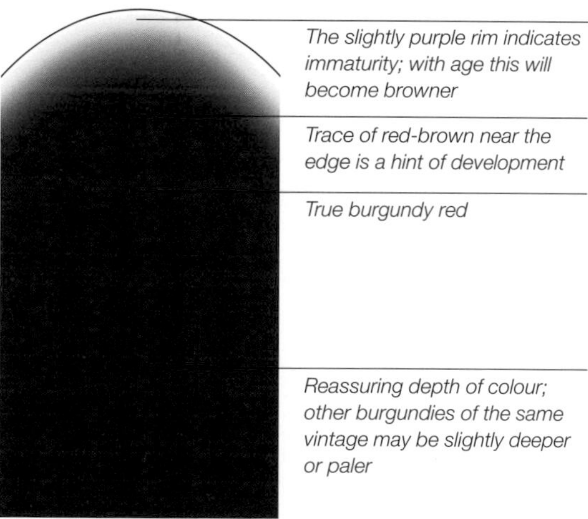
The slightly purple rim indicates immaturity; with age this will become browner
Trace of red-brown near the edge is a hint of development
True burgundy red
Reassuring depth of colour; other burgundies of the same vintage may be slightly deeper or paler

Burgundy tends to mature more quickly than claret. It is less tannic and enjoyable when young. However, a little bottle-ageing can work wonders. The producer's name is highly important: read and take advice.

Mature burgundy

A thirty-year-old Côte de Nuits, of excellent vintage and from a well-known négociant house

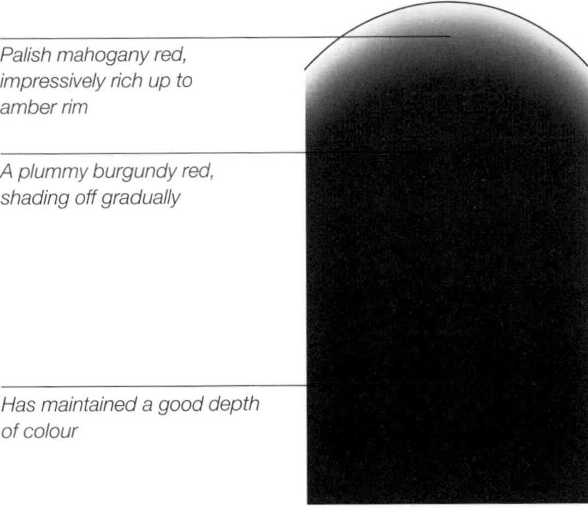

At this age definitely at its peak, its initial Pinot Noir aroma will now be a subtly developed fragrance, but it is the warmth of the mouth that will bring out the flavour, opening up beautifully like a peacock tail.

Very old burgundy

A sixty-year-old, fully mature *grand cru* burgundy of a classic vintage

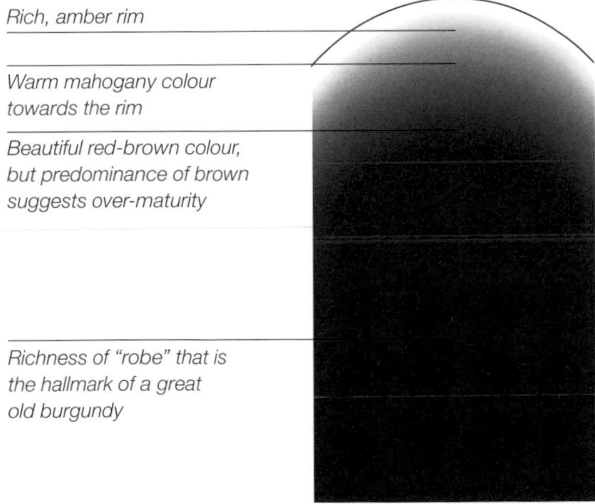

Only the finest burgundies will survive this sort of age but they can be a revelation: mellow looking, with a fragrance which bears no relation to grapes, and a softness and warmth beyond description.

Fino and manzanilla sherry

A young, lightly fortified wine, best drunk freshly bottled. Should be dry and zestful

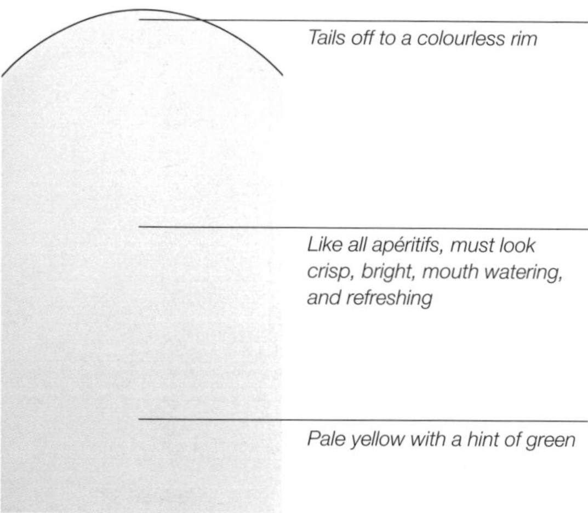

The perfect apéritif, dry, tangy, and refreshing. Only a degree or two of alcohol more than white burgundy and mini top class table wines. Also the least expensive of all the classic wines on the market.

Amontillado

A good, commercial, medium-dry sherry

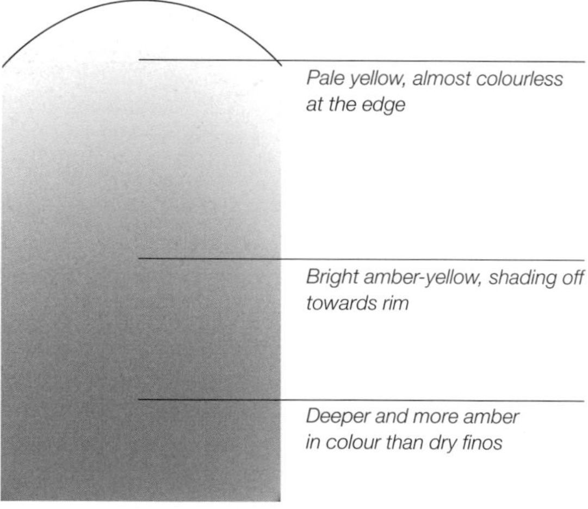

Not sweet, not too dry. In a modest price range, the sort of sherry that one used to keep in a decanter to offer the parson! The older blends have more character and an inimitable "nutty" flavour.

Old oloroso

A high-quality oloroso sherry, cask-matured in Jerez

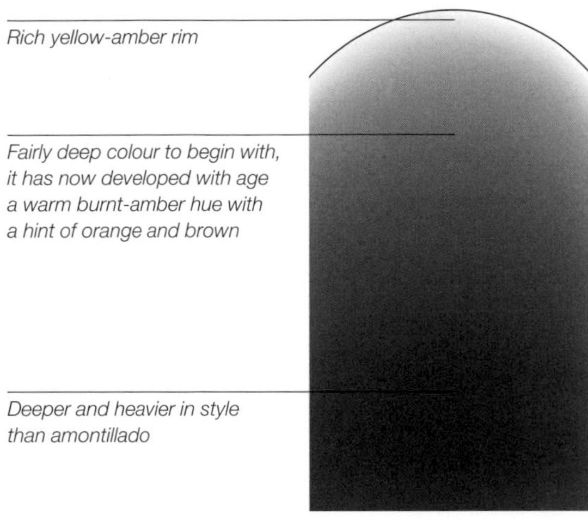

Behind, beneath, the intensely rich, tangy bouquet lurks an uncompromisingly dry, powerful wine. Superb but something of an aquired taste.

Finest old brown sherry

Old-fashioned style of sherry, very sweet and concentrated in flavour after considerable age in cask

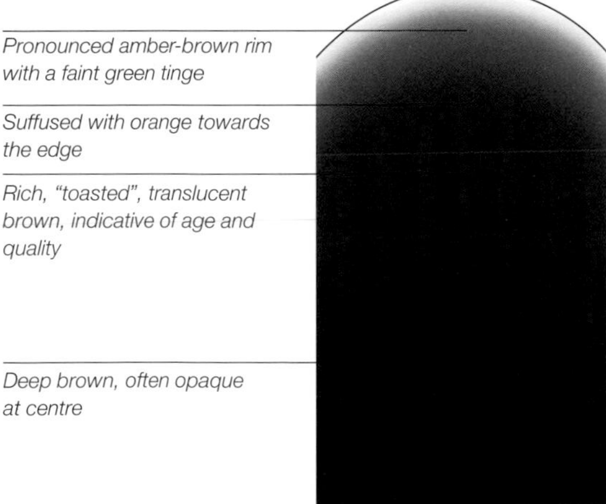

Rich golden sherry and old browns were immensely popular in Queen Victoria's time. Dark and deep with a rich taste of chocolate and burnt caramel and superb length.

Immature vintage port

Taken from a sample two years in cask. Classic shipper, good vintage. Will take fifteen years to mature; capable of lasting fifty years or more

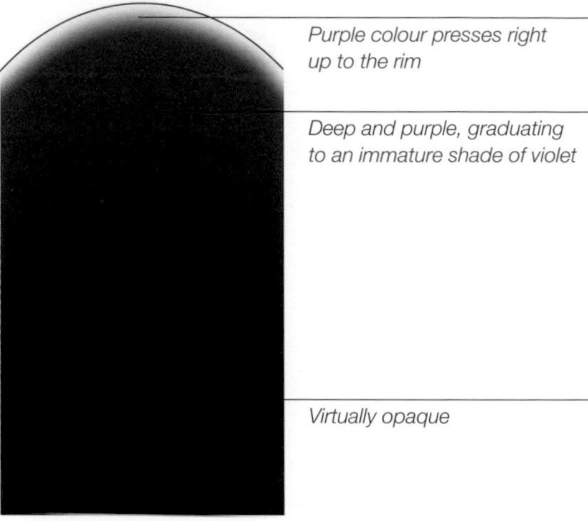

Easy to admire, difficult to taste – sweet, rich, peppery, and laden with tannin. The brandy which had been added to arrest the fermentation very much in evidence. But what a miraculous future!

Late-bottled vintage

Minimum four years in cask, bottled, ready for drinking

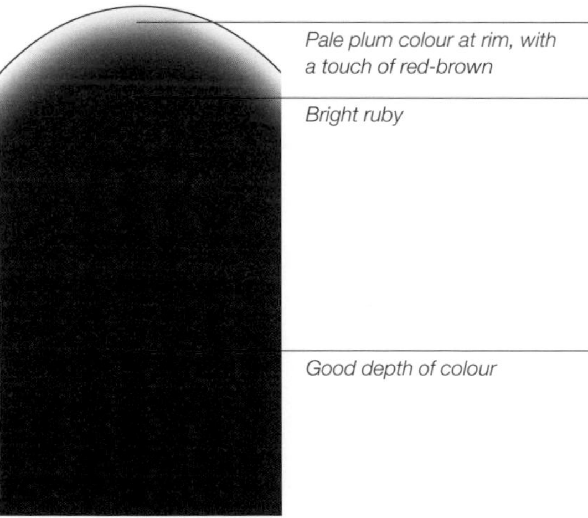

A half-way house, much more amenable because it has spent extra time in cask which hastens its maturity. Also less expensive and perhaps more versatile than a classic vintage port.

Mature vintage port

A great vintage from a top shipper; bottled after two years; matured in bottle for thirty years. Fully mature now but will keep for longer

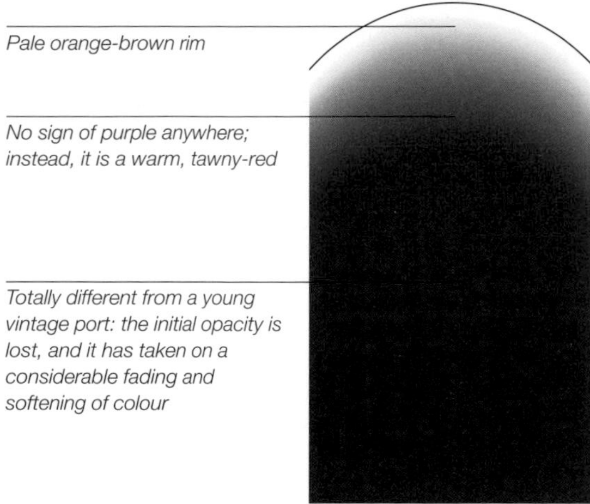
Pale orange-brown rim
No sign of purple anywhere; instead, it is a warm, tawny-red
Totally different from a young vintage port: the initial opacity is lost, and it has taken on a considerable fading and softening of colour

What is the point of keeping port twenty or thirty years? Those who drink only young vintages will never experience the beauty, the subtlety, and harmony of a perfectly mature port.

Twenty-year old tawny port

Matured in wood, then bottled in Oporto at its peak of maturity; perfect now

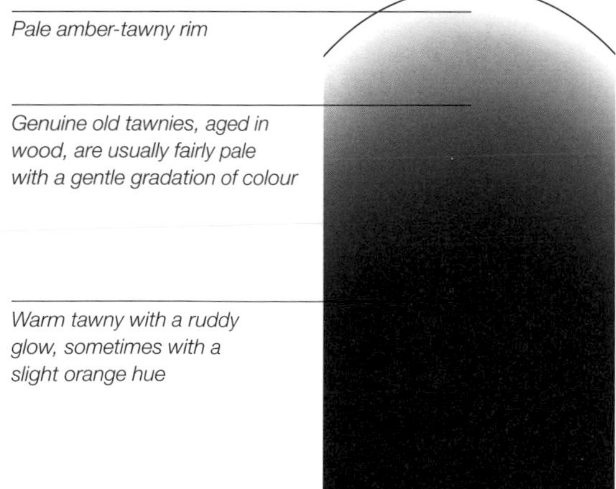
Pale amber-tawny rim
Genuine old tawnies, aged in wood, are usually fairly pale with a gentle gradation of colour
Warm tawny with a ruddy glow, sometimes with a slight orange hue

This is the style of wine that the shippers drink in Oporto: mellowed by ageing in wood, sweet, soft, with fragrant hazelnut bouquet, perfect flavour and finish. One of the world's great tastes.

Young Mosel wine

A three-year-old Riesling Spätlese of good vintage, from a top vineyard in the Middle Mosel Valley

Fades to a colourless rim

Pale lemon, with a mouth-watering hint of green; this wine can be drunk now or kept for further development, probably at best five to seven years after the vintage

Still pale, even at its deepest, but will gradually, almost imperceptibly, gain colour with age

Wines from the Mosel-Saar-Ruwer can in fact vary from virtually colourless to an entrancing pale-lemon yellow. What they all have in common is a touch of sweetness, low alcohol, and refreshing acidity. Delicious when young.

Mature Rhine Wine

A twenty-year-old Auslese of a major, classic vintage, from a leading estate in the Rheingau

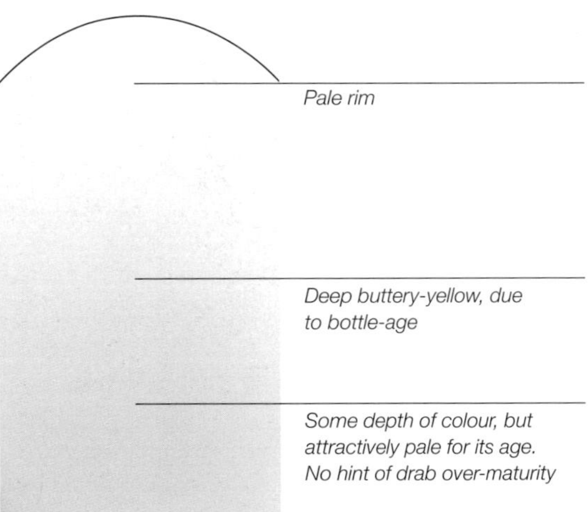

Classic Riesling demonstrating its depth of flavour, honeyed bouquet, combining bottle-age and a touch of botrytis, and the gifted wine maker's aim; a perfect balance of fruit and acidity.

Over-mature white burgundy

From a great and classic vintage, but after thirty years it has lost its initial zest, becoming rather flabby

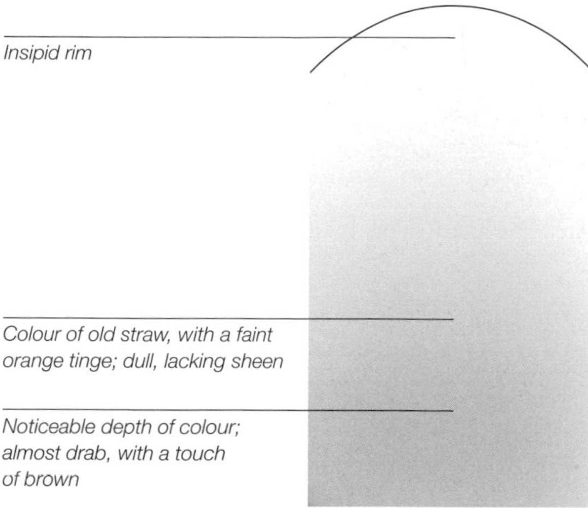

White burgundy begins life pale in colour, perhaps with a touch of yellow. Signs of over-maturity are exhibited first by its deepening colour, tired bouquet, and lack of zest. Only the finest are worth keeping.

Australian muscat

An intensely sweet, fortified dessert wine from northeast Victoria, long aged in cask

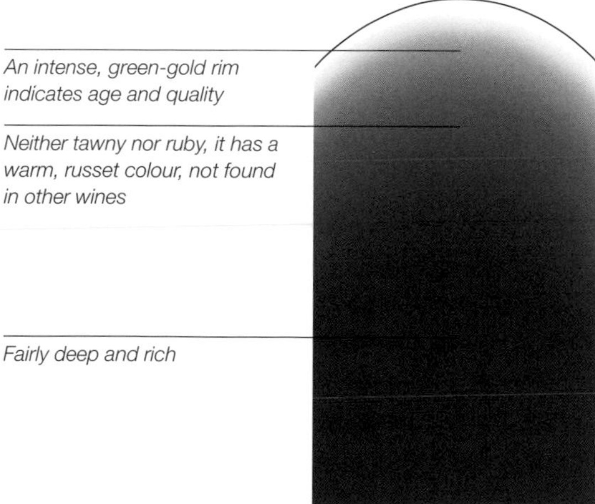

This is one of the world's lesser-known classics: sweet, smooth, rounded, delicious, with a distinct old muscatelle/raisiny flavour. Available from specialist importers.

Napa late-harvest Zinfandel

Almost a caricature of a great California red: a three year old, from very ripe, late-picked grapes, high strength, slightly sweet, with long life ahead

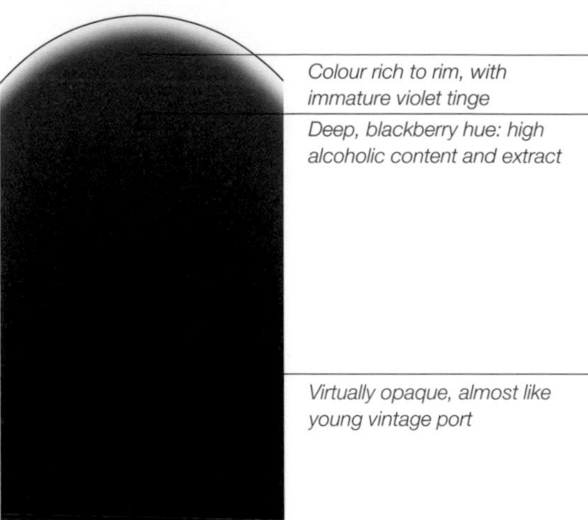

Very distinctive and fairly rare, worth seeking out and perfect with fruit, even more so with cheese, taking the place of port with Stilton.

Napa Cabernet Sauvignon

A top vintage from a relatively new winery. At five years of age, it has a long future, during which colour loss and changes will be very gradual

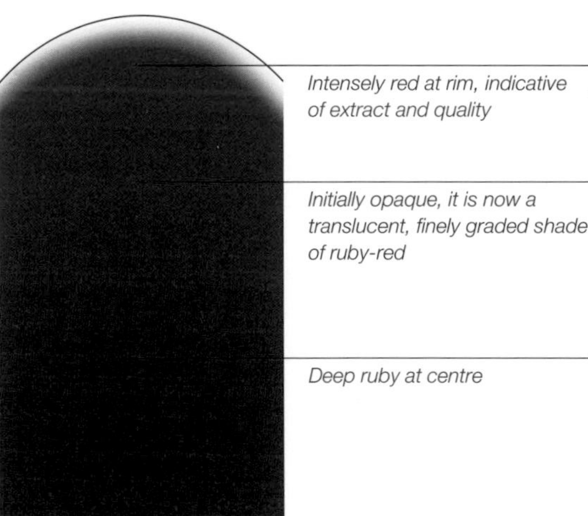

The original American answer to Bordeaux but, because of the climate, fuller, riper, and higher in alcohol than claret. Once one hundred per cent Cabernet Sauvignon, now often blended with Merlot and Cabernet Franc.

Semi-mature Châteauneuf-du-Pape

A ten-year-old wine from one of the best vineyards

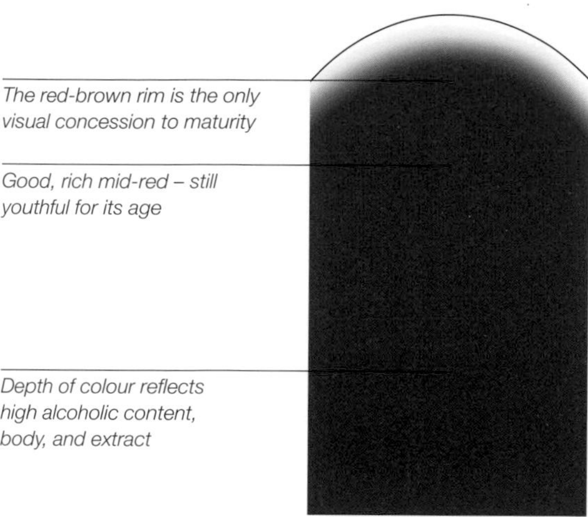
The red-brown rim is the only visual concession to maturity
Good, rich mid-red – still youthful for its age
Depth of colour reflects high alcoholic content, body, and extract

The Rhône Valley, with its hot summers and wide range of grape varieties, produces archetypal rich reds – not sweet but robust.

Maturing Australian red

A four-year-old "claret -style" wine from one of the oldest-established wineries in the Barossa Vallley

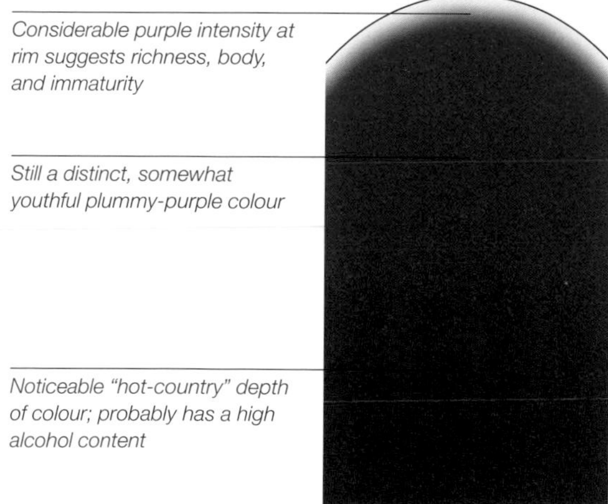
Considerable purple intensity at rim suggests richness, body, and immaturity
Still a distinct, somewhat youthful plummy-purple colour
Noticeable "hot-country" depth of colour; probably has a high alcohol content

Deservedly popular, rich, ripe, red table wines often, confusingly, a blend of different grapes, Cabernet Sauvignon and Shiraz for example, grown in different districts.

Five-year-old sercial madeira

A standard commercial blend of sercial from an old-established madeira shipper; but does not improve in bottle. For immediate consumption

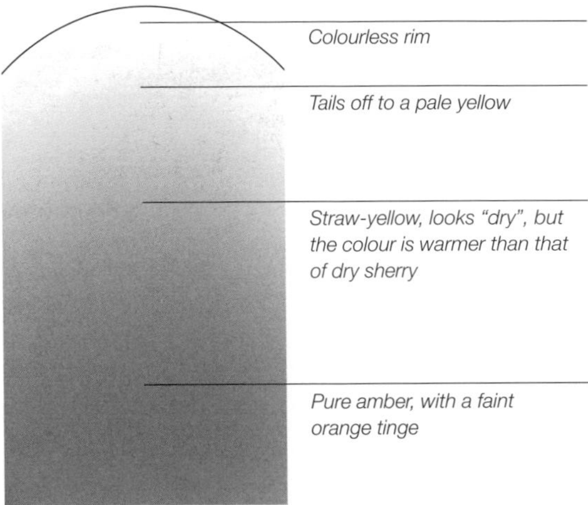
Colourless rim
Tails off to a pale yellow
Straw-yellow, looks "dry", but the colour is warmer than that of dry sherry
Pure amber, with a faint orange tinge

Madeira, a Portuguese-owned island, has – since the eighteenth century – produced a classic range of "fortified" wines of which Sercial is the palest and driest.

Old vintage madeira

A "straight" vintage from pure bual grapes, with at least fifty years in cask, forty years in glass demijohns, and about fifteen years in bottle; superb

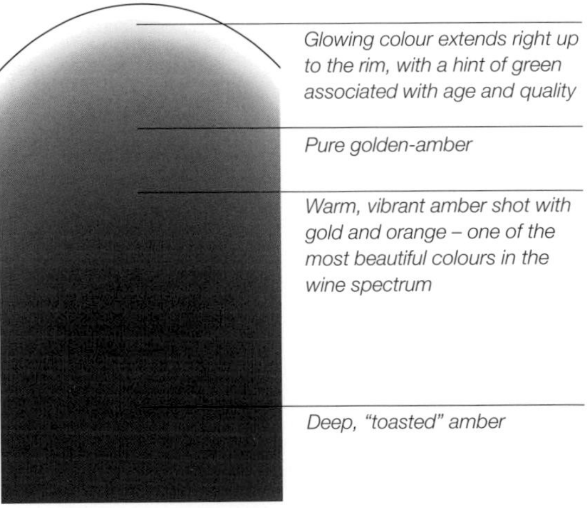
Glowing colour extends right up to the rim, with a hint of green associated with age and quality
Pure golden-amber
Warm, vibrant amber shot with gold and orange – one of the most beautiful colours in the wine spectrum
Deep, "toasted" amber

The wines of Madeira were in fact the creation of British merchants in Funchal and were shipped in enormous quantities to England and the British colonies. Bual grapes have a tangy richness. Long lasting.

Appendix

FOR FURTHER READING AND INFORMATION

The following is a fairly comprehensive list of books written, mainly in English, on the subject of tasting, from the lightly instructive to the deeply academic. In this edition, wine books of a general nature, whether discursive or factual, have been omitted, for to include them all would be tedious and confusing, and to select only those I rate highly would, I am afraid, offend a few friends and some literary acquaintances.

Some of these books are out of print, so I list selected specialist wine-book dealers who either stock, or can find, them; also some libraries that house major wine-book collections.

I currently receive wine magazines and journals from all over the world so I have greatly extended this section, including only those, however, which regularly feature tasting notes.

There is nothing to beat tasting itself, for practice and experience cannot be gleaned from books. The only short cut I recommend is to attend a well-organized wine course with competent tutors. This appendix ends with some useful addresses.

THE SCIENTIFIC APPROACH TO TASTING

Modern Sensory Methods of Evaluating Wines by Maynard A. Amerine, Edward B. Roessler, and F. Filipello (Hilgardia, University of California, June 1959). A scholarly pamphlet dealing with the senses; chemical components; statistical tasting techniques and the mathematical scoring systems. One of the first modern treatises on the organoleptic examination of wine. Not for amateurs, even if they managed to obtain a copy.

Sensory Evaluation of Wines by Maynard A. Amerine and Edward B. Roessler (Wine Institute, San Francisco, 1964). A follow-up of *Modern Sensory Methods* but still concerned with the academic approach to product-testing.

Wines, Their Sensory Evaluation by Maynard A. Amerine and Edward B. Roessler (W H Freeman & Company, New York and Oxford, 1976; revised and enlarged 1983). Putting "wines" first, introducing the Christian names of the authors, and including an odd New Yorker cartoon or two is a clear indication of intent: to present two distinguished professors in assimilable form. However, whereas at least half the book is still too complex for non-academics, the remainder is a must. Though some curious prejudices are exhibited, it is scholarly, informative, and impressive.

ON THE SENSES

Odour Description and Odour Classification by R. Harper, E. C. Bate-Smith and D. G. Land (J. and A. Churchill, London, 1968). Very scientific review of systems and classifications.

Gustation and Olfaction edited by G. Ohloff and A. F. Thomas (Academic Press, London and New York, 1971). Proceedings of an international symposium sponsored by Firmenich et Cie, Geneva.

The Human Senses in Action by Roland Harper (Churchill Livingstone, Edinburgh and London, 1972). Reveals the structure of sense organs, nature of stimuli, methods of measuring perception; with an exhaustive bibliography. Dr. Harper, of Reading University, writes for fellow scientists, but really keen wine students might well find the book fascinating, as I did.
Le Nez du Vin by Jean Lenoir (Ed. Lenoir, Paris, 1990. Translated). With miniature scent bottles.

FOR WINE BUFFS

The Flavour of Wine by Dr. Max Lake (Jacaranda Press, Sydney, 1969). An attractive, original, and sometimes complex little book by an erudite Australian surgeon-cum-winery-owner.
Gustation and Olfaction by Ohloff and Thomas (Academic Press, New York, 1970).
How to Test and Improve Your Wine Judging Ability by Irving H. Marcus (Wine Publications, Berkeley, California, 1972). A small paperback by the former owner-editor of *Wines and Vines*. The first part compact and helpful, the second a potted version of the Amerine-Roessler evaluation tests.
Initiation into the Art of Wine Tasting by Puisais and Chabanon (Vacaro, 1974).
The Taste of Wine by Emile Peynaud (J. Wiley, New York, 1987).
Understanding Wine by Michael Schuster (Mitchell Beazley, 2000). Accurate, logical, attractively produced, highly recommended.
The Wine Taster's Notebooks by Tom Stevenson (Stevenson, 1989).
Wine-Tasting Journal International des Sciences de la Vigne et du Vin (1999). Outstanding: Series of essays by French authorities covering "The Taster", "Tasting methods", "Components of taste and smell"... etc.
Wine Taster's Logic by Pat Simon (Faber, London, 2000).

FOR BEGINNERS

Wine Taster's Secrets by Andrew Sharp (Horizon, Toronto, 1981). Extremely unoriginal – as admitted by the author.
Enjoying Wine, a Taster's Companion by Pamela Vandyke-Price (Heinemann, 1982).
Master Glass by Jancis Robinson (Pan, 1983). A sensible, "jolly hockey-sticks" approach with unnecessarily complicated layout. However, effective, and recommended.
Start to Taste Wine by Max Lake (1984).
The Wine Taster's Notebooks by Tom Stevenson (Stevenson, 1989).
Académie du Vin Wine Course by Steven Spurrier and Michel Dovaz (Mitchell Beazley, London, 1990).
Lateral Wine Tasting by Rosemary George (Bloomsbury, 1991). Basic information, unoriginal. Clever but quirky. Mosel does not appear in the index (Nahe does) but alphabetically in the text alongside Bernkastel.
The Taste of Wine by Jilly Goolden (BBC Books, 1994). Deals with table wines only and is as unoriginal as its title. Sound, though written in a cosy, journalistic style. On the other hand, its aim – to describe individual types of wine – is achieved pretty well.
The Wine Experience by Gérard Basset (Kyle Cathie, London, 2000)

Winetasting by Nicolle Croft (Ryland, Peter, and Small, London, 2002). Uneven and unoriginal.

IN FRENCH

Le Physiologie du Goût by Brillat-Savarin (1825).
La Dégustation des Vins by Raymond Brunet (Bureau du Moniteur Vinicole, Paris, c. 1930).
Les Caractères des Vins by Raymond Brunet (Bureau de Moniteur Viticole, Paris, c. 1935).
Précis d'Initiation à la Dégustation by Puisais and Chabanon (Institute Technique du Vin, 1969).
Essai sur la Dégustation des Vins by Vedel, Charle, Charnay, and Tourneau (INAO, 1972).
Un Initiation à la Dégustation by Max Leglise (DIVO, 1976).
La Dégustation by S. Spurrier and M. Dovaz (Bordas, 1983).
La Dégustation des Vins by Norbert Got (Sodiep, 1985).
Le Goût Juste by Jacques Puisais (Flammarion, 1985).
Le Vin, Pratique de Degustation by J-C Buffin (ed. Syntheses, Paris, 1987).
Le Goût (L' Amateur de Bordeaux Cahiers, 1992).
Le Livre des Millésimes Les Grands Vins de France by Michael Broadbent (Scala, 1993).
L'Ecole de la Degustation by Pierre Casamayor (Hachette, Paris, 1998).
La Dégustation des Vins by Yves Meunier, Alain Rosier (Nathan, Paris, 1998).
La Dégustation (Journal International des Sciences de la Vigne et du Vin, 1999).

IN OTHER LANGUAGES

DANISH **Vinsmagning** by Michael Broadbent (Gyldendal, 1999).
DUTCH **Vijn proeven** by Michael Broadbent (Het Spectrum/ Utrecht, 1999).
GERMAN **Weine, Eheben & Geniessen** by Rolf Kriesi and Peter Osterwalder (Vinum, 1994).
Broadbent's Weinnotizen (Hallwag, 1994).
Weine, richtig, geniessen, lernen by Ambrosi and Swoboda (Falken, 1995).
Weine prüfen, kennen, geniessen by Michael Broadbent (Hallwag, 1995).
Wein Degustieren by Kurt Gibel (Hallwag, Bern, 1999).
JAPANESE **Winetasting** by Michael Broadbent, translated by Nobuko Nishioka (Shibata Shoten, Tokyo, 1996).
SPANISH **Cómo se disfruta y se entiende la degustación del Vino** by Michael Broadbent, translated by Ing Juan B. Morales Doria (Editorial Regina de los Angeles, Mexico City, 1981).
Guía para conocer y degustar Los Vinos by Michael Broadbent (Guias de bolsillo, Folio, Barcelona, 1982).
SWEDISH **Vinprovarens Handbook** by Michael Broadbent, translated by Professor Nils Sternby (Norstedts Forlag, Stockholm, 1986).

TRANSLATED FOR AMERICANS

Initiation into the Art of Wine Tasting by J. A. Vaccaro (Interpublis, Madison, Wisconsin, 1974). A rather laboured version of the *Précis...* by Puisais and Chabanon, well-illustrated and interesting, but including the original irrelevant apple and cream-cracker score sheets and information about French hotel school courses.

BOOKS WITH TASTING A MAJOR FEATURE

Notes on a Cellar-book by George Saintsbury (Macmillan, London, 1920). Detailed reminiscent jottings, which had a seminal influence on wine writing and connoisseurship (new edition with Yoxall preface, 1979).

The Physiology of Taste by Brillat-Savarin (Peter Davies, London, 1925). A famous classic: discursive, civilized. Translated from the French *Physiologie du Goût*, 1825.

A Matter of Taste, Wine and Wine Tasting by Jack Durac (André Deutsch, London, 1975). Also published as *Wines and the Art of Tasting* (Sunrise, E. P. Duitton and Co, New York, 1974). A New York book reviewer incorrectly credited Mr Durac (London University research scientist) with being "the first" to make "a systematic attempt at explaining how a wine should be tasted...".

A Taste of Wine by Pamela Vandyke-Price (Macdonald and Jane's, London, 1975). Sixty pages of somewhat idiosyncratic taste classifications, and other general matter – winemaking, maps etc.

Gorman on Californian Premium Wines by Robert Gorman (Ten Speed Press, Berkeley, California, 1975). Thoughtful approach to tasting, with model notes.

Harry Waugh's Wine Diaries (Christie's Wine Publications, 1975, 1976, 1978, and 1981). A series of travel journals and tasting notes.

The Great Vintage Wine Book II by Michael Broadbent (Mitchell Beazley, London, and Knopf, New York, 1991). A complete record of vintages of all the major classic districts, good, bad, and indifferent, and the reasons why; illustrated; 5,000 tasting notes.

Académie du Vin Wine Course by Steven Spurrier and Michel Dovaz (Century Publishing in association with Christie's, London, 1983). The complete study course in wine appreciation of the *Académie du Vin*, Paris. Recommended.

The Taste of Wine by Emile Peynaud (Macdonald, London, 1987 and Wiley, New York, 1996). Conscientious translation by Michael Schuster of the original 1980 French version. Recommended.

Carte Blanche by Albert Givtan (Turnagain Enterprises, Vancouver, 1999) Idiosyncratic wine diaries.

Bacchus & Me by Jay McInerney (The Lyons Press, New York, 2000). Serious fun.

Vintage Wine by Michael Broadbent (Websters Little Brown, London 2002, Harcourt, New York 2002).

WINE LIBRARIES

The Guildhall Library, in the City of London, houses the Library of the Institute of Masters of Wine, which in turn incorporates the old Wine Trade

Club Library, founded and amassed by André Simon (reference library open to the public).
Harvey Wine Museum in Bristol (this is well worth a detour – by appointment only).
The Fresno State College Wine Library, California, incorporating the extensive library collected by Roy Brady, a former editorof Wine World.
The A. J. Winkler Library in the Department of Viticulture and Enology, University of California, Davis.
Public Libraries: most public libraries in the United Kingdom have a food and wine section, and titles not stocked can usually be obtained, on request, through inter-library loans.

SPECIALIST WINE BOOKSELLERS

Janet Clarke, Antiquarian Books (3 Woodside Cottages, Freshford, Bath, BA3 6EJ, UK; fax: 00 44 (0)1225 722 063).
MM Einhorn Maxwell, Books (At the Sign of the Dancing Bear, 80 East 11th Street, New York, NY 10003, USA.)
The Wine & Food Library, Janice B Longone (1207 West Madison, Ann Arbor, Michigan 48103, USA).
John Roberts, Antiquarian and out-of-print wine books (130 St Leonards Road, London SW14 7NJ, UK).
Cooks Books, Tessa McKirdy (34 Marine Drive, Rottingdean, Sussex BN2 7HQ, UK; fax: 00 44 (0)1273 301 651).
Libraire Mollat (15 rue Vital-Carles, 33080 Bordeaux Cedex, Beaune, France; fax: 00 33 5 565 640 88.)

WINE MAGAZINES

Decanter (583 Fulham Road, London SW6 5UA, UK.) The best English monthly.
Wine International (6–14 Underwood Street, London N1 7JQ, UK.) Monthly. Lively, with regular tasting reports.
Wine Spectator (387 Park Avenue South, New York, 10016, USA.)
Quarterly Review of Wines (24 Garfield Avenue Winchester, MA 01890, USA.)
Which? Wine Guide (2 Marylebone Road, London NW1 4DF, UK.) Notes and recommendations for consumers.
Wine & Food. The annual journal of The International Wine and Food Society. (Discontinued but earlier annuals worth seeking out, from 1934 to 2001.)
Wine & Food Society, Journal of. Founded by André Simon in 1934 and, alas, discontinued after 2000. Civilized writing and mentioned because back numbers and sets worth pursuing (*see* specialist booksellers).
Wine Tidings (Suite 414, 5165 Sherbrooke Street West, Montreal, Quebec H4A 1T6, Canada.)
La Revue du Vin de France (10 Rue Guynemer, 92136 Issy-Les-Moulineaux, France.) Five issues per annum. Old-established and high-grade.
Le Nouveau Guide Gault-Millau (22 bis, Rue des Volontaires, 75738 Paris Cedex 15, France.) Stimulating, often provocative, always lively critique of food, wine, and restaurants.

Cuisines & Vins de France (Groupe Marie-Claire, 10 Bd des Frères Voisin, 92792 Issy Cedex 09 Reculettes, France.)
Wineglass (Wineglass Publishing, PO Box 9527, Newmarket, Auckland, New Zealand.)
Vinum (Klosbachstrasse 83, Postfach 8030 Zürich, Switzerland.) German language. Monthly. Excellent.
Falstaff Magazin (A–3400 KLOSTERNEUBURG INKUSTRASSE 1–7/STG 4/2 OG, Austria.) Monthly.
Vini (Via Sudorno 44, 24100 Bergamo Alta, Italy.) A glossy and lively wine and food monthly.
Alles über Weine (Woschek Verlag, Wilhelm-Theodor-Römheld-Strasse 34, D-55130 Mainz, Germany.) Excellent bimonthly.
L'Amateur de Bordeaux (22 Rue des Reculettes, 75013 Paris, France.) Monthly, excellent.
International Wine Cellar (New York Stephen Tanzer's excellent consumer guide.)

SUBSCRIPTION WINE NEWSLETTERS

Clive Coates, The Vine (76 Woodstock Road, London W4 1EQ, UK.) Clive Coates' in-depth reports and tasting notes.
The Wine Advocate (1002 Hillside View, Parkton, Maryland 21120, USA.) Robert Parker Jr.'s influential bimonthly tasting notes.

WINE COURSES/ACADEMIES

Vini-viticultural schools, sometimes departments of universities, have for many years existed in major wine-producing countries: Geisenheim in Germany, Roseworthy in Australia, Montpellier in France, the University of California, Davis and at the University of Bordeaux, to mention just a few. The following establishments run regular structured courses open to all; in the listing they are followed by some of the firms and organizations which specialize in one-off tutored tastings. Their effectiveness depends partly on the class of wine and quality of individual tutors. Naturally these vary, but the overall level is surprisingly high and keen amateurs as well as beginners will certainly gain a lot from attending them.
Christie's Wine Course in association with *L' Académie du Vin* (Christie's Education, 5 Kings Street, St James's London, SW1Y 6QS). Regular evening courses from introductory to advanced.
Sotheby's (34 New Bond Street, London W1, UK.) Lecture/tastings.
Wine & Spirit Education Trust (Five Kings House, 1 Queen Street Place, London EC4R 1QS, UK.) Day and evening courses for the trade but open to all. Three levels: elementary, intermediate, and advanced (for Diploma).
Wine & Spirit Education Centers of America Inc. (Frank H Stone, PO Box 20450, Atlanta, Georgia 30325, USA.) Operates with franchises of Wine & Spirit Education Trust (UK).
International Wine Center (144 West 55 Street, New York, NY 10019, USA.) Regular classes. Wine bar below lecture rooms.
Windows on the World Wine School (Marriott Marquis in Times Square New York, USA.) Quite long-established and highly regarded.
"Wine Captain's Seminar" (The Sommelier Society of America, 435 Fifth Avenue, New York, NY 10016, USA.)

Independent Wine Education Guild (AC Hirons, PO Box 883, Station Q Toronto, Ontario, M4T 2N7, Canada.)

KWV Wine Courses (Laborie Wine Centre, PO Box 528, Suider Paarl 7624, South Africa.)

Centre d'Information, de Documentation et de Dégustation (45, rue Liancourt, 75104 Paris, France.) Evening courses.

Flemming Hvelplund's Wine School (Magstrade 7, 1207 Copenhagen, Denmark.) Effective, open to all.

German Wine Academy, at Kloster Eberbach.

Wijnacademie (Postbus 1840, 2280 DV Rijswijk, Netherlands.)

EXHIBITIONS

Vinopolis "City of Wine" (1 Bank End, London SE1 9BU, UK.) Wine odyssey tour of wine regions; tastings, wine shop, accessories, wine restaurants, art gallery.

Index

C

K

L

M

N

O

Y

Z